The Power of Prophecy

Ronald D. Graybill

The Power of Prophecy

Ellen G. White and the Women Religious Founders
of the Nineteenth Century

Ronald D. Graybill

Baltimore, Maryland: PhD Dissertation
The Johns Hopkins University, 1983
Eastvale Press, 2019

For information contact:
Ronald D. Graybill
3290 E. Yountville Drive, Unit 13
Ontario, CA 92761

Cover design: Oak & Acorn

First Edition: October 2019

10 9 8 7 6 5 4 3 2 1

Contents

Preface to this 2019 Book

This book is a reproduction of my 1983 dissertation. I have not revised or updated it. It is published as an historic document in order to represent what I said in the dissertation in 1983. The only changes I have made is to correct typographical and other technical errors. These changes in no way alter the meaning of the original text, although they do make this text appear to be more carefully copy-edited. I have also inserted, in several places, bracketed notes to update or correct certain passages. Each of these is identified as a "2019 note." These notes are preceded by the exact 1983 text. My views on most of the topics covered in this dissertation have not changed much over the past 36 years. But they can be seen, along with more recent research, in my newly published book, *Visions and Revisions: A Textual History of the Ellen G. White Writings* (Westlake Village, CA: Oak & Acorn Publishing, 2019). The publisher of this copy of my dissertation, "Eastvale Press" is simply a name I've chosen to list, a "virtual press" if you please.

Abstract

Ellen G. White (1829-1915) used her charisma, based on the belief that she received divine revelations, to help her husband James establish the Seventh-day Adventist Church in 1863. Her career is comparable to that of other nineteenth century women religious founders such as Mary Baker Eddy, "discoverer" of Christian Science; Catherine Booth who, with her husband William, built the Salvation Army; and Alma White, who started the Pillar of Fire denomination. Ellen White and Catherine Booth both shared their leadership with their husbands. At first, James explained and defended Ellen's prophetic gifts while she provided divine endorsement of his leadership initiatives. Later she emerged as an independent leader when ill health limited his activities. After his death in 1881, she sought emotional and practical support from her son, William, although he was accused of unduly influencing her.

The charisma of Ellen White and Mary Baker Eddy gave them the ability both to establish order and, when necessary, to defy established procedure and introduce innovation in their churches. However, Mrs. White's supernatural gifts were negatively related to feminism, since they said nothing about the potential of ordinary women and gave little encouragement to women to move out of traditional roles.

During her younger years, Ellen White's revelations were conveyed in trance-like visions which were a part of the enthusiastic religious experience all Adventists shared. When that emotional environment cooled in the 1860's, the visions calmed into prophetic dreams, and Adventist apologists ignored their earlier ecstatic setting. Although these revelations taught the importance of the Bible and urged its study, they also gave Mrs. White a doctrinal authority that was never fully harmonized with the Adventist belief that Scripture alone must establish doctrine. Furthermore, her trance experiences implied that her revelations were in no sense influenced by her surroundings. Thus when the scope of her writing expanded and she began to draw on literary sources to enrich her work, she was either unable or unwilling to admit these influences. Early and late, then, her charisma was enhanced by efforts to isolate it from every human influence and negative association.

Preface

Millions of her books are sold every year. Royalties from English editions total more than $100,000 annually. Four million church members consult her writings for wisdom on theology, family life, health and nutrition, business, education, and church administration. Yet until recently, Ellen G. White (1827-1915) has been almost unknown outside the Seventh-day Adventist Church which she and her husband founded.[1]

This dissertation examines how Mrs. White exercised her leadership and established her authority. Her charisma fits Max Weber's classic definition, being that "certain quality of an individual personality" by virtue of which one "is set apart from ordinary men and treated as endowed with supernatural, superhuman, or at least specifically exceptional powers or qualities."[2] In the present case, this endowment was believed to consist of direct revelations from God. Thanks to the processes I will describe, Adventists came to share Ellen White's deep-rooted belief in her divine calling. The quality of "charisma" and the role of "prophet" are intended here to connote that she was thought to be literally the bearer of divine messages.

What difference did it make that Ellen White was charismatic in this radical sense? Did she exercise leadership in a manner different from leaders who claimed no prophetic gifts? I have tried to answer these questions by comparing and contrasting her career with those of other female religious founders. Through comparative biography I conjure with otherwise imponderable questions, asking, for instance, what if Ellen White had not claimed the gift of prophecy? The experiences of Catherine Booth, co-founder of the Salvation Army, and Alma White, founder of the Pillar of Fire, may help answer such questions. Like Ellen White, these women were reared as Methodists and came to lead religious movements, yet neither claimed divine revelations. What if Ellen White had not endeavored to share her leadership with her husband? Here, Mary Baker Eddy's experience is relevant. Like Ellen White, she claimed divine revelations, yet made no attempt to share leadership.

This study bears the weaknesses of all comparative history: the examples are few, the variables are many. But most historical statements are comparative, if only because they affirm change over time, comparing one condition with another which preceded or followed it. I have, of course, compared Ellen White's early career with her later experience, but contrasting her with other women gives us additional reference points.

Ellen and her twin sister Elizabeth were born Nov. 26, 1827, in Gorham, Maine. Her father, Robert Harmon, a hatter and sometime farmer, moved his family to Portland, Maine, during Ellen's early childhood.[3] There she was reared a Methodist until William Miller's preaching persuaded the family that Christ was coming in the near future. Cast out of the Methodist communion, Ellen devoted her energies to converting young friends to the new message. After Christ failed to appear, her religious dreams were transformed into ecstatic visions. In 1846 she married a young Adventist preacher, James White. Together with the former abolitionist Joseph Bates, the three founded the Seventh-day Adventist Church in Michigan in 1863.[4] By the time of her death in 1915, the church had grown to 136,000. Today it has four million members world-wide, with more than 650,000 in North America.[5]

While this is a study of "authority"—how it was defined, shaped, established, exercised and threatened—Ellen White would have preferred the term "influence." In fact, "influence" better describes her informal exercise of power. Formal authority within her movement belonged to others; her power rested on charisma and moral appeal. For Ellen White, influence seemed a form of authority particularly appropriate to women. A mother's influence, she said, was "as abiding as eternity." Its power was, next to God's, "the strongest known on earth."[6] Influence was quiet, yet inexorable: "Throw a pebble into the lake, and a wave is formed, and another and another; and as they increase, the circle widens, until it reaches the very shore. So with our influence. Beyond our knowledge or control it tells upon others in blessing or in cursing.[7]

This "silent witness" of a "true, unselfish, godly life" was, for Ellen White, "almost irresistible." So precious was such power that if one injured another's influence in any way, forgiveness must be sought.[8] To be sure, Ellen White warned those who rejected her counsel that they were, in effect, rejecting the counsel of God. But at the same time, she worked constantly to extend, protect and defend her own influence.

Ellen White was particularly sensitive to two potential threats to her influence. One was the suggestion that, rather than God, her environment influenced her—those people she knew and the books she read. The other was the possibility that her influence might be neither effective nor good. Her family relationships exposed her to both these hazards. At the same time, both her husband and younger son supported her authority. Early in the marriage James White explained and defended his wife's divine gift even while assigning her a more limited role than other prophets played. Later, James's poor physical and emotional health inhibited her authority because her efforts to care for him kept her away from public labor, while his failings rendered him a poor example of the fruits of her work.

Ellen's two sons also influenced her developing role in the church. Edson, the eldest, became a liability because of his unstable religious experience and criticisms of his brother, Willie. The genial, obedient, younger son worked with his mother after James's death and did much to support and extend her power. But Ellen paid a price for her close cooperation with Willie—allegations that he unduly influenced her were frequent.

In the early part of her career, the revelations Mrs. White claimed as the basis of her authority occurred during visionary trances. Later, vivid dreams served the same purpose. I have shown here that these trances were part of the enthusiastic worship experience of Adventism. They gained credibility not because they were unique but because they resembled the spiritual exaltations of other believers. Once Adventist worship grew sedate, Ellen's trances ceased, and her early visions acquired a miraculous aura.

Like the other women founders, Ellen White reinforced her authority with a heavy use of the Bible. In her case however, the claim to special gifts of the Spirit created a tension between the authority of Scripture and her own authority as one of its inspired interpreters. Still, she defended and elevated the Bible more vigorously than her counterparts, thus laying a foundation on which Adventists could rest their fundamentally conservative doctrines.

Ellen White's charisma had a significant impact on the organizational development of her church since it enabled her both to "make the rules" which established order and "break the rules" when innovations seemed necessary. However, that same charisma seems to have been negatively related to feminism. Since the gifts Ellen White enjoyed were thought to be supernatural, they did not demonstrate the potential of women, but merely proved God's power. What is more, the charismatic leader's burden of doctrinal deviance may have inhibited cultural deviance in the area of women's rights.

Mrs. White's authority expressed itself chiefly through her writings. Her extensive correspondence put her in touch with the developing church and provided the raw material from which her secretaries assembled articles and books. As the volume and scope of her writing increased, she sometimes utilized the work of other authors, a fact that has become more apparent and more controversial in the years since the 1970's than it ever was in her lifetime. Bound by her self-image as an inspired messenger, Mrs. White rarely recognized or admitted that human sources influenced her, and Adventists who read her writings for spiritual benefit seemed little concerned when critics accused her of plagiarism. For them, her originality mattered less than the assurance and direction she offered.

In this study, the careers of Mary Baker Eddy and Catherine Booth are understood from their excellent recent biographies: Robert Peel's three volumes on the founder of Christian Science,[9] and Catherine Bramwell-Booth's account of her grandmother's life.[10] The fact that sympathizers authored these books does not limit their usefulness for factual data. Indeed, believers often revel in details and provide the extensive quotations more dispassionate scholars would omit. Alma White's five-volume autobiography is similarly useful because it is so full and often so naively revealing that it approximates the value of original letters and diaries.[11] In her case, a small collection of correspondence confirmed my impression that her life story, although self-serving, is also reliable. I consulted many other sources, but these, in the end, proved most fruitful.

A professor once inquired whether Ellen White was going to be the soloist or merely a singer in this quartet of women founders. She clearly stands in the foreground of this dissertation. As the first student to have immediate and unlimited access to her personal and unpublished papers. I am both blessed and burdened—blessed by an abundance of intimate detail, and burdened because others have beaten few clear paths through this thicket. Her personal papers include some 60,000 pages of letters, sermons, articles, and diary and journal entries.[12] As I have used these I have been fully aware of the keen interest of her immediate descendants and of Seventh-day Adventists in general in maintaining Mrs. White's authority and protecting her reputation. Even so, such considerations have not consciously affected my choice of materials or my interpretation of them. I write an insider's account, but hopefully one which is disciplined by my training as a historian, my scruples about candor, and my distaste for special pleading.

After the experience of writing a doctoral dissertation, I am less inclined to begrudge Ellen White the literary assistants who polished her prose. My own work would be much poorer without the helpful historical criticisms and editorial suggestions of Gary Ross, Bonnie Casey, Roy Branson, Viveca Black, and John Kelley. My professor, Timothy L. Smith [2019 note: (1924–1997)], was more than generous in his painstaking efforts to improve my history as well as my writing. Professor Ron Walters introduced me to family history and offered cogent suggestions as well. My wife, Gerte, gave the dissertation a final reading, but her help was far greater through years of patient support and encouragement.

At various archives and libraries, others also gave of their time and expertise. Tom Johnsen, a fellow graduate student, answered many questions about Mrs. Eddy and introduced me to his colleagues at the Christian Science headquarters, Robert Peel and Steven Gott-shchalk, each of whom granted helpful interviews. Lee Johnson oriented me to the Christian Science Archives. At Pillar of Fire headquarters, Rev. E. J. Lawrence, himself a historian, arranged for me use of the church's library facilities, where Gladys Hill shared sources as well as insights concerning Alma White. In England, Lieut. Col. Cyril Barnes of the Literary Department of the Salvation Army, shared his knowledge of the Army "Mother," Catherine Booth, and allowed me to copy a number of historic photographs. Major James Northey arranged my visit with Catherine Bramwell-Booth and even drove me to her Berkshire County home. Closer to home, Timothy L. Poirier, who worked with me as a research assistant, facilitated my progress in the final stages of this work. I am also indebted to Warren H. Johns for his extensive research into Ellen White's use of literary sources.

---

[1]C.C. Goen, "Ellen Gould Harmon White," in Edward T. James, ed., *Notable American Women*, 1607-1950, vol. 3 (Cambridge, Mass., 1971), 585-588; Ronald L. Numbers, *Ellen G. White: Prophetess of Health* (New York, 1976); Arthur L. White, *Ellen G. White: The Early Elmshaven Years*, 1900-1905 (Washington, D.C., 1981), and *Ellen G. White: The Later Elmshaven Years*, 1905-1915 (Washington, D.C., 1982), and Ellen G. White: *Messenger to the Remnant* (Washington, D.C., 1969); Ellen G. White, *Life Sketches* (Battle Creek, Mich., 1880}, and *Life Sketches* {Mountain View, Calif., 1915).

[2]S. N. Eisenstadt, *Max Weber on Charisma and Institution Building* (Chicago, 1968), 48.

[3]Ron Graybill, "Ellen G. White: The Hidden Years," (unpublished manuscript, Washington, D.C., 1974).

[4]James White, *Life Incidents in Connection with the Great Second Advent Movement* (Battle Creek, Mich., 1868); Joseph Bates, *The Autobiography of Elder Joseph Bates* (Battle Creek, Mich., 1868); Godfrey Anderson, *Outrider of the Apocalypse* (Mountain View, Calif., 1972).

[5]Constant H. Jacquet, Jr., ed., *Yearbook of American and Canadian Churches, 1982* (Nashville, Tenn., 1982), 235; Donald Yost, comp., *120th Annual Statistical Report—1982* (Washington, D.C., 1982), 2.

[6]Ellen G. White, "The Work of Parents," *Good Health*, vol. 15 (Mar., 1880), 76-77, quoted in Ellen G. White, Adventist Home, (Washington, D. C., 1952), 240.

[7]Ellen G. White, *Christ's Object Lessons* (Nashville, Tenn., 1941), 340, first published, 1900.

[8]Ellen G. White, *Thoughts from the Mount of Blessing* (Washington, D.C., 1956), 59, first published, 1896.

[9]Robert Peel, *Mary Baker Eddy: The Years of Discovery* (New York, 1966); *Mary Baker Eddy: The Years of Trial* (New York, 1971); *Mary Baker Eddy: The Years of Authority* (New York, 1977); See also Steven Gottschalk, The *Emergence of Christian Science—American Religious Life* (Berkeley, Calif., 1973).

[10]Catherine Bramwell-Booth, *Catherine Booth: The Story of Her Loves* (London, 1970).

[11]Merrit Cross, "Alma Bridwell White," in *Notable American Women*, vol. 3, 581-583; Alma White, *The Story of My Life*, 6 vols. (Zarephath, N.J., 1919-1934); Alma White, *The Story of My Life*, 5 vols. (Zarephath, N.J., 1935-1943); Alma White, *Looking Back From Beulah* (Denver, Colorado, 1902, Zarephath, N.J., 1929).

[12]At the time my dissertation was written, other scholars have been required to request particular documents on the basis of a subject-index which is a good deal less than comprehensive. Research policies of the Ellen G. White Estate are discussed in Arthur L. White, "The Literary Resources of the Ellen G. White Estate and Policies Governing Their Use," (duplicated, Washington, D.C., 1973).

CHAPTER ONE

Wife and Husband

F ew nineteenth century women had husbands who fully supported them in the pursuit of public careers. Abolitionist Angelina Grimke and her husband Theodore Dwight Weld both believed in the equality of the sexes, but Weld's practice of forcing others into his own image of Christlikeness meant that after their marriage Angelina virtually retired from public life in order to curb what Weld saw as her "sinful pride." His criticisms laid upon her a "crushing sense" of her own inferiority.[1]

Julia Ward Howe, a budding poet who later wrote *The Battle Hymn of the Republic*, discovered that although her husband, Samuel Gridley Howe, favored reforms in many fields, women's rights was not one of them. He deeply resented her public success and demanded she withdraw from literary pursuits. She published her first book of poems anonymously and without his knowledge.[2]

Henry Stanton was generally tolerant and occasionally supportive of the feminist activities of his wife, Elizabeth Cady Stanton. But as he became more active in politics, he absented himself from home for long periods. Even when at home, he was often "staid and indifferent," according to one of Mrs. Stanton's recent biographers.[3] Neither of them shared the other's career.

If anything, the combination of religious leadership and marriage was even more difficult. Of the 37 women designated "religious founders and leaders" in the biographical dictionary, *Notable American Women*, many were nuns, and only three besides Ellen White can be said to have had husbands who aided their movements or shared their careers. These three, like Ellen White, were reared in one or another of the Wesleyan denominations: Maud Ballington Booth, Myrtle Page Fillmore, and Barbara Ruckle Heck. Another Methodist, Phoebe Palmer, should be added to this list, although she is absent from this biographical dictionary.[4] Catherine Booth, of British extraction, is yet another child of Methodism who combined marriage with religious leadership. The fact that Methodism had always made some allowance for female leadership doubtless made it easier for Methodist husbands to grant their wives public roles, at least in the religious sphere.[5]

In their brief study of differences among female religious and secular leaders, Barbara and John Maniha found women religious leaders twice as likely as secular leaders to marry. However, the marriages of religious leaders were also twice as likely to end in failure.[6] Certainly many male leaders also had unsuccessful marriages, but the popular expectation that wives would be subordinate supporters of their husband's careers made marriage for male leaders less problematic and, by the standards of the time, more "successful."[7]

Of the women given special attention here, only Ellen White and Catherine Booth shared their leadership roles with equally talented and important husbands. Mary Baker Eddy's first husband died tragically, and she divorced her second when he was unfaithful. Her third husband, Gilbert Eddy, never held a significant leadership position in her movement, although he was a revered teacher of her doctrine.[8] Alma White's husband became more and more estranged from her as she assumed a public role, finally fleeing to England where he remained until shortly before his death.

James White's contribution to Ellen White's leadership can be summarized by saying that during the first two decades of their marriage, he did much to legitimate her claim to prophetic gifts and to expand her influence, while at the same time channeling her into a less prominent role than other persons claiming divine inspiration had sometimes played. In the last sixteen years of their marriage Mrs. White grew more independent of her husband as his problems came to threaten her authority.

Ellen met James in Orrington Maine as she travelled across that state telling of her early visions. Although she believed God had commissioned her to share what she had seen with others, the assignment looked impossible at first. When they were able, various family members accompanied her to nearby towns. When James became interested in her messages he joined her and her sister as they journeyed further. When ugly (and unfounded) gossip sprang up that the two were travelling alone together, James decided Ellen needed a "legal protector" and offered his hand in marriage.[9]

When the couple married on August 30, 1846, James had just turned 25. Born in Palmyra, Maine, in 1821, he was the fifth of nine children. Because of poor eyesight he was unable to attend school until he was 19. Having studied on his own, he then entered a nearby academy and by working 18 hours a day, earned a teaching certificate in four months. Another stint of 17 weeks concluded his formal education, and he went to work as a teacher.[10]

At 15, James had been baptized into the Christian Connection a New England sect with beliefs similar to those of Alexander Campbell and the early Disciples of Christ.[11] In 1842 he heard William Miller, left his teaching position and, armed with a prophetic chart, began to preach that Christ would return to earth sometime in 1843. White claimed some 1,000 converts in his first winter of preaching. On his return to Palmyra, he was ordained to the ministry of the Christian Connection.[12]

By the time of their marriage, then, both James White and Ellen Harmon had been deeply involved in religious activities for a number of years. They had the advantage that both knew from the outset that their marriage would not be the typical Victorian arrangement in which the wife was expected only to care for children, nurture her husband, and physically maintain the home.[13] Thus James did not have to adjust after their marriage to a totally unexpected role for his wife.

Although James and Ellen doubtless had come to love each other, romance would have been a far too selfish motive for marriage. In view of the imminent end of the world, James had recently condemned marriage as a "wile of the devil." The trend of the times was toward partnerships based on mutual affection, but since they both still believed that Christ's coming was liable to occur at any moment, they needed more than romantic interests to justify their marriage in their own minds and in the minds of their fellow-believers.[14]

Ellen White conceived of herself and her husband as a sort of leadership team, each with a special calling and mission, but each

with a duty to support and maintain the other. James' support of Ellen was both practical and ideological. On the practical side, he seems
to have been endlessly patient with her illnesses, fainting spells, and
periods of depression. More skilled as a writer, he served as her copy
editor, literary agent, publisher, reviewer, and advertising manager.
James "acted as a helper and counselor" in the publication of her messages. "We examined the matter together," she wrote, "my husband
correcting grammatical errors, and eliminating needless repetition."[15]
James insisted that Ellen's books be "polished" before publication
by the "last touches of the old gentleman's [his] pencil."[16] His correspondence was often filled with the tedium of choosing typefaces,
formats, papers, bindings, and prices for his wife's books. Given the
struggles which some nineteenth century female writers endured, it
was no small advantage—financially or emotionally—for Ellen White
to have James as her agent.[17]

James helped shape the church's concept of Ellen's "prophetic
gift," and defended her work against critics and doubters. She first
came to public notice in 1845 when he wrote a Millerite paper in
Cincinnati, Ohio, of "one Sister in Maine who has had a clear vision
of the Advent people traveling to the City of God," adding, "I think
the Bible warrants us in looking for visions in the last days of time."[18]
Three months passed before Ellen sent in her own account of what
she had "seen."

While promoting her visions, however, James urged a limited
view of their authority. The Bible was "a perfect and complete revelation," the "only rule of faith and practice," he wrote. True visions
would lead believers to God and the Bible. But he saw no reason why
God could not "show us the past, present, and future fulfillment of his
word, in these *last days*, by dreams and visions," as the Apostle Peter

had predicted.[19] The place of Mrs. White's visions in Adventism was, therefore, much less powerful than the one Joseph Smith's revelations occupied in the Church of Jesus Christ of Latter-day Saints. Although Mormons felt Smith's revelations did not contradict the Bible, from the outset his writings had equal authority to it, and soon included doctrines he did not claim were found in Scripture.[20] James White, perhaps with Smith in mind, said that any vision "given for a new rule of faith and practice, separate from the Bible, cannot be of God, and should be rejected."[21] To highlight his belief in the harmony between Ellen's visions and Holy Writ, James provided scores of Scriptural footnotes when he republished her early revelations in 1847.[22] When accusations continued that Adventists based their faith on visions instead of the Bible, James, for several years, left Ellen's testimonies out of the *Review*.[23]

James observed that the American people were "a nation of Lords," who prided themselves on their right to "think, speak, and act independently." Thus it was difficult for them to "waive private judgment and take testimony coming from another." Nevertheless, he said, there were several reasons why they should accept his wife's visions as being from God. Among these was the fact that the Bible promised visions in the last days. Furthermore, White argued, true prophets pointed out sins while false ones cried "peace." His wife's visions must be genuine revelations, he argued; for twenty years they had consistently exalted God, reinforced his commandments, and comforted the desponding. Moreover, he wrote, "the brethren at Battle Creek," the church headquarters where the Whites lived, were acquainted with the prophetess, had seen her in vision and heard her "talk with power," and had been "baptized with the same Spirit," and had said that the evidence was sufficient to prove her divine credentials.[24]

James defended the style as well as the content of his wife's messages by putting her sharp rebukes in the best possible light. She called the congregation in Wright, Michigan, together one afternoon in 1867 to hear her read fifty-one pages of "testimony" she had written concerning various church members. "Those reproved," James reported, "were, of course, surprised to hear their condition described, and were thrown into great trial."[25] Later, his ingenious defense of his wife's reproofs offered the condemned members a way to save face. Most of them were not willing to reject Ellen's testimonies out of hand, but neither could they believe that they were as guilty as she seemed to think. James accepted that as an honest position, and protected their dignity by noting that since the rebukes came as a surprise to them, they were not hypocrites, but had been "sincere in error and wrong."[26]

James White's autobiography, *Life Incidents*, published in 1868, included descriptions of Ellen physical state while in trance. He stressed that the visions occurred under a variety of circumstances and argued that her health was actually better immediately after a vision. He also took the occasion to refute slanders which had been directed at his wife and the movement, and to present his scriptural arguments in favor of the perpetuity of "spiritual gifts" beyond the apostolic age.[27] In 1880, while revising the book, he spent an afternoon in the Battle Creek Church answering objections to her testimonies. When someone asked whether her messages were influenced by her reading or conversations, he observed that for her to have written her thousands of pages of private testimonies and her many books all on the basis of what church members had told her and what she had read, while at the same time traveling, raising a family, and constantly attending meetings, would have required a wonderful memory and a "philosophic mind beyond any person that lives." She was not educated, he said, had been sick a large part of the time, and did not have the intellectual capacity to frame "the beautiful theories" presented in her writings. Reporting the meeting to Ellen, James said he realized "why the Lord chose one in feebleness, and without a mind strengthened and disciplined to reason by study. From these facts will be our strongest appeal to the people."[28]

Since the Whites functioned as a leadership team, Ellen's support of James was also crucial to the success of their movement. In the early days of their marriage, her visions gave him guidance and encouragement. This was no typical case of a Victorian wife providing her husband with the spiritual nurture he lacked because he was an aggressive male.[29] At least during the first half of their marriage, they accepted each other as spiritual equals. Ellen simply had special access to divine revelations. Her visions directed their travels: "Ellen has seen in vision that we should go west before the Lord comes; therefore I believe we shall go," James wrote a friend in 1847.[30] And again: "Since I have been writing the brethren have flocked in and Ellen has had a most glorious vision. She has seen in vision that we shall go father before we return to Maine."[31]

In 1849, when the visions encouraged James to start a "little paper," the *Present Truth* was launched in Middletown, Connecticut. Yet Joseph Bates, who, along with James and Ellen White, is also designated a "founder" of the Seventh-day Adventist Church, was against the publishing project. Early in 1850 he convinced James to give it up. While her husband was in a "depressed, miserable state of mind" over this failure, Ellen was "taken off in vision" again: "I saw that paper, and that it was needed," she said. "I saw that God did not want James to stop yet; but he must *write, write, write, write,* and speed the message."[32] James took heart and wrote Bates, confident that the vision would make him "see a little differently on some things."[33]

On many such occasions Ellen's visions rescued James from deep discouragement. After eleven numbers of *Present Truth* appeared at irregular intervals, she encouraged him to establish the *Second Advent Review and Sabbath Herald* in Paris, Maine, in November of 1850. The paper moved to Saratoga Springs, New York, in 1851, and to Rochester in 1852.[34] Times were hard in Rochester. James complained when two fellow ministers were given $30 apiece while he, Ellen, and their houseful of workers were living on turnips. But, when tempted to bitterness, he wrote: "I have some encouragement through visions. Ellen sees that I must trust in God, and take care of myself."[35]

Ellen was just as supportive of James's authority and he was of hers. She declared she had seen in vision how God had given James "experience and placed him in the [publishing] Office to manage the work." Insofar as she was concerned, there was no one who could fill his place in the work.[36] God had inspired the confidence the people placed "in his ability to manage and they felt safe to entrust means to his care to appropriate and dispose of according to his judgment." God had thus chosen her husband and herself "to bear burdens, to reprove individual wrongs, and to act a prominent part in the cause of God."[37] Ellen said that in visions she had been "pointed back" to the beginning of the movement and "shown" that God had pushed James forward in order that "he might obtain an experience to fill the place He designed for him to occupy as one to manage His cause, to forward the work, to take responsibilities, and to risk something on the success of this message." God, she said, had made him His agent to "stir up to zealous action."[38]

Mrs. White had the greatest adoration for her husband's abilities and dedication. She believed God had given him a "giant intellect." and "penetrating insight" together with "executive ability in a large degree."[39] Years later, she looked back over her husband's career and wrote:

> He started in the ardor of youth and devoted the tireless energy of his manhood to the service of Christ, seeking to warn sinners and to proclaim the last note of warning to the world. …God united us that he might be a helper to me to bear the reproach I should suffer for the truth's sake. He has had unabated zeal in the great work in which he has been engaged. He has sought to inspire others with the earnestness and energy which has characterized his own life.[40]

Given their symbiotic relationship, all that Ellen did to advance James's leadership also strengthened her own position.

Up until the last decade of their life together, Ellen defended James against the two major criticisms which surfaced repeatedly throughout his life: that he was too harsh and plain-spoken in his rebukes, and that, obsessed with greed, he mishandled church funds and used his position for personal financial gain. These criticisms of James first emerged in 1850 during the White's stay in Paris, Maine, where they boarded for a time with the family of Edward and Sarah Andrews. While there, James vigorously rebuked some of the Paris Adventists and acquired the reputation for harshness and severity which would stay with him throughout his life.[41] These incidents were especially important because the Andrews's son, John, eventually married a woman from Paris, Angeline Stevens, and went on to become the church's leading Biblical scholar and a much-respected writer and evangelist. Angeline's sister, Harriet, married Uriah Smith who later served for many years as editor of the *Review and Herald*. The Stevens family was, if anything, even more critical of James White's style than were the Andrews. Since he always supported Ellen's visions, and since Ellen always defended his rebukes, the Andrews and Stevens families both doubted Ellen's visions and criticized James's leadership.[42]

In the summer of 1860, Mrs. White wrote Harriet Stevens Smith a stinging letter complaining of her bad influence on her husband. "I was pointed back to Paris in a vision," Ellen said. The Paris Adventists were wrong to feel that James was "censorious and severe." The vision indicated that the Andrews and Stevens families were "linked together" and "strengthened each other's hands against Brother White."[43] Individuals were watching James White with jealousy and suspicion, Mrs. White wrote. They did not like his "plain testimony" because it did not suit their "natural feelings." When everything went along smoothly, "then past dissatisfactions and difficulties [originating] in Paris lie dormant, but when reproof is given, the same warfare commences." When this letter arrived, Harriet was visiting her parents in Iowa, where they had moved in 1856. She was so upset that she returned to Battle Creek immediately. It was several years before relations between the Whites, Andrews and Stevens improved, but Ellen would not let the matter rest until James was vindicated and confessions were received from the offenders.

Late in 1860, the Whites' fourth child, an infant just three months old, died. The blow, added to the criticisms of fellow believers, devastated them. At the depth of their despair, Ellen had another vision, and now ventured to defend her husband in print for the first time in a *Testimony for the Church*. James, who had "faithfully met error and wrong" was "grieved and wounded" when he did not receive "the fullest sympathy of his preaching brethren" she said. He became so discouraged "in discharging such painful duties" that he was withholding the "very testimony God designed should live in the church."[44] God would not accept the "smooth testimony" that some of the Adventist ministers gave. Instead, they must "cry aloud and spare not." The "living, pointed testimony" was meant to develop character and purify the church.[45] All along, she said, there had been those who were ready to speak "smooth things, daub with untempered mortar" and destroy the influence of their own work. The ministers of the "nominal" churches, she said, already did enough "scringing and crippling, and wrapping up pointed truths." Adventist ministers should let the truth "tear off the garment of security, and find its way to the heart."[46] Satan was working to get people jealous and then dissatisfied "with those at the head of the work." Consequently, her own testimony came to have "but little weight. Instructions given through vision are disregarded."[47]

She and James were especially distressed because those who had been "closely connected" with them in the work, [doubtless J. N. Andrews and Uriah Smith] and had "witnessed the manifestations of the power of God many times," during her visions, still allowed Satan to control their minds" with doubts.[48] While brooding on his difficulties one Saturday as he was entering the church, James was so overpowered with a "sense of injustice" that he stopped and wept aloud while the whole congregation waited. At moments like this, Ellen was not above appealing to the emotions of her fellow believers in an attempt to win sympathy for herself and her husband:

The cause of God is a part of us. Our experience and lives

are interwoven with this work. We have had no separate existence. It has been a part of our very being. The believers in present truth have seemed as near as our children. When the cause of God prospers we are happy, but when wrongs exist among the people of God we are unhappy, and nothing can make us glad. The earth, its treasures and joys, are nothing to us. Our interest is not here. Is it strange that my husband, with his sensitive feelings, should suffer in mind?[49]

Harriet Smith called James White's style "cutting and slashing."[50] J. N. Andrews put it more gently: "certainly no one is so faithful in plainness of speech."[51] Yet Ellen defended him steadily, appealing sometimes to the example of Moses to demonstrate her husband's relationship to the laity as well as to church leaders. Moses' brother Aaron, "with his amiable disposition, so very mild and pleasing," would seek to conciliate Moses when the Israelites committed great sin. Aaron, she wrote, thought Moses "too unyielding" and wished he had been "less firm, less decided" in order to avoid trouble with the people.[52]

For those familiar with the personalities of the leaders in Battle Creek, it was clear that Uriah Smith was Aaron to James White's Moses. Ellen imagined church members saying: "What an easy, happy time we were having. The church was in a pleasant condition. We were doing well. But lo! Here comes Elder White and his wife, the disturbers of Israel.... If they only had the sweet spirit of Elder Smith; he never hurts anyone's feelings, he never says sharp and cutting things."[53]

It is hard to imagine that James White could have been any more "sharp and cutting" than Ellen herself, yet few criticisms of this sort were leveled at her. Perhaps James provided a kind of lightning rod for criticism which was attracted as much by her words as his. Given the belief that Ellen was only passing on what God had told her people were probably afraid to criticize her directly. One layman said that though he had "never felt fully satisfied" in regard to the validity of her visions, he had "tried not to harbor any feelings against them, "lest he be fighting against God."[54] The principal complaint about Ellen seems to have been that she embarrassed people by publicly issuing her messages to individual members. J. N. Andrews confessed that the visions were such a source of "terror and distress" to him that he could not "make that use of them that is such a blessing to others." For those who felt this way, James White was a less formidable target, yet one just as satisfying to strike since James's prestige and authority was so closely linked to Ellen's.[55]

Aside from the charge of harshness, the most frequent criticism of James White involved his handling of money. Seventh-day Adventists, from their earliest days, had attracted a disproportionate number of prosperous farmers and other rural people in their ranks.[56] Perhaps it offended them to see a minister so frequently involved in complex financial transactions. But paper and printing presses cost money; travelling ministers needed cash for food, clothing and transportation. Before the church instituted any regular system of financial support, most of these needs were met by James White's appeals or supplied from his generous pocket. He floated one fundraising scheme after another, raising money to build homes for half a dozen ministers, to buy tents for evangelistic meetings, to purchase books for theological and historical research, and to buy printing presses and build an office for the publishing association.[57]

Ellen insisted James was not a selfish schemer.[58] "He has encouraged liberality.... and has censured selfishness," she argued. "He has pleaded for donations to the cause of God and, to encourage liberality in his brethren, has led off by liberal donations himself."[59] Ellen said that James' aptness for business had in fact led many of his fellow ministers to give him responsibilities which they should have born themselves.[60] Moreover, he had also been eager to "stand in defense of the widow and the fatherless, to be kind to the poor, to help the needy."[61] Charges of "dishonest dealing" simply did not stand against him.[62]

It was not merely the sharing of careers that made the early years of the White marriage remarkable. One study, which included James and Ellen along with other reform couples in the mid-nineteenth century, indicated that several reformers married like-minded individuals and shared careers.[63] However, the same study noted that in several cases, these successful marriages were preceded by unsuccessful ones. There is also a substantial difference between sharing a career in reform and sharing the top leadership of a movement. Leadership involves much deeper ego and identity dynamics since leaders must call for people to follow them, not just to accept a concept or cause.

The experience of Alma and Kent White demonstrates all too well the difficulties of would-be church leaders who are not compatibly wedded. After an unhappy Kentucky childhood, Alma Bridwell was teaching school in Montana when Kent arrived to preach in the local Methodist Church.[64] She had already decided to marry no one but a preacher, and the two struck up a friendship. After corresponding for several years, they were married in 1887.[65] At the time, Kent was studying religion at the University of Colorado. According to Alma's autobiography, their conflicts started almost immediately when he persuaded her to go to the local opera house to see Edwin

Booth in *Hamlet*. She came away feeling terribly guilty and began to distrust her new husband's religious experience. When Kent's mother moved in with the young couple, matters worsened. Alma's account of these events was written through the painful memory of a failed marriage, but even her childhood memories reflect a deep fear of losing the love of those close to her. At any rate, she soon suspected her mother-in-law of "poisoning" Kent's mind against her.[66]

Soon after Kent took his first parish, Alma began to play a more public role than he had anticipated. She took his pulpit and initiated her own revival in 1894, followed by several school-house meetings.[67] Kent was not only disturbed by her assertiveness, he also took strong exception to her free-wheeling Biblical interpretations.[68] He soon discovered he had married a woman whose religion was less sophisticated and whose loyalty to the Methodist church was less strong than his. Alma resented Kent's efforts to organize her converts into Methodist classes.[69] They worked together with varying degrees of friction for some five years in the Colorado Holiness Association, although near the end Alma suspected Kent of conspiring with the leaders to freeze her out of speaking appointments at the annual camp meeting. Undaunted, she asked for a chance to preach, then literally seized the pulpit while the perplexed leaders were huddling over her request.[70]

Alma White appears to have had more native talent than her husband, and despite his opposition, she organized the Pentecostal Union Church in December of 1901, later changing the name to the Pillar of Fire.[71] According to Alma, Kent was tormented by his own lack of spirituality as well as by her independent spirit.[72] Soon after she moved her headquarters to New Jersey in 1908, he found a way to assert his independence: he began to advocate the new "Pentecostal" idea of speaking in tongues.[73] Although Alma's religion was vigorously emotional, she joined other leaders of the holiness movement in rejecting tongue speaking a device of the devil and "nothing more than gibberish such as Mormons and Spiritualists have used in their deceptive arts for many years."[74]

About this same time, Alma began to suspect Kent was ambitious to take over the leadership of her movement.[75] He was obviously frustrated by his minor role in it, and bristled when newspapers referred to him as "Mrs. Alma White's husband."[76] For her part, Alma insisted she had never disputed his headship of "home government," but she believed God had called her, not him, to lead the Pillar of Fire.[77]

Soon after this, in the fall of 1909, he left for England where he joined the Apostolic Faith Movement.[78] In spite of Alma's numerous efforts to affect a reconciliation, Kent did not return to his family until shortly before his death in 1940. His son believed that he "stood in combined awe, admiration and fear" of Alma, and at the end of his life "seemed amazed and pleased at all the progress and influence of the Pillar of Fire."[79]

Ellen White was more fortunate, at least in the early years of her marriage. James knew from the beginning that she would be more than a submissive wife. In their mutual efforts to shape the disordered remnants of the Millerite movement into a viable church, each was able to support the other when discipline had to be administered. If people thought them unnecessarily severe, each could count on defense from the other.

The cases of Mary Baker Eddy and Alma White suggest that had James White not been at Ellen's side to handle administrative and promotional duties, her role in the movement might have been much more prominent than it was. Instead, in the early days of the movement it was possible for Seventh-day Adventists, even a leading minister such as Uriah Smith or J. N. Andrews, to have serious doubts about the validity of Ellen White's gift, yet still remain in the church. When a new church was organized in Wisconsin, she herself did not want members excluded who had never seen her, had little knowledge of her visions, and were skeptical of them.[80]

———————

[1]Katherine DuPre Lumpkin, *The Emancipation -of Angelina Grimke* (Chapel Hill, N.C., 1974), 184-185.

[2]Doborah Pickman Clifford, *Mine Eyes Have Seen the Glory* (Boston, 1978), 63-64, 82-83, 118-119, 162-164, 167, 177.

[3]Lois W. Banner, Elizabeth Cady Stanton: A Radical for Woman's Rights (Boston, 1980), 33-38, 111.

[4]Richard Wheatley, *The Life and Letters of Phoebe Palmer* (New York, 1876), 22-24, 133,141-144; Timothy L. Smith, *Revivalism and Social Reform* (New York, 1957), 116-117, 122-124; Ernest Wall, "I Commend Unto You Phoebe," *Religion in Life*, vol. 26 (Summer, 1957), 396-408. Wall's article is largely based on Wheatley's book, but does contain some comparisons between Palmer and Catherine of Siena. Assuming it was in part a more prestigious role for the wife than for the husband that made the marriages of nineteenth century female leaders problematic, the Palmers had the advantage that the husband, Walter, carried on a successful and lucrative career of his own as a physician.

[5]On Methodism's encouragement of women leaders, see Lucille Sider Dayton and Donald W. Dayton, "'Your Daughters Shall Prophesy:' Feminism in the Holiness Movement," *Methodist History*, vol. 14 (Jan. 1976), 68-70.

[6]John Maniha and Barbara B. Maniha, "A Comparison of Psychohistorical Differences Among Some Female Religious and Secular Leaders," *The Journal of Psychohistory*, vol. 5 (Spring, 1978),523-549.

[7]For example, William Lloyd Garrison's "successful"" marriage entailed no public role for his wife. John L. Thomas, *The Liberator: William Lloyd Garrison, A Biography* (Boston, 1963), 179-181; Russel B. Nye, *William Lloyd Garrison and the Humanitarian Reformers* (Boston, 1955), 150-151.

[8]Robert Peel, *Mary Baker Eddy: The Years of Discovery* (New York, 1966), 72, 200-203, 357; *Mary Baker Eddy: The Years of Trial* (New York, 1971), 19, 65.

[9]Ron Graybill, "The Courtship of Ellen Harmon" *Insight*, vol. 4 (Jan. 23, 1973), 4-7; Ellen G. White, *Life Sketches* (Battle Creek Mich., 1880), 238.

[10]Virgil Robinson, *James White* (Washington, D.C., 1976), 13-18; Don F. Neufeld, ed., *Seventh-day Adventist Encyclopedia*, rev. ed. (Washington, D.C., 1976), s.v. "James White".

[11]Winfred Garrison and Alfred T. DeGroot, *The Disciples of Christ: A History*

(St. Louis, 1948), 87-92; David Millard, "Christians, or Christian Connexion," in I. Daniel Rupp, ed., *An Original History of the Religious Denominations at Present Existing the United States* (Philadelphia, 1844), 166-170; N. Summerhill, *History of the Christian Church* (Cincinnati, 1873).

[12]James White, *Life Incidents*, 72-120; Virgil Robinson, *James White*, 18-32.

[13]Carl Degler, *At Odds: Women and the Family in America from the Revolution to the Present* (New York, 1980), 26.

[14]James White to "My Dear Brother Jacobs," *Day Star*, vol. 7 (Sept. 27, 1845), 47; Carl Degler, *At Odds*, 8-19, discusses the shift toward marriages based on mutual affection during this period.

[15]Ellen G. White, Writing and Sending Out of the Testimonies to the Church Sanitarium, Calif., [1913], 4.

[16]James White to Willie White, May 7, 1876.

[17]Martha Saxton, *Louisa May: A Modern Biography of Louisa May Alcott* {Boston, 1977),301-302,317; Helen Papashvily, *All The Happy Endings: A Study of the Domestic Novel in America* (New York, 1956), 118.

[18]James White to "Dear Bro. Jacobs," *Day Star*, vol. 7 (Sept. 6, 1845), 18.

[19]Ibid., 13.

[20]James B. Allen and Glen M. Leonard, *The Story of the Latter-day Saints* (Salt Lake City, Utah, 1976), 65-70; Leonard J. Arrington and David Bitton, *The Mormon Experience: A History of the Latter-day Saints* (New York, 1979, 30-32.

[21]James White, *A Word to the "Little Flock"* (Brunswick, Maine, 1847), 13.

[22]Ibid.

[23]Infra, 103.

[24]James White, "Report from Bro. White. No. 3," *Review and Herald*, vol. 29 (Jan. 29, 1867),87.

[25]Ibid., 86.

[26]Ibid., 87.

[27]James White, *Life Incidents*, x, 271-274, 312-313, 318-320, 324-331.

[28]James White to Ellen G. White, March 20, 1880.

[29]Carl Degler, *At Odds*, 30,38.

[30]James White to Sister Hastings, Aug. 22, 1847.

[31]James White to "My Dear Brother," July 1, 1848.

[32]Ellen G. White, Manuscript 2, January 9, 1850 (written at Oswego, NY).

[33]James White to Brother Hastings, Jan. 10, 1850.

[34]Don F. Neufeld, ed., *Seventh-day Adventist Encyclopedia*, rev. ed., s. v., "Review and Herald."

[35]James White to Brother Abraham [Dodge], July 31, 1853

[36]Ellen G. White, "The Review Office," c. 1864, Ms. 1, 1864.

[37]Ellen G. White to Brother Ingraham, c. 1864, Letter 15, 1864

[38]Ellen G. White to Brother Byington, c. 1864, Letter 14, 1864.

[39]Ellen G. White to James White, July 2, 1874, Letter 38, 1874; Ellen G. White, "Trials of James White," c. 1875, Ms. 4, 1875.

[40]Ellen G. White to Brother [Diggins], Dec. 18, 1872, Letter 22, 1872

[41]Ron Graybill, "J. N. Andrews as a Family Man," (duplicated, Washington, D.C., 1979).

[42]Ellen G. White to Harriet Stevens, June, 1860, Letter 8, 1860; A. S. Andrews to Brother and Sister White, Jan. 30, 1862; Almira Stevens to Brother and Sister White, Jan. 23, 1862; P. R. Stevens to Sister White, Jan. 27, 1862; Edward Andrews to Brother and Sister White, Jan. 25, 1863.

[43]Ellen G. White to Harriet Smith, June, 1860, Letter 7, 1860.

[44]Ellen G. White, *Testimonies for the Church*, vol. 1 (Mountain View, Calif., 1948), 213, first published in Testimony for the Church, No. 6 (Battle Creek, Mich., 1866). The currently published nine volumes of *Testimonies for the Church* (1948), originally appeared in 37 separately numbered pamphlets and books, beginning in 1855. I will indicate the date when the original appeared, but cite the current edition.

[45]Ibid., 216.

[46]Ibid., 249.

[47]Ibid., 236.

[48]Ibid., 246.

[49]Ellen G. White to Lucinda Abbey, Apr. 5, 1861, Letter 5a, 1861.

[50]Ellen G. White to Sisters Harriet, Cornelia, and Martha, Sept. 24, 1869, Letter 13, 1869.

[51]J. N. Andrews, "The Labors of Brother and Sister White," *Review and Herald*, vol. 31 (Mar. 3, 1868), 184.

[52]Ellen G. White, *Testimonies for the Church*, vol. 3, 298, first published 1873.

[53]Ellen G. White, *The Judgement* (Battle Creek, Mich., 1879), 13.

[54]Jonathan Chase, in "Extracts from Letters," *Review and Herald*, vol. 7 (Mar. 6, 1856), 183.

[55]J. N. Andrews to Brother White, Feb. 2, 1862.

[56]Ron Graybill, "Millenarians and Money: Adventist Wealth and Adventist Beliefs," *Spectrum*, vol. 10 (Aug., 1979), 31-41. Adventists were, on average, wealthier than their neighbors, but concentrated in independent occupations like farming, probably because this enabled them to observe Saturday as the Sabbath. Already in 1860 they had more lawyers and doctors among them than the general population, but far fewer laborers.

[57][Uriah Smith, et. al.], *Vindication of the Business Career of Elder James White*, (Battle Creek, Mich., 1863).

[58]Ellen G. White, *Testimonies for the Church*, vol. 3, 89, first published 1872.

[59]Ibid.

[60]Ibid., 95.

[61]Ellen G. White, *The Judgment*, 14.

[62]Ibid., 21; The worst that could be said of James—and this was an isolated incident—was that once, while raising money for a Book Fund, he decided how much money certain families could afford to pledge and, in a few cases, changed

pledges already made. He then set the list in type and mailed out the proofs seeking approval (prior to publication) from all those whose pledges he had assigned or changed. This obviously created a fair degree of pressure on would-be donors. It would have been embarrassing to anyone of them to request that their pledge be lowered. [J. N. Andrews, et. al.], *Defense of Eld. James White and Wife; Vindication of Their Moral and Christian Character* (Battle Creek, Mich., 1870), 15-18.

[63]Donald R. Kennon, "'A Knit of Identity,' Marriage and Reform in Mid-Victorian America" (Ph.D. dissertation, University of Maryland, 1981).

[64]Alma White, *Looking Back to Beulah* (Zarephath, N.J., 1929), 61-63,77-78; *The Story of My Life*, vol. 1 (Zarephath, N.J., 1935), 11-90, 229.

[65]Alma White, *Looking Back to Beulah*, 113, 120; *The Story of My Life*, vol. 1, 235, 285, 292, 299.

[66]Alma White, *The Story of my Life*, vol. 1,302,316

[67]Ibid., 29, *The Story of my Life*, vol. 2 (Zarephath, N.J., 1935), 35.

[68]Infra., 120-121.

[69]Ibid., 83, 122.

[70]Ibid., v, 117, 132-133.

[71]Ibid., v, 201.

[72]Ibid., 208, 218, 226.

[73]Alma White, *The Story of My Life*, vol. 3 (Zarephath, N.J., 1936), iii, 96-97, 115-116, 125.

[74]Ibid., 21.

[75]Ibid., 116.

[76]Ibid., 144.

[77]Ibid., 117,146.

[78]Ibid., 147, 164; Alma White, *My Heart and Husband* {Zarephath, N.J., 1923), 4, 67, 83. This book contains some correspondence which, even in edited form, seems naively revealing of the sources of conflict between Kent and Alma.

[79]Arthur K. White, *Some White Family History* (Denver, Col., 1948), 400-402.

[80]Ellen G. White, *Testimonies for the Church*, vol. 1, 327, first published 1862.

CHAPTER TWO

Charisma in Conflict

The last decade and a half of the White's marriage—till James's death in 1881—saw Ellen emerge as the dominant figure in the home and an independent leader in the church. This process was necessary because several cerebral hemorrhages impaired James's physical and emotional health and because James problems finally began to threaten Ellen's influence. Although the Whites shared many expressions of affection during these years, Ellen's defense of James was muted, and there were agonizing conflicts between them as she began to criticize his course. Neither of them had an adequate understanding of the psychological damage strokes often cause.[1] Both suffered as they saw the harmony of their early years erode.

In Mary Baker Eddy's contrasting experience, there was no struggle for independent leadership. Her first two marriages were virtually over by the time she launched her movement. By the time she married again she was, in Robert Peel's words, "inseverably wedded to an idea so that her marriage was primarily a means of carrying on more effectively the great task to which that idea had committed her."[2] Her third husband, Asa Gilbert Eddy, was a salesman for the Singer Sewing Machine Company when, in 1876, he sought the then Mrs. Patterson for relief from a chronic heart ailment. In his middle forties, he was a mild man with a kindly smile and a fondness for children. When his heart difficulties abated under the new treatment, he committed himself totally to Christian Science and became a healer himself. A few months later, when he called Mary out of a violent seizure, she felt a sudden affection for him. "Never before had I seen his real character, so tender and yet so controlling," she said.[3] He proposed marriage, and Mary, encouraged by a dream, accepted. The vows were solemnized by a Unitarian clergyman.[4]

The new husband gave up his private practice of Christian Science healing to devote himself wholeheartedly to his wife. His role and hers were exact reversals of the typical nineteenth century marriage. At times, he even took over the cooking and sewing.[5] His position aroused some jealousy among other Christian Scientists until they saw that he served as Mrs. Eddy's lieutenant rather than her mentor and supported her decisions totally. In 1879, when she was pastor and president of the Mother Church in Boston, he attended services in his faultless Prince Albert, helped as an usher, and chatted with interested newcomers. He was aptly described by one observer as part of "a necessary background."[6]

James White, however, had always been in the foreground of Ellen White's career. When his problems came in conflict with Ellen's charismatic calling, he had to be moved. As early as 1863, Ellen saw in a vision that James was violating the laws of health through overwork, and that this was not pleasing to God. In the fall of 1865, following a particularly exhausting and anxiety-ridden trip west, James and Ellen were taking their usual early morning walk. As they stopped to chat with a neighbor and inspect his corn, James made a strange noise. Ellen turned to see his face flushed and one arm hanging helpless at his side as he staggered, about to fall. He had suffered a serious stroke.[7] Always before, Ellen had been the invalid of the family, and James had nursed and cared for her. Now the roles were reversed, not only in the home but, from this point onward, more and more in public life as well.

At first Ellen was terrified at the thought that her husband might die. Fighting back these fears, however, she refused to let James even consider the possibility of his death. When he called for a lawyer to put his affairs in order, she would not allow it.[8] For three weeks she did not leave his side, exhausting herself in prayer and attempts to administer water treatments. James improved slightly, but very slowly. After five weeks, Ellen concluded it would be best to take him to Dansville, New York, for treatment at Dr. James Caleb Jackson's water cure, "Our Home on the Hillside." There her devotion to his health continued. He was so nervous he could not sleep nights, and she would often be roused to massage his limbs and pray him into peaceful slumber.[9] When, after more than two months at Dansville, he took a turn for the worse and began to think again that he might die, she decided to take his case into her own hands. She feared Dr. Jackson was confusing James by urging him to get his mind off religious things. Like other conservative Christians at Jackson's establishment, the Whites were troubled by the dancing, card playing, and theatrical entertainment there. Ellen decided it would be best to return to the company of their "tried and true friends" in Battle Creek. She believed their prayers could revive James's courage and determination to live. The journey was undertaken in stages, and after a three week lay-over in Rochester, the Whites came home to a warm house and a hot meal prepared by their friends.[10]

All winter James remained an invalid. Ellen somehow sensed that he needed activity, exercise, and something to take his mind off himself. When the Michigan snow lay deep around their house, she led him on daily walks, making tracks for him to follow. She drug him along on a trip to Wright, Michigan, against the tearful protests of his aged parents who lived nearby. "That brain," she told them, "that noble, masterly mind, shall not be left in ruins . . . You will yet see us standing side by side in the sacred desk."[11]

Prior to James's illness, Ellen had not conducted preaching services as such. The usual practice was for James to preach in the morning and Ellen to give her "testimony" at the "social meeting" in the afternoon. But now, with her husband incapacitated, she began preaching and her articles began to appear in "The Sermon" section of the church paper.[12]

During the six weeks in Wright, Michigan, Ellen continued to nurse James. She sat dutifully by, pen in hand, while he dictated reports of their meetings for the *Review*. He began to preach again, and she thought he was growing "stronger and more connected" in his subjects. Finally, when he spoke clearly for an hour, Ellen was overcome with tears of joy.[13] For the first time, though, her accounts begin to refer to him as her helper. As she counseled church members in the area, she found that "no other two of our ministers" could have rendered her the assistance that James did.[14] As success began to attend her efforts as a preacher, she "became fully convinced" that she "had a testimony for the people" which she could bear "in connection with"

James. Still, she felt dependent upon him in her new role.[15]

Even though she had willingly nursed him during his illness, her gratitude was unbounded now that she would be "unfettered" to go back to work "standing by the side" of her husband. Her published testimonies began to imply he was giving up leadership duties to work more closely with her. "Our gifts are needed in the same field in writing and speaking. While my husband is overburdened, as he has been, with an accumulation of cares and financial matters, his mind cannot be as fruitful in the word as it would be."[16] At the beginning of the work, Ellen wrote, someone was needed to lead out, but now that the church had become a fully organized body, it was time for her husband to cease to act alone as a leader.[17]

James continued to have his physical ups and downs, however. In 1866, the family moved to a little farm near Greenville, Michigan, in order to escape the turmoil of Battle Creek and in hopes that outdoor life might aid in James's rehabilitation.[18] When the time came to get the hay in, Ellen persuaded him to drive the horses while she and their 12 year old son Willie pitched it on the wagon. Then she got him to pitch the hay off while she stacked it. Neighbors who had heard this little woman preach in church on the weekend were "curious and amazed" to see her out in the field pitching hay as well, but she was "not at all troubled" by this. "Little by little I was, by the help of God, able to lead my husband to exercise and thus lead him to forget himself."[19]

James White's illness crippled the family's finances. In order to purchase the farm in Greenville, he sold property in Battle Creek. When the buyer failed to pay, he had to sell off furniture and household goods to make ends meet. He pressed hard to get the church's new water-cure establishment, the Western Health Reform Institute, to purchase his house in Battle Creek.[20] Soon grumblings about his sharp financial dealings began, and on trips back to Battle Creek the Whites encountered a barrage of critical rumors.[21] Ellen was devastated. She wept aloud for hours.[22] She finally called church leaders together and replied to the charges brought against her and her husband. Eventually harmony was restored. Then she issued an 80-page *Testimony for the Church* in which the unhappy history of the period was recounted.[23] Included was a confession of apology from the Battle Creek Church. Included also was an article designed to set straight those who had assumed that James White illness was a punishment for the "cutting and slashing" style of his verbal reproofs. Ellen did, however, issue some gentle rebukes for his tendency to recall past injustices and not be as forgiving as he should have been.[24]

Life was not easy for Ellen during this period. Sometimes she had to apologize to her husband for the way she had "felt or spoken."[25] James was so wrapped up in his own difficulties that he could not always help with her problems:

> No one, not even my husband, can have an understanding of my mind. He is a stranger to my trials, my temptations, my conflicts and buffetings. His own case occupies his mind, and I ought not to expect that appreciation of my peculiar position my spirit so earnestly craves. I long to lean upon someone, but God sees perhaps this is not best, and breaks my hold from everyone that I shall cling to Him alone.[26]

Before his illness, Ellen had sometimes cautioned James privately about certain weaknesses. He dwelt too much on the past, she said, and did not have the same "spirit of forgiveness" that Jesus possessed. He should delegate responsibilities and not think that everything had to be done up to his own standards of perfection. After his illness, for the first time, she began to allude to some of his failings in print, though at first she excused them. "My husband has sometimes, under the pressure of care, spoken without due consideration and with apparent severity" she said in one *Testimony*. At the same time, she criticized him for "living over the unhappy past."[27] On the charge of harshness, she admitted James might be "in danger of not being so careful in his manner of reproving as to give no occasion for reflection, but quickly added that some of those who criticized him also used "cutting and condemnatory language."[28] Finally, in 1875, she spoke clearly: "I was shown that my husband's course has not been perfect. He has erred sometimes in murmuring and in giving too severe reproof.[29] This was her first clear, public admission of James White's harshness. It was also her last. After this her published *Testimonies* were virtually silent about him. Ellen's public comments about her husband had thus moved from spirited defense through veiled criticism to explicit rebuke and finally silence.

In private letters and diaries a richer interplay was developing. At times, James's emotional problems were so acute that Ellen almost despaired of their further usefulness together. In spite of the fact that J. N. Andrews and others had apologized profusely for their criticism of him, James continued to harbor his wounded feelings and, in 1871, apparently proposed to publish an account of the errors of Andrews and other church leaders. Ellen told him his imagination was diseased, that God had forgiven these men and that she could not "go one step" with him in his plan. "I dare not do it," she said, "even for your love and confidence." James accused her repeatedly of having more sympathy for Andrews and others than for him. "I know that is not true," she said. She begged him to "take his hands off these men and leave them with a little spark of courage and of their manhood."[30]

Although Ellen had joined James in his suspicions and criticisms in the late 1860's, by the early 70's she had come to feel he had been more at fault. Still, she stood by him in every way she could. She even offered to join him in retirement:

> Let us step quietly from the work, cease writing and laboring, and then see how we feel. I will be a true and faithful wife to you. But I cannot violate my conscience in pursuing a course which will please you when I have the clearest evidence that God would not be honored.[31]

While Ellen interpreted James's failings primarily in spiritual terms, she was always alert for physical explanations as well. She held to the then-popular phrenological concepts of brain function which taught that for a person to be "well-balanced" he needed to give equal exercise to all of the "higher powers" or "organs" of the brain while he kept the "animal passions" or "lower powers" in strict subjection. She spoke of how his "cautiousness, conscientiousness, and benevolence" had been "large and active." These had "been special blessings in qualifying him for his business career," but during his illness, these "special developments, which had been a blessing to him in health, were painfully excitable, and a hindrance to his recovery."[32]

Early in 1872, Ellen sometimes went weeks without a full night's rest. James would be "threatened with paralysis in his right arm and limb" and would "not be able to exercise his brain in the least perplexing matters."[33] In all likelihood, James was still suffering mild strokes from time to time, and these upset his emotional as well as physical health. At other times Ellen was able to announce that James

was "very cheerful and like his own self again." He was preaching "to the point" and "had nothing discouraging to say."[34]

By December of 1872, James was down again. For two weeks he could not walk without dizziness and great weakness. During an intensive two-hour prayer session, "the healing power of God came upon him," Ellen believed, and James seemed much improved. He issued a pamphlet in which he reviewed his case, confessed his failings, and suggested that others ought to do the same. "I find," he said, "that my wrongs have grown out of not being suitably affected by what God has shown my wife, especially what she has been shown of *my* dangers and wrongs." He had never doubted her visions, though he admitted he had not given those affecting him the "reflection and attention" he should have.[35]

James gradually recognized that the husband-wife relationship in his family had been an anomalous one. "It was my duty to stand by the side of Mrs. W. in her work of delivering the reproofs of the Lord," he wrote in 1873, accepting a reversal of the traditional husbandly role.[36] He explained that for the past two years a "terrible weight of discouragement and gloom" had afflicted him much of the time, but one December night he had gone out to the barn and there "fell into the hands of Christ." Then he "had a view of how terrible was the sin of those who profess to believe that God speaks to them through vision, yet from heedlessness receive no lasting impression when reproved."[37] His convictions, he said, "grew into an agony that for a time wrung my whole being. Finally, he was able to make a "full surrender of all to God" and "hope, courage, peace, and joy" took the place of his despair.[38] He saw clearly enough that it was no longer his duty to be responsible for the publishing association; rather, he would serve as counselor, if only those at the head of the work were "humble enough to ask our counsel in matters where we have experience, instead of despising it as some did in 1866-1869."[39]

Ellen was delighted with the improvement in her husband. "He is like a new man," she wrote her son. "He can exercise without painful weariness. His food does not distress him. He is cheerful and happy. He has thrown off the cares of Battle Creek to a great degree, and there is now some chance for his life.[40] Back in Battle Creek in March of 1873 Ellen was at first pleased to see that church leaders respected her husband's judgment.[41] Her happiness was short lived, however, and in May she was again reproving Uriah Smith for his ambivalence toward James. "Those who have brought reproach upon the cause of God have your pity and your sympathy," she complained.[42] Dr. John Harvey Kellogg revived the old charge that James was a "monomaniac on money matters." Discouraged, the Whites retired to the mountains of Colorado where one sleepless midnight found James roaming the cold damp streets of Black Hawk, a little mining town.[43]

By 1874 James White's continued problems were making it increasingly difficult for him and Ellen to work together. In the middle 70's she was often torn between the obligations she felt to him and the desire to exercise her own talents in public ministry: "Oh, how unreconciled I feel to be doing nothing of any account, when I know I have a testimony for the people! I long to be at work and say or do something that will advance the cause of God."[44] She wondered whether it might not be her duty to go alone on a forthcoming tour, but was fearful that James would not do as well if she left him. "We ought to labor unitedly together," she said.[45]

A month later, she decided to leave anyway.[46] James was not happy and followed her with his letters of complaint and criticism. Her response pointedly rejected his perspective on their problems:

> Don't let the enemy make you think only of my deficiencies, which are, you think, so apparent, for in trying to fix me over you may destroy your usefulness, my freedom, and bring me into a position of restraint, of embarrassment, that will unfit me for the work of God.[47]

> You must not accuse me of causing the trials of your life, because in this you deceive your own soul. It is your brooding over troubles, magnifying them, and making them real which has caused the sadness of your life. Am I to blame for this?

> I must be free from the censures you have felt free to express to me. But if I have to bear them, I shall try to do it without retaliation. I never mean to make you sad. Your life is very precious to me and to the cause of God.[48]

For the time being she had broken decisively from any feeling of subjugation to her husband. Yet even if she thought her judgment better than his, she defended her position as one of submission to God rather than defiance of her husband. Thus, like other religious women, she was able to appeal to a higher authority in order to assert herself against the tradition of male dominance.[49] She told James that her orders would henceforth come from God:

When we can work the best together we will do so. If God says it is for His glory we work apart occasionally, we will do that. But God is willing to show me my work and duty and I shall look to Him in faith and trust Him fully to lead me.[50]

"I long for perfect union," she told James, but she assured him she would not buy harmony at the expense of her conscience. She was certain James was not "led of the Lord" in the things he was saying in his letters, and she told him she was determined not to allow her own usefulness to be destroyed by his "erroneous" view of her. If they had to "walk apart the rest of the way," she hoped that at least they would not try to "pull each other down." "I do believe it is best for our labors to be disconnected and we each lean upon God for ourselves."[51]

In spite of these difficulties, James and Ellen were back together visiting mid-western camp meetings in 1875. "My husband will not let anything depress him. We have been harmoniously working with armor on," she wrote.[52] The next year, however, differences over their respective duties separated them again. Ellen stayed in Oakland, California, while James went east to Battle Creek. Apparently Ellen wanted to persuade James that she was doing the right thing to remain in Oakland.[53] She wrote him almost every day telling how her writing was progressing. He was missed "very, very much," but she was so buried in her work she had "no time to be lonesome while thus engaged," but, she added, "when gathered about the fireside, then there is a great miss."[54] James and Ellen kept protesting to each other that they were contented and happy, but tension was evident nevertheless:

You are happy and never so free. Thank the Lord for this. . . .

I am happy and free and I thank the Lord for this. You are in the line of duty. God blesses you. I am in the line of my duty and God blesses me. It may never be as well as now for me to write....Should I leave now to go east, I should go on your light, not on mine.[55]

Three weeks later, the situation had reached a nadir. Ellen wrote Lucinda Hall, a close friend in Battle Creek, that she was glad James was so cheerful, but she was afraid his mood might change at any moment. Then too, James had said some things she deeply resented, most notably that they should not attempt to control each other. "I do not own to doing it, but he has, and much more," she complained:

I never felt as I do now in this matter. I cannot have confidence in James's judgment in reference to my duty. He seems to want to dictate to me as though I was a child. . . . I hope God has not left me to receive my duty through my husband. He will teach me if I trust in him.[56]

Two days later she wrote with a tinge of sarcasm:

I have decided to remain here. I dare not go east without an assurance that God would have me go. The Lord knows what is best for me, for James, and the cause of God. My husband is now happy. Blessed news! If he will only remain happy I would be willing to ever remain from him. If my presence is detrimental to his happiness God forbid I should ever be connected with him. I do not think my husband really desires my society. He would be glad for me to be present at the camp meetings but he has such views of me which he freely has expressed from time to time that I do not feel happy in his society and I never can till he views matters entirely differently. He charges a good share of his unhappiness upon me when he has made it himself by his own lack of self-control.[57]

That same day she wrote James, saying:

In regard to my independence, I have had no more than I should have in the matter under the circumstances. I do not receive your views or interpretation of my feelings on this matter. I understand myself much better than you understand me.[58]

Meanwhile, James turned his pen against his wife:

I shall use the old head God gave me until he reveals that I am wrong. Your head won't fit my shoulders. Keep it where it belongs, and I will try to honor God in using my own. I shall be glad to hear from you but don't waste your precious time and strength in lecturing me on matters of mere opinions.[59]

Mrs. White's first reaction to this was indignation, but soon she softened.

It grieves me that I have said or written anything to grieve you. Forgive me and I will be cautious not to start any subject to annoy and distress you. We are living in a most solemn time and we cannot afford to have in our old age differences to separate our feelings. I may not view all things as you do, but I do not think it would be my place or duty to try to make you see as I see and feel as I feel. Wherein I have done this, I am sorry. I want a humble heart, a meek and quiet spirit. Wherein my feelings have been permitted to arise in any instance, it was wrong.

I wish that self should be hid in Jesus. I wish self to be crucified. I do not claim infallibility, or even perfection of Christian character. I am not free from mistakes and errors in my life. Had I followed my Saviour more closely, I should not have to mourn so much my unlikeness to His dear image.[60]

The next day she wrote again to Lucinda, asking her to burn the earlier letter, and four days later she was on the train traveling eastward.[61]

Things went tolerably well for James and Ellen for a time, and in the fall of 1877 she reported that they "never had greater influence in Battle Creek than at present."[62] Their difficulties started again when James suffered another mild stroke. After working till midnight on articles for the *Review*, he suddenly became confused at the breakfast table. He would take things from the serving dish and place them on the table beside his plate instead of on it. He was rushed to the Sanitarium, but he was unable to walk without assistance. A deep gloom settled over him.[63] Nevertheless, a week later he went to Massachusetts with Ellen for camp meetings. In South Lancaster, at the home of S. N. Haskell, a close friend and fellow minister, another ecstatic prayer session led to what seemed a slight improvement in James's health. His attitude toward Ellen also changed: "He seems to feel that he has wronged me very much. He goes back to the letters he wrote me. He feels that he has committed a great sin and the Lord can hardly forgive."[64] More and more, James's role was being subordinated to Ellen's. She assumed a mothering stance: "My work is to comfort him and pray for him; to speak cheerful, loving words to him and soothe him as a little child."[65]

Shortly after, Ellen reported that James had "unlimited confidence" in her judgment and felt very bad that he had been "so wild and unreasonable in his feelings" toward her.[66] It seemed to her that his attitude toward her was better than it had been for ten years. "The scales have fallen from his eyes. We are in perfect harmony in views and feelings. I never enjoyed his company so much in years as I do now."[67]

James's health continued to suffer, however, and care of the invalid fell principally on Ellen. The burden, born willingly at first, became more frustrating as the months went by. The couple moved to Healdsburg, California, in late 1877, where they purchased a "little bit of a house."[68] As she had done 10 years earlier, Ellen vowed to nurse her husband back to health.[69]

Seeing how "perfect harmony" had now been restored between them, Ellen believed that James's affliction has been a great blessing to him spiritually. He depended on her, she said, and she would not leave him "in his feebleness."[70]

She thought he would surely improve in the "quiet repose" of their little Healdsburg home, safely away from the urban bustle of the Adventist centers in Oakland and Battle Creek.[71]

Before six weeks had passed, however, Ellen was frustrated. James was not sleeping well. He began to exhibit strange symptoms such as excessively hot hands and feet. Ellen decided she had made a mistake in trying to care for her husband alone. It was "no little sacrifice" for her to have no one to share the burden. She complained that her soul was "weighed down," her hands tied. She couldn't leave James alone but she couldn't take him along either because he had "habits of eating and sleeping" that did not "impress the people correctly."[72]

She was determined that when spring arrived she would attend camp meetings. "God has given me a testimony which I must bear. I cannot let Satan triumph over us," she declared.[73] As time went by, James's problems became more difficult to handle. He could not keep his food down. He was agitated and nervous. To cool his burning hands he took to dipping them repeatedly in water. This only dried them out and aggravated the problem. He wanted a stiff breeze blowing on him constantly. He took to sleeping in a tent in the yard with the flaps open even in furious winds. He abandoned his wool socks for cotton, then left both and went barefooted. Ellen confessed she was at her wit's end to know what to do. Over and over she said to herself: "Left alone, no Lucinda, no Mary, no Sister Ings."[74]

Ellen counseled, pled and talked with James, but it was difficult, she said, to "break up his peculiar habits" without giving him the impression that she wanted to rule him rather than act as an "advisor, a counselor."[75] One night she dreamed a "celebrated physician" had visited James, and through this visionary physician she was able to give him some pointed views on his case. The "physician" informed James that he was keeping not only himself but his wife from doing the work to which God had called them. "She has too tender sympathy for you and is inclined to favor and pet your notions too much," he added. "If you have no power of self-control, then give yourself up to be controlled by those who have judgment." The dream was, after all, Ellen's.[76]

Once she became convinced that James was not going to improve enough to attend the season's camp meetings with her, she broached the subject of her going alone. "He wept like a child as I mentioned it," she told her son. "This will never do. I shall not leave him if he feels thus." She thought that perhaps she should spend the summer writing instead.[77] She secured a man to serve as his nurse and to take James on his daily carriage rides. She was yearning to be back at work. "Elder Loughborough is pleading for me to go to Oregon. He says my testimony is greatly needed there and I shall have a woman to accompany me. I think I may go, but I have not decided fully."[78] In June, 1878, James was sent east to Battle Creek where he could have treatment at the Sanitarium, and Ellen left for the Northwest.

Her letters from Oregon show she was uneasy about being away from him, yet delighted to be at work again. "I miss James, O, so much," she wrote, "and I have feelings of indescribable loneliness, but yet I am among friends who do all for me that they can."[79] She said she could "feel the testimony within her, and had been thinking for some weeks that it was really not her duty to write when she had such a good opportunity to be out preaching. "The truth is like fire shut up in my bones and I must speak that I may be relieved . . . . God has given me a testimony that no other one has and I am responsible for the great gift." "Work!" she exclaimed delightedly, "I need not cross the plains to find it. It is heaped up everywhere." She assured James that he need have no fears that her judgment would conflict with his. "God will teach us," she said. "Trust in Him. But my work must be here on the coast till I get marching orders."[80]

In Oregon her conviction grew that she should work independently of James became all the more settled; yet it generated some conflict in her mind. She told James that she loved him and missed him "very, very much," yet she felt that for the present she belonged to God. She claimed that it had been a "great sacrifice" to be separated, but since it seemed to be God's will, she "must be reconciled." She had "wept and prayed and pondered and wept again," but the "steady conviction" forced itself upon her that she was doing the right thing. "Separated as we are, we shall not be influenced by each other but we shall look to God separately and do our work in His fear and to His glory."[81]

Meanwhile, James White had improved and was beginning to take an active role in church affairs in Battle Creek.[82] His concerns naturally seemed more important to him than Ellen's activities on the West Coast. He wanted her with him. Others also wanted her in Battle Creek, he said. "There is no person to whom our people look ... as they do to you .... It would be the greatest disappointment that our people everywhere could meet with to have you remain the entire winter in California."[83]

In the fall of 1879 James and Ellen worked diligently through a number of camp meetings in spite of some friction.[84] On October 23, 1879, Ellen experienced a vision which dwelt at considerable length on James's case. The vision revived many of the old defenses and discussed many of the old charges against James.[85] His "firmness and decision" were needed at the beginning of the work, Ellen noted, but he would have had greater influence if he had cultivated "gentleness, kindness, and charity" as well.[86] Although the vision praised James's contributions, it also claimed Ellen should have a great deal of the credit for these achievements. James had been "highly favored in being connected with one whom God is leading, counseling, and teaching." His success was due, "in a great measure," to this.[87] James's voice, Ellen now said, should not have "absolute control."[88] James published this lengthy testimony along with a short response. He admitted that "under great grief I have sometimes spoken rashly and imprudently." Still, he found "great relief in those passages in the testimony which give me credit for endeavoring to be true and honest."[89] Things being as they were, he had decided to give up all responsibilities in Battle Creek and spend his time writing.

James did not remain long contented with this decision. From Oakland, Ellen frankly admitted that she had arranged with the local church leaders to prevent his coming to the West Coast. His letters had convinced her that for him to come "would result badly" for himself and for the "future prosperity of the cause of God." Her love for him was "deep and firm," but she did not want him to injure his reputation or her authority:

> My influence at times will be more favorable alone than if you are with me. I shall be with you when I can, but in the future we both may have to endure the trial of separation more in our labors than in the past. You do not mean to do it, but many times you lessen faith in my testimonies by unguarded expressions and views and feelings which you manifest.[90]

Believing as he did in Ellen's divine inspiration, James had to accept the restrictions she laid down; but he did not accept them graciously. He announced in the *Review* that he would "leave the positions of trust and responsibility to those who have found it easier to criticize our course than to point out a better one."[91] Ellen as much as assumed James's work was over: "It is time cares were laid off of your shoulders and you sweetening up, elevating, refining, and preparing for the day of God," she wrote him.[92] Cut off by his own problems and his wife's strictures from a more active role, James warmed to the idea of writing, and wanted Ellen to join him: "I must still plead that we take time to get out certain books," he said. "With the increased demand for our writings…. there will be an income of several thousand dollars annually, besides the immense amount of good our writings will do."[93] Ellen, however, did not feel it was her "duty" to take up writing again at this point. "I have no burden of writing more than I can do from time to time and bear my testimony. My way is always hedged up when I attempt to write. I am settled in the matter that I have written when it was my duty to visit the churches."[94] Back in 1876, James had wanted Ellen with him on speaking tours but her "duty" to write had kept them apart. Now, when he wanted her to write, her "duty" to speak in the churches necessitated a separation. The choice of occupations may say something about how difficult it had become for her to deal with James and still meet her public responsibilities.

James was a sad figure now. His former colleagues in the leadership of the church no longer consulted him, his wife told him to retire from responsible positions, and he felt that even his son Willie was infringing on his private affairs.[95] "I am so far broken down in nerve," he wrote, "that my mind is easily turned about by such positive temperaments as are in my own family." James felt he was losing his sense that he was a "responsible individual." He knew his son had not meant to, but he told Willie, "You have hurt me terribly."[96]

Willie and his talented wife, Mary Kelsey, were editing the paper James had started on the West coast, *The Signs of the Times*. They were eager to get Ellen's articles, but did not care for James's. This hurt him also:

It is possible that if Mary wished me to write, while using ink to express her appreciation of mother's articles, as in her last letter, she would have said a word about MY writing, or even mentioned my name. There was a time, when I had money plenty, that my labors were prized on the *Signs*.[97]

Sourly he noted: "I have made mistakes, and it seems to me that my friends are disposed to make the most of them, and make me fully realize them and that perpetually."[98] When he thought he might again take a leadership position, Ellen told him that although it would be hard for him to cease being "General," he would have to get used to it.[99]

As long as he remained around Battle Creek, James inevitably got embroiled in denominational affairs. The younger leaders—Kellogg, Haskell, and George I. Butler—took to using Ellen White's statements to keep him at arms length. This put her in an embarrassing position. After all, she did agree with James on some things, and the lack of harmony between him and the other leaders was "killing her."[100] When the family's old friend, Lucinda Hall, began to criticize James, it was more than Ellen could bear. She started to feel that James's accusers were little better than he when it came to harshness. She dreamed Kellogg took her to a room in his house where he had many stones systematically laid out, each one numbered and named. These, Kellogg announced in the dream, were the sins of James White. "I am going to stone him with them. Stone him to death," the doctor announced self-righteously. Then she saw her husband collecting a similar pile of stones.[101]

Kellogg, she believed, was "prompted by Satan if a man ever was," but she confided in Haskell that she dared not do anything in

camp meetings in the 1881 season for fear James would make matters worse.[102] When James sensed that Ellen agreed with Butler and
Haskell against some of his positions, he tried to enlist evangelist D.
M. Canright in an effort to break the undue influence he thought the
younger leaders had over his wife.[103] Meanwhile, Butler and Haskell
had the same suspicions about James. Ellen feared this even more:

> I told them I had been in continual fear that my husband's
> mistakes and errors would be classed with the testimonies of
> the Spirit of God and my influence injured. If I bore a plain
> testimony against existing wrongs they would say, "She is
> moulded by her husband's views and feelings." If I reproved
> my husband he would feel I was severe and others had preju-
> diced me against him.[104]

There were still a few bright spots in the couple's life together.
In the Spring of 1881, James and Ellen held a successful revival at
the church's college in Battle Creek, and had a pleasant visit to camp
meetings in Iowa and Wisconsin. However, after weekend meetings
in Charlotte, Michigan on July 23 and 24, James began to have pains
in his limbs. He became very sick and was taken to the Sanitarium.
On Saturday, August 6, 1881, he died.[105]

In the end then, Ellen White, like Alma White and Mary Baker
Eddy, failed to sustain both a happy, egalitarian marriage and a
shared leadership role in her church. This was not only because she
could not care for her ill husband and pursue a public career at the
same time. Every aspect of Ellen White's leadership turned on the
question of influence, and when James, by his unseemly health habits and harsh criticisms began to erode her influence, she drew away

from him and curtailed his activities in every way she could. Her leadership credentials were, she believed, issued by God in the form of revelations. Her "testimonies" to these revelations must be free of human influences, they must not be tarnished by negative associations. Ellen was pained by James failure to provide her with the companionship and understanding she longed for, but that could be endured. It was when he became a liability to her leadership that he had to be restrained. His death ended the struggle, and Ellen emerged as an independent leader.

---

[1] Arthur L. Bention, ed., *Behavioral Change in Cerebrovascular Disease* (New York, 1970), 169-218.

[2] Robert Peel, *Mary Baker Eddy: The Years of Discovery* (New York, 1966), 278.

[3] Mary Baker Eddy to Hattie Baker, July 14, 1876. https://tinyurl.com/y6ceqbbl

[4] Robert Peel, *Mary Baker Eddy: The Years of Trial* (New York, 1971), 16, 19.

[5] Ibid., 20, 65.

[6] Ibid., 63.

[7] n.a., "Sickness of Bro. White," *Review and Herald*, vol. 26 {Aug. 22, 1865), 95; Ellen G. White, "Our Late Experience," *Review and Herald*, vol. 27 (Feb. 20, 1866), 90.

[8] Ellen G. White, "Reminiscent Account of the Experience of James White's Sickness and Recovery," c. 1882, Ms. 1, 1867.

[9] Ellen G. White, "Reminiscent Account," Ms. 1, 1867; "Our Late Experience," *Review and Herald*, vol. 27 (Feb. 27, 1866), 97.

[10] Ellen G. White, "Reminiscent Account," Ms. 1, 1867. 10

[11] Ibid.

[12] R. Edward Turner, *Proclaiming the Word* (Berrien Springs, Mich., 1980), 18-19, 21.

[13] Ellen G. White, Testimonies for the Church, vol. 1, 574, first published 1867.

[14] Ibid., 571.

[15] Ibid., 575.

[16] Ibid., 85-86.

[17] Ibid., 501.

[18] Virgil Robinson, *James White* (Washington, D.C., 1976), 179-190.

[19] Ellen G. White, "Reminiscent Account," Ms. 1, 1867.

[20] Ellen G. White, Testimonies for the Church, vol. 1, 582-595, first published

1867.

21Ibid., 579.

22Ibid., 593

23First issued as *Testimony for the Church*, No. 13 (Battle Creek, Mich., 1867), now in Ellen G. White, *Testimonies for the Church*, vol. 1, 569-628.

24Ellen G. White, *Testimonies for the Church*, vol. 1,609,620, first published 1867.

25Ellen G. White, "Diary," March 31, 1868, Ms. 14, 1868.

26Ibid.

27Ellen G. White, *Testimonies for the Church*, vol. 3, 86, 96-97, first published 1872.

28Ibid., 507.

29Ibid., 508.

30Ellen White to James White, Sept. 2, 1871, Letter 13, 1871, 5.

31Ibid., 6.

32John P. Davies, *Phrenology, Fad and Science: A 19th Century American Crusade* (New Haven, Conn.: 1971); Ellen G. White, "Our Late Experience," *Review and Herald*, vol. 27 (Feb. 27, 1866), 98; James White to Ira Abbey, June 27, 1873.

33Ellen G. White to Brother Bell, April 11, 1872, Letter 4, 1872.

34Ellen G. White to Edson and Emma White, June 19, 1872, Letter 5, 1872.

35James White, *A Solemn Appeal to the Ministry and the People* (Battle Creek, Mich., 1873), 5.

36Ibid., 7-8.

37Ibid., 9.

38Ibid.

39Ibid., 15.

40Ellen G, White to Willie White, Jan. 25, 1873, Letter 4, 1873.

41Ellen G. White to Brother and Sister Stockton, Mar. 28, 1873, Letter 30, 1873.

42Ellen G. White to Brother Smith, May 14, 1873, Letter 10, 1873.

43Ellen G. White to Edson White, Aug. 9, 1873, Letter 11, 1873.

44Ellen G. White to [Willie] Clarence White, Mar. 20, 1874, Letter 17, 1874

45Ellen G. White to [Willie] Clarence White, May 15, 1874, Letter 27, 1874.

46Ellen G. White to James White, June 21, 1874, Letter 34, 1874.

47Ibid.

48Ellen G. White to James White, July 2, 1874, Letter 38, 1874.

49Nancy F. Cott, *The Bonds of Womanhood: "Woman's Sphere" in New England, 1780-1835* (New Haven, Conn., 1977), 140; Barbara Harris, Beyond Her-Sphere: Woman and the Professions in American History(Westport, Conn., 1978), Helen Papashvily, *All the Happy Endings* (New York, 1956), 106.

50Ellen G. White to James White, July 2, 1874, Letter 38, 1874.

51Ellen G. White to James White, July 8, 1874, Letter 40,. 1874.

52Ellen G. White to G. I. Butler, June 6, 1875, Letter 16, 1875.

53Ellen G. White to Lucinda Hall, June 17, 1875, Letter 46, 1875; James White to Willie White, May 7, 1876.

[54]Ellen G. White to James White, April 18, 1876, Letter 9, 1876.

[55]Ellen G. White to James White, April 20, 1876, Letter 11, 1876.

[56]Ellen G. White to Lucinda Hall, May 10, 1876, Letter 64, May 10, 1876

[57]Ellen G. White to Lucinda Hall, May 12, 1876, Letter 65, 1876

[58]Ellen G. White to James White, May 12, 1876, Letter 25, 1876.

[59]Quoted in Ellen G. White to Lucinda Hall, May 16, 1876.

[60]Ellen G. White to James White, May 16, 1876, Letter 27, 1876.

[61]Ellen G. White to Lucinda Hall, May 17, 1876.

[62]Ellen G. White to Edson and Emma White, Aug. 21, 1877, Letter 9, 1877.

[63]Ibid.

[64]Ellen G. White to Willie and Mary White, Sept. 3, 1877, Letter 13, 1877.

[65]Ibid.

[66]Ellen G. White to Willie and Mary White, Sept. 5, 1877, Letter 14, 1877.

[67]Ellen G. White to Edson and Emma, Sept. 7, 1977, Letter 16, 1877.

[68]Ellen G. White to Willie [White], Jan. 12, 1878, Letter 4b, 1878.

[69]Ellen G. White to Willie and Mary White, Jan. 22, 1878, Letter 4d, 1878.

[70]Ibid.

[71]Ellen G. White to Children, Jan. 25, 1878, Letter 6, 1878.

[72]Ellen G. White to Children, Feb. 10, 1878, Letter 7, 1878.

[73]Ibid.

[74]Ellen G. White to Willie and Mary White, c. Mar. 1878, Letter 20, 1878.

[75]Ellen G. White to Children, Feb. 10~ 1878, Letter 7, 1878.

[76]Ellen G. White to James White, Apr. 5, 1878, Letter 22, 1878.

[77]Ellen G. White to Willie and Mary White, Apr. 11, 1878, Letter 23, 1878.

[78]Ellen G. White to Willie and Mary White, May 5, 1878, Letter 27, 1878.

[79]Ellen G. White to Lucinda Hall, June 19, 1878, Letter 29, 1878.

[80]Ellen G. White to James White, June 20, 1878, Letter 31, 1878.

[81]Ellen G. White to James White, June 24, 1878, Letter 32, 1878.

[82]James White to Ellen G. White, June 24, 1878.

[83]James White to Ellen G. White, June 30, 1878.

[84]James White to Willie White, Mar. 10, Apr. 10, 1879.

[85]Ellen G. White, *The Judgment* (Battle Creek, Mich., [c. 1879]), 7.

[86]Ibid., 8-9.

[87]Ibid., 27.

[88]Ibid., 37-38.

[89]Ibid., 43.

[90]Ellen G. White to James White, Apr. 6, 1880, Letter 19, 1880.

[91]James White, "Personal," *Review and Herald*, vol. 55 (Apr. 29, 1880), 280-281; see also James White to Ellen G. White, Apr. 16, 1880, and Feb. 7, 1881.

[92]Ellen G. White to James White, Apr. 17, 1880, Letter 23, 1880.

[93]James White to Ellen G. White, Apr. 18, 1880.

[94]Ellen G. White to James White, Apr. 19, 1880, Letter 24, 1880.

[95]Ellen G. White to Willie and Mary White, Oct. 30, 1880, Letter 45a, 1880.

[96]Ellen G. White to Willie and Mary White, Oct. 30, 1880, Letter 45a, 1880.

[97]James White to Willie White, Nov. 3, 1880.

[98]James White to Willie White, Dec. 12, 1880.

[99]Ellen G. White to James White, c. July, 1880, Letter 53, 1880.

[100]Ellen G. White to Willie and Mary White, June 14, 1881.

[101]Ellen G. White, "A Dream," n.d., Ms. 2, 1880.

[102]Ellen G. White to S. N. Haskell, June 28, 1881, Letter 2, 1881.

[103]James White to D. M. Canright, May 24, 1881.

[104]Ellen G. White to Willie and Mary White, July 27, 1881, Letter 8a, 1881.

[105]J. H. Kellogg, "Fallen at His Post," *Review and Herald*, vol. 58 (Aug. 9, 1881), 104-105.

CHAPTER THREE

Sons of the Founders

I f leadership duties sometimes placed women "at odds" with their husbands, their relationship to their sons provided them both masculine support and an acceptable female role—that of a Mother. In Victorian culture, a dominant mother was more acceptable than a dominant wife, sometimes making the sons more helpful to the women founders than their husbands.

Of the four figures compared in this study, only Catherine Booth had daughters, yet it was on her son Bramwell that she leaned most heavily in her later years. Alma White's two sons, Arthur and Ray, offered emotional support and practical assistance in their father's absence, and Arthur headed the church after her death. Unable to rear her own child, Mary Baker Eddy legally adopted an adult man as her "son." She also relied heavily on her male secretary, Calvin Frye. Two of Ellen White's sons survived to adulthood. Her favorite, William Clarence, served as her assistant after James died in 1881. However, she felt the attitudes and actions of her older son, James Edson, undermined her authority.

Prominent nineteenth century women often sought practical and emotional support from persons other than husbands. In the case of unmarried leaders, this help came from other women. Early in her career, Jane Addams relied on Ellen Gates Starr. A close friend from her school days, Starr gave Addams the support and affection she needed to break away from her family.[1] Later, Mary Rozet Smith, gentle and self-effacing, devoted herself to Addams' every need, loving her "without question and without criticism."[2] Francis Willard's friend, Anna Gordon, was fond of saying she mended her heroine's gloves and washed her stockings so that Miss Willard could make speeches and write books.[3] Earlier in the century, the "Public Universal Friend," Jemima Wilkinson, a prophetess who headed a small sect in Western New York, was well served by Sarah Richards, and later, by the Malin Sisters.[4] Ellen White and other married religious leaders drew this type of support chiefly from their sons.

To hear her granddaughter tell it, Catherine Booth was the most remarkable Mother in the group considered. Her success in reaching her goals bears out this positive assessment. Her eight children all remained fervent Christians and all but one became effective leaders in the Salvation Army. Some Salvationists believed that had Catherine lived longer she might have been able to prevent the organizational rifts which developed between some of her children and their father.[5] Although Catherine took pride in all the children, she leaned most heavily on her eldest son, Bramwell. Once William began his work in the slums of Whitechapel, Catherine felt he was too overwhelmed to bear her burdens as well. If problems over money, ill-health, or William himself arose, she confided in Bramwell. She also dominated him. When the boy reached 18, his Mother was much more certain than he was that he should become a preacher. The longer he held back from a decision, the more intensely she pressured him. "I have thought very much about you," she wrote, "your future harasses me considerably."[6] At 21, Bramwell still had not committed himself. "Do you think your *circumstances* are the result of chance?" his mother asked. "Were we, your earthly proprietors, sincere when by the side of your natal bed we held you up in our arms to God and gave you to Him for an *evangelist*? Yes, if any act of my life was thorough and real, *that* was."[7] Catherine didn't hesitate to play on the feelings of her affectionate son: "No matter what I *say* I *cannot* believe that you care about me as you ought till you are willing to yield a little and meet my wishes on this question of work."[8] Needless to say, Bramwell eventually capitulated, became his father's "Chief of Staff," and the "prophet and teacher" his mother always wanted him to be.[9] Catherine also decided when it was time for Bramwell to marry: "You want a wife," she informed him, "one with you in soul, with whom you could commune and in whom you could find companionship and solace...God will find you one, and I shall help Him."[10] This time Bramwell accommodated this wish of his Mother's more easily, choosing Florence Soper, a friend of his sister's. Florence submitted cheerfully to her mother-in-law's continued domination. Catherine decided that Bramwell's home would have no mirrors in the closets because it was too ostentatious. She even insisted on a custom-made bed for the new couple.

When Catherine discovered she had a serious swelling in her breast, she confided in Bramwell, not William. Bramwell arranged her visit with the specialists who diagnosed cancer. In her last days he brought her "quietness of spirit when no other could," her granddaughter wrote. "Her very love for William made her want to spare him." When her distress seemed beyond endurance, she called for her son.[11]

Mary Baker Eddy was so devastated by her first husband's death and her own physical and emotional problems that she was not able to care for her son, George Washington Glover. He was eventually placed in the care of a young friend of the family, Mahala Sanborn, who became his surrogate mother. When Mahala married and moved west, George went along, eventually seeking his fortune in the Black Hills gold rush. Except for a few visits, some correspondence, and an unseemly lawsuit later in life, Mrs. Eddy had little contact with him; he played no role in her movement. [12]

Other young men took the place of the son Mrs. Eddy never really had. In the mid-60's George Barry served her every way he could— running errands, performing chores, hunting rooms, and copying and recopying her manuscripts. He was the first of her students to call her "Mother." At one point she wrote a will, gratefully leaving him everything she owned.[13] When Gilbert Eddy arrived on the scene and began to take over Barry's role, the latter became jealous and turned against Mrs. Eddy, finally suing her for what he thought his five years of service had been worth.[14]

From the death of Gilbert Eddy in 1882 until his own death twenty-eight years later, Calvin Frye served Mrs. Eddy as private secretary. Meticulous and dogged, Frye faithfully performed his duties as secretary, steward, aid, coachman, spokesman, and confidant. Frye had the indispensable ability to understand, or at least accept his leader's mercurial moods and sudden decisions, her mixtures of emotion and reason, girlishness and authority. In his tedious diary, he occasionally lapsed into shorthand to record his private frustration with some difficult demand or painful rebuke. Yet for all of his devotion to her,

Frye was a little too stiff to fill the role of a surrogate son.[15]

In Ebenezer J. Foster, M.D., Mrs. Eddy found not only devotion but some of the warmth Frye lacked. A quiet, kindly man who loved music and flowers, Foster attended one of Mrs. Eddy's classes in 1887. Although he was already in his 40's, he quickly took to calling her "Mother," and referring to himself as "your child."[16] In 1888 Mrs. Eddy legally adopted him, changing his name to Ebenezer J. Foster Eddy. During her years at Concord, New Hampshire (1892-1908), Frye stayed at home to take care of a thousand details while "Bennie" Foster Eddy served as messenger between Concord, Boston, and points farther afield. On her "darling Benny," Mrs. Eddy lavished her frustrated maternal affection, declaring him to be the "dearest and sweetest of all the earth."[17]

Although Foster Eddy was for some time heir apparent to Mrs. Eddy, in the end he proved too ambitious and too lacking in discipline to qualify for leadership. He offended her by teaching a class in Boston without her prior approval, then scandalized the movement by a questionable relationship with his secretary. He and Calvin Frye were jealous of each other. Against his preference, Mrs. Eddy sent him to form a new church in Philadelphia. Eventually, the church he established expelled him. Mrs. Eddy forbade him to visit her for three years. Finally, in 1897, she ceased to regard him as her son.[18]

In the end, Mrs. Eddy settled for the help and support provided by Calvin Frye and the female members of her household, but her life-long quest for a "son" shows that she dearly wanted an arrangement such as other female founders enjoyed.

Neither Catherine Booth nor Mary Baker Eddy experienced much conflict between the demands of their careers and those of their children. This was partly because they did not travel as extensively as did Alma and Ellen White. Then too, Mrs. Eddy's early inability to care for her child meant that by the time she began her career she had no family obligations.

Alma and Ellen White, like most career women who attempt to rear a family, often found their twin responsibilities in conflict. Yet their sense of divine calling helped them cope with the guilt of leaving their children behind. When Alma's first child, Arthur, was still an infant, she suffered a serious, life-threatening illness. Naturally she prayed for God to spare her, at first arguing that she needed to live for the child's sake. But this prayer seemed selfish to her: "There was a greater work for me than simply to live for my own child ... People were everywhere in tombs of spiritual death and needed the gospel preached to them."[19] Three years later, a second son, Ray, was born. When this baby became ill, it seemed to Alma that her resolve to go out and preach was being tested:

> As I stood looking into the face of the little one whose life was slowly ebbing away, the Lord spoke to my soul: "If I spare him will you devote your life to the ministry of my Word?" Hope revived as I yielded to the Holy Spirit's entreaty. Gradually his pulse grew stronger. [20] When the same experience occurred again, Alma concluded: "The Lord made it clear to me that he would let the baby stay with us if I would preach the gospel, otherwise he would take him."[21]

Exactly the same solution had released Ellen White for public work half a century earlier. A year after her marriage to James White, she bore her first child, Henry. The poverty-stricken couple had just set up housekeeping with the Howland family of Topsham, Maine, when letters arrived from various states begging them to visit, instruct, and encourage the Adventist believers. Mrs. White replied that she was unable to do so because she could neither leave her child nor travel with him. "But little Henry was soon taken very sick," she recalled. In spite of crude remedies and fervent prayers, the child grew rapidly worse. The problem, Ellen concluded, was that they had "made the child an excuse for not traveling and laboring for the good of others, and we feared the Lord was about to remove him."[22] Once more the desperate Mother prayed, this time promising to travel if only God would spare the child's life. "From that hour he began to amend," she noted. The daughter of their landlord volunteered to care for Henry, and the Whites were soon on their way to Connecticut.

Leaving children behind was never easy; both Alma and Ellen White tell of homesick longings. Still, their conviction that God had called them enabled them to escape the guilt which tortures any parent sensitive to the needs of children when that parent chooses to pursue a public career. These women resolved that guilt at its most powerful moment: the sickbed of a child.

The lives of both of Ellen White's surviving sons were dominated by their relationship to their mother. In both cases, these relationships had their impact on her authority and influence. With Edson, the question was whether his failings reflected so poorly on his mother as to impair her influence. Edson further threatened his mother's authority by accusing his brother Willie of influencing her.

Edson acquired his problems in an understandable way. During his earliest years, his parents were poverty-stricken itinerants, struggling against impossible odds to forge a church out of the ragtag remnants of the Millerite movement. Edson often found himself left in the care of one family and then another. When his parents

were with him, they interpreted his frequent illnesses as a part of
Satan's attack on the fledgling movement and his healings as evidence of God's endorsement of their public efforts. Thus even in his
sufferings he was only an adjunct to their careers.[23]

His brother Willie's childhood was more fortunate. At the time
he was born in 1854, Ellen's visions had ceased temporarily and she
had concluded that it was her duty to settle down and attend to her
family.[24] The visions resumed the next year after Adventist leaders
repented of their neglect of her prophetic gift, but by this time the
family had moved into their first permanent home in Battle Creek.
Thereafter, when the parents travelled, the boys could stay at home
in familiar surroundings, cared for by resident housekeepers. In later
years, Ellen sensed that these early experiences might account for the
differences between her two sons. She told Willie that he had been
too severe toward Edson: "The circumstances of his birth were alto-
gether different from yours. His mother knows, but everyone does
not."[25]

A nomadic childhood was not Edson's only burden. He also
chafed under the constant unfavorable comparisons which his parents made between him and his brother Willie. From the time Willie
was born, Edson received constant reproof and condemnation, while
his little brother got constant praise and encouragement. Willie was
a "good natured" baby who seldom cried; Edson had "more life and
roughery."[26] When Edson was 11, his father urged him to "love and in-
dulge Willie" for he was the "best boy" Edson would ever see.[27] When
he was 12 his mother told him she had awakened weeping because
she had dreamed he was dying and had no evidence that he "loved
God" and was "prepared to die." "You may ask," she wrote, "why does
Mother think I am not a child of God? One evidence is, you do not

love to attend meetings on the Sabbath." Once he was in church Edson fixed himself in an "easy position," and took a nap instead of listening to the sermon. During family prayers, he kept his eyes wide open, staring at the floor around him.[28] Meanwhile, to her younger son Ellen wrote: "Willie, dear boy, you have been our sunshine, and Oh, how I prayed that you might always be the same pure sweet Willie."[29] In another letter she told Edson to watch against his "besetments," and a few lines later: "My dear little Willie, may the Lord bless you."[30]

Edson was not what his mother would have called a "profligate," or even a "rowdy," but his shortcomings seemed endless. She urged him to conquer his "passion" for reading story books and to stay away from the local amusement arcade where the "air gun" was kept to extract money from idle youth. He must spend his evenings at home instead of "down the street," and stop trying to keep secrets from his parents.[31] When he began courting, Ellen did not feel that his "riding out" with a girl was a "grievous sin," but she thought age 16 was too early to show "partiality to any young miss." She scolded him for spending his money carelessly on a gold watch chain and on such needless indulgences as fish and "dandelion coffee."[32] She rebuked him for leaving tools laying around, for not cleaning the horse's stable, for joining the Good Templars without permission, and—again and again—for his spendthrift ways: "How could a sleigh ride cost you 70 cents? Do tell me. Did you settle the entire cost? Keep out of sleigh rides." She advised him to split wood if he needed exercise.[33]

Meanwhile, Edson was supposed to "love Willie, be very kind to him, love to please him" and not to "leave too many burdens upon his young shoulders." "Set him a good noble example," Ellen urged.[34] "You know your Master's will," she wrote Edson in a letter addressed to both sons, "only do it." Then she added: "Willie, my dear boy, love is a part of your nature. Cherish it, for it is the most precious gift of heaven."[35]

James White finally wrote Edson off as a lost cause. He had hoped his son's "bright intellect" might enable him to grow up to be a physician or businessman rather than a "plodding" farmer. But he despaired of Edson ever making a success of anything because he "wouldn't be advised." When the young man turned 20, James promised to give him $1,000 worth of land if Edson could accumulate an equal amount in cash, but he told Ellen ruefully: "He will never earn it. He can't keep means."[36]

Edson seems to have been caught in a vicious cycle. Because he often failed, he was expected to fail, and probably because he was expected to, he failed again and again. Doubtless he was plagued by guilt as well; for the advice and rebuke he received was overlaid with a heavy sense of sinfulness and neglected "duty." Ellen often reminded him that his life was "a mistake, worse than useless" and "a failure."[37] James White said he would always be a burden to his parents.[38] Again and again he was assured he was in danger of losing his soul. When Edson was 17, Ellen wrote him: "Should you now be snatched away and lie down in the grave, I could not feel you were prepared."[39] He was, after all, not just a preacher's son but the son of a prophet. Many a religious parent in the nineteenth century might have written: "Don't forget, dear children, that evil deeds and wrongs are faithfully recorded, and will bring their punishment unless repented of and confessed, and washed away by the atoning blood of Jesus."[40] But Edson's mother could go on to say: "I have written you letters dictated by the Spirit of God, and I beg you not to disregard my efforts."[41] Not only did she urge him to study his Bible, she also recommended her book, *Spiritual Gifts*, as one which should be studied "carefully, candidly, prayerfully."[42] "God has taught your mother, and she has taught you your wrongs," she told him.[43]

Edson's burden of guilt might identify him with the eighteenth century "evangelical" children Philip Greven described, children for whom guilt was an expected part of the maturation process.[44] But it is more difficult to fit one person's life into Greven's categories of "evangelical," "moderate," and "genteel" than it is to find episodes that fit in each category. For all his guilt, Edson never experienced the kind of "new birth" Greven posits as an integrating factor in the personalities of evangelical children. Rather, he passed through a series of spiritual regenerations and declensions, never achieving any stable, consistent approach to life. Nor did Ellen White fit Greven's model of a parent who believed in "breaking" her child's will, at least so far as her stated theories were concerned. On this issue she sided with his "moderates," who sought to bend, not break the will.[45] Even if it could be argued that her actual treatment of Edson did break his will, what are we to make of her treatment of Willie? And what becomes of an "evangelical" style of child-rearing when one parent rears two children in different ways?

Edson coped with his parent's badgering the way many adolescents do: with secrecy and silence. Naturally, Ellen was all the more frustrated:

> When I have tried to counsel you kindly and reason with you, you have sat and made no response, as though you were a piece of machinery I was talking to instead of a reasoning being....You continue to keep your secrets, to have your notions and plans and fancies, and to hide them from your father and mother.[46]

"You do not take the least notice of the letters I write you," she complained. "Are they unworthy of an answer?"[47] At one point in 1869, Edson must have lashed out, telling his mother how unwelcome were her constant reminders of his past failures. Ellen responded with a weak promise not to burden him further. "When you wish to hear from me" she added, "read the letters I have written you the past year."[48] The respite was brief.

However misguided her approach might have been at times, some of Ellen's efforts in Edson's behalf indicate that it was more than self-interest and family pride that sustained her drive to bring him up to her ideal of Christian manhood. Whenever he showed the slightest inclination toward diligence and responsibility, she encouraged him, defended him, and lent him money—money which James and Willie were sure was all but wasted. Especially in the 1870's she sometimes defended Edson so stoutly that James was offended, feeling she was taking Edson's side against him.

As Edson grew to manhood, he made his living primarily from publishing ventures. From 1877-1880 he held a shaky tenure as business manager for the publishing house his father had founded in Oakland, California, then returned to Battle Creek to start his own establishment, handling books on etiquette, cookery, and business forms. He also wrote hymns and with his cousin, Frank Belden, published a number of hymnals. Edson's business career tended to bear out his parents' misgivings about his financial ability, but he plunged ahead, borrowing from one person to pay off another, trying desperately to prove himself and overcome his poor reputation.[49]

By the early 1890's Edson had moved his business to Chicago and had grown indifferent toward religion. Ellen White, in Australia at the time, was all the more concerned about Edson because she had begun to feel that his neglect of her counsels was undermining her influence, and that of his brother, Willie:

> The confidence of our brethren in our judgment, and in the testimonies the Lord has given, has been shaken. They know not the letters of appeal, of reproof and warnings given your Mother for you, and therefore they have judged me from outward appearance. I am compelled to bear testimony against the course some in responsible positions have taken, and your pursuing your own course of action independent of Willie's and my advice and counsel, has made of little effect my work in Battle Creek.... You were too blind to perceive to where these things were tending—to uproot the confidence of my brethren in me.[50]

At the time this letter arrived, Edson was seething with resentment because he felt Willie's actions had resulted in his losing his business in Battle Creek. He wrote his mother a letter which devastated her: "I have no religious inclinations now in the least," he told her. He planned to reform, but only when he had paid off $500 in debts.[51]

Ellen replied with a long, anguished letter, attaching a note begging Edson not to "cast it aside or burn it." The night after she got Edson's letter she had had a dream. She was at the beach where she noticed Edson and four other young men playing in the surf. "The waves were rolling up nearer and still nearer and then would roll back with a sullen roar." She called to him at the top of her lungs: "The undertow! The undertow!" But Edson was already caught. A rope was tied to a would-be rescuer who tried to make his way out to save him, but

Edson made fun of the whole effort. Ellen awoke as he uttered a "fearful shriek." The undertow, she told Edson, represented the "power of Satan" and Edson's own "set, independent, stubborn will."[52]

Edson's phrase, "not at all religiously inclined," had seared his mother as nothing else could: "These are the words of Satan, not my son," she wrote. Then she complained again that he was weakening her influence:

> There is nothing more sacred on earth than for a child to defend and shield his mother from any taint of misapprehension and reproach, a widowed mother who has felt so much alone, dependent upon that help which her sons could give her and which they promised to give her at the death of the husband and father. Your Mother's worth, and the goodness, verity, and truth of her mission were assailed, her judgment questioned, her discernment pronounced unreliable, her influence limited. Should not her sons rally around her then, and give evidence of the fact of the untruthfulness of these statements? . . . Should they not throw over her a protecting shield?[53]

"Woe is me," she exclaimed, "that I have brought into the world a son that helps to swell the rebel's ranks, to stand in defiance against God." As she often did on such occasions, she reviewed the story of Edson's delirious fever as an infant: "I found you fighting with both arms and hands an invisible foe" she recalled. "And now I see that invisible foe [Satan], lurking, alluring, and deceiving your soul to ruin."[54] Sometimes, Ellen confessed, she lay awake all night, reviewing all her dealings with Edson, trying to discover where she had "made a mistake" so that one of her children would "not be a recommendation of the efforts, the prayers, the appeals, the counsels of the mother."[55]

In spite of the self-interested tone of some of her arguments, Ellen's letter apparently moved Edson. In reply, he announced: "I have surrendered fully and completely, and never enjoyed life before as I am now.... I have left it all with my Saviour, and the burden does not bear me down any longer."[56] Indeed, it was a new beginning for him. He wrapped up his business affairs in Chicago and went to Battle Creek to attend a training class for ministers. Intrigued by reports he heard from Northern missionaries working among Blacks in the South, he decided to dedicate his life to that work, a decision which was confirmed when he discovered a printed copy of a lecture his mother had given two years earlier, calling for just such endeavors.[57]

Edson's mission, which Ellen supported vigorously, was really the Adventist church's first systematic effort to evangelize Blacks. He built a riverboat, *Morning Star*, to use along the twisting waterways of the Mississippi Delta, and in January, 1895, arrived in Vicksburg with a small crew of volunteers to open his campaign. For five years he labored in Mississippi, assisting Blacks with job training and other educational opportunities even as he invited them to become Seventh-day Adventists. He founded several churches and schools, established a periodical, *The Gospel Herald*, to promote work among Black people, and organized the Southern Missionary Society to oversee various philanthropic, educational and evangelistic projects.[58] From beginning to end his mother's testimonies were a major source of encouragement, guidance, and defense against church leaders who, remembering his checkered early life, were reluctant to support his efforts.

Although Ellen was delighted to have Edson back in the fold, and although she supported his Mississippi project, she had really preferred that he join her in Australia where she too was pioneering Adventist work. She and her two sons, she said, should be a "threefold cord."[59] When Edson showed no inclination to come, she wrote:

> I have not been able to get over this disappointment without tears.... I cannot expect to have many more years of life; and when I am mostly surrounded with those who are of no kith or kin for the most of my time, a longing desire is begotten in my heart to have my children united with me in the work.[60]

Edson was willing to use his mother's authority to support his own work, but having achieved at last a measure of success, he was not about to work as her underling in Willie's shadow. Edson continued to resist the suggestion that he come to Australia, and Ellen did not insist further. As the end of the century approached, increasing racial tensions and mounting violence against Blacks and their benefactors made it impossible for Edson to continue his work in Mississippi. He left it in the care of Black pastors and moved on to Nashville, Tennessee, where he founded the Southern Publishing Association.

Edson's years in Mississippi had been marked by several serious clashes with the church leaders in Battle Creek. In Tennessee he became ever more bitter and vocal against them. Before long, his mother's fears about him returned. A. G. Daniells, a close ally of Ellen White's younger son, Willie, had been elected president of the General Conference in 1901. As time went on, Edson became suspicious of both Daniells and his brother Willie. The latter estrangement troubled Ellen terribly. "In your hatred for your brother—for it is nothing less than this—you certainly have shown that you have not been led and controlled by the Spirit of God." W. C. White, she said, was "an honorable, unselfish man."[61]

Meanwhile, a rift developed between the medical leaders, notably John Harvey Kellogg, and the General Conference officers. Edson made a trip to Battle Creek and soon reports reached Ellen that he was charging Willie with manipulating her writings. Her reaction was strong:

> What kind of a move was it that you made in rushing to Battle Creek and saying to those there that W.C. White, your own brother, for whom you should have respect, manipulated my writings? This is just what they needed to use in their councils to confirm them in their position that the testimonies the Lord gives your mother are no longer reliable .... I stand where I cannot vindicate your course any more, for God forbids .... If you and W. C. White should both turn from me I should not turn from the counsels God has given me.

> I cannot and will not suffer reproach to come upon the cause of God and my work that God has given me to do, by your saying he [Willie] manipulates my writings. It is falsehood— but what a charge is this! Not one soul manipulates my writings.[62]

In order for Ellen White to preserve her own influence, she felt she needed to resist the suggestion that she was influenced by anyone other than God. Although she had designated Willie as her "counselor," she would not concede that he influenced her any more than she would admit that her writings were influenced by the things she had read. For her son Edson to make such charges was almost more than she could bear: "I am cut to the heart when I think that my son gives occasion for disbelief in the testimonies that God has given me for his people, causing the confidence of some to be shaken."[63] Again she appealed to him to consider the sorrow and sleepless nights he was causing, then added: "If you do not decidedly change your course of action, you will do more to weaken the confidence of the church in the integrity of the Testimonies than all other influences combined can do."[64]

If Edson threatened Ellen White's influence, her younger son, Willie, did all he could to extend it. Willie was everything Edson was not—stable, frugal, congenial, and cooperative. During her husband's sickly years, Willie had moved easily into the role of assistant to her: "Willie waited upon me in the desk and took a seat there with me, and placed a fur around my shoulders after I ceased speaking. He seems to understand his part."[65] During the last decade of James's life, Ellen often confided in Willie things she could not share with James. Willie's wife understood and accepted the fact that he was to take his father's place "as much as any man could."[66]

A little more than a year after James's death, Willie's role was confirmed by a vision. Ellen had migrated to Healdsburg, California, where, in October, 1882, a state-wide camp meeting was held. She had been ill for some weeks, but was remarkably restored during the meetings. A vision followed shortly in which she was impressed that God still had a special work for her to do and had provided her son Willie to assist her:

The Mighty Helper said: LIVE, I have put my Spirit upon your son, W. C. White, that he may be your counselor. I have given him the spirit of wisdom, and a discerning, perceptive mind. He will have wisdom in council . . . . He will be kept and will be enabled to help you bring before my people the light I will give you for me. . . . I will be with your son, and will be his counselor. He will respect the truth that comes through you to the people.[67]

. . . .

The Lord has selected him to act an important part in his work. For this purpose was he born.[68]

The role Ellen envisioned for Willie provided him ample opportunity to influence her as well as to extend her influence. Willie became counselor, confidant, literary agent, travel manager, spokesman, apologist, personnel manager, and business agent for his mother. "I have instructed him to labor untiringly to secure the publication of my writings in the English language first, and afterword to secure their translation and publication in many other languages."[69] Like his father before him, Willie became an expert on type styles, papers, bindings and every aspect of printing. As her attendant, he was "thoughtful and attentive, neglecting nothing."[70] Ellen found him not only "a great comfort" but "a wise counsellor."[71] Her role as prophet left Ellen precious few individuals with whom she could be close emotionally. Willie provided the warmest human bond she had. Shortly after James's death, he assured his "dearest Mother" that he wanted to be her "comfort and support." "I long to be near you and have your society," he wrote. He and his wife Mary loved her and promised to care for her feelings. "I will do what I can for the advancement of your interests cheerfully and for nothing." Willie pledged.[72] In the years that followed, Ellen frequently expressed her loneliness when Willie was away.[73] "I prize his kindly attentions," she wrote.[74] "I do want to see my Willie every day."[75] When discouragements came, Mother and son would sometimes weep together. [76]

For all his ties to his Mother, and partly because of them, Willie managed a career of his own as a minister and church administrator. He was only 21 when elected board chairman and business manager of the church's west coast publishing house. Although he had precious little formal education, he served on the board of Battle Creek College and was for a time director of the Battle Creek Sanitarium. He also established Healdsburg (now Pacific Union) College, and served on the General Conference Committee during his entire adult life.[77]

Ellen was proud of his achievements, though often frustrated by his absences.

"We have to do the best we can, we, women, alone," she sighed. "It is sad that I cannot have any help from Willie. He is full of work, early and late."[78] When Willie was away, she wrote: "I have no one to counsel with. I dare not move without counsel."[79] She and Willie, she believed, could accomplish ten times as much together as they could alone.[80] Willie agreed: "My work alone, is of little account, but as connected with mother, it is important."[81]

Ellen paid a price for her more or less-public doting on Willie. Edson was not the only one who accused him of undue influence over her. Since the charge grew more insistent as Ellen grew older, it may be that as an aging widow she was seen as more vulnerable, more helpless, and thus more susceptible to Willie's influence than she had been as an energetic young wife. The mere fact that Willie served as Ellen White's "counselor" and that both she and he felt free to thus define his role suggested that he would have some influence with her. "Willie does all my business," she wrote, "I should not make any trade without his advice or counsel for he is my business agent."[82] He had free access to all her mail: "Open any letters you please that arrive for me, and read them, then send them on afterward without delay."[83]

Willie made no apologies for controlling the information coming to his mother:

> When the last American mail came, she was so feeble she did not dare open it and read it at once. I persuaded her to let me read it first, and then I sorted the letters, and gave her the most encouraging first .... The same mail brought us some letters from California, giving a catalogue of crimes. I have begged mother to leave these with me, and I shall write to the parties sending these epistles that I know that God is able to reveal to mother that which he wishes her to know about these matters.[84]

"I must thank you most heartily for writing this to me instead of laying it before Mother," he wrote to one correspondent. "I shall take every pain in my power to prevent this coming to her attention. If the Lord wants her to write .... on this point, he will direct her what to write."[85] To another correspondent, he wrote: "Whenever I find that Mother's mind has been drawn to this matter, then I will read your letter to her."[86]

In addition to controlling the information coming to his mother, Willie sometimes influenced decisions on when and whether certain testimonies should be released. In 1903, she had condemned the theological sentiments of Dr. John Harvey Kellogg's book, *The Living Temple*. Then, in May, 1904, an important conference was held in Berrien Springs, Michigan, pitting Kellogg and his supporters against Daniells and his party, which included Ellen White. Daniells was apparently looking forward to a confrontation in which Kellogg would be publicly forced to yield. His colleague, W. W. Prescott, was planning a full-scale public attack on Kellogg's alleged pantheism. Ellen White had at first given her consent, but then she changed her mind. She felt "deeply impressed" that it would be a mistake to attack Kellogg from the platform. She penned a note to the church leaders advising them "to speak upon some subject that will touch and tender hearts."[87] But Willie White intervened to prevent this counsel of restraint from being copied and delivered. Prescott went ahead with his attack, and Kellogg was further alienated from the General Conference leaders. Two years later, Willie tried to explain his action by saying that although his mother had "no human help in the writing of the Testimonies, in the decision as to when and to whom she shall send the messages written," she often took counsel. In this case, Willie had gone to her, reminded her of how she had been saying that a strong stand needed to be taken and asked her permission not to deliver the letter to Prescott. Ellen had yielded to his pleading.[88]

Willie White's power in deciding when things should be published seems to have been great enough that Ellen White's literary assistants sometimes sought his counsel even when they had clear instructions from her. Clarence Crisler, who joined her staff in 1901, was once instructed by Mrs. White to publish one of her manuscripts "at once, without a day's delay." Crisler tried to dissuade her but she was, he wrote Willie, "positive and firm in her declaration that it must be published immediately," and that they were not to wait until they could consult with Willie. Reluctantly, Crisler went ahead, but he instructed the publishing house to delay presswork so that he could fire off a letter to Willie asking him to wire instructions. Crisler felt that Mrs. White did not understand the situation fully.

> We cannot make her understand it; therefore we are trying to get out of the dilemma as best we can. We do not want to hurt her feelings by going directly contrary to her imperative directions; on the other hand, we do not know what disposition you may wish to make of the article.[89]

Whether Crisler succeeded in his attempt to circumvent Mrs. White's instructions is not known. That he would appeal so openly to Willie for help in doing so suggests that, at least on some occasions, Willie had considerable power in his mother's affairs.

Whether Ellen White was influenced by supernatural means is something historians cannot determine, but on a human level, Willie White, her son and counselor, obviously influenced her. On the other hand, she doubtless influenced him even more profoundly. It is difficult to weigh the extent of such interaction at this distance. Clearly, however, Willie's life-long dedication to his Mother greatly expanded and extended her influence in the church.

Although Ellen White trusted and depended on her son, she made no attempt to pass her charismatic authority on to him. His prestige in the church was derived almost exclusively from her living presence. He was designated as one of five members of the Board of Trustees she established to administer her estate, but it was an insignificant post. In fact, Willie was all but forgotten in the years immediately following her death. Although he remained a member of the General Conference Committee, he was rarely able to travel from his California home to attend meetings in Washington. The other members of the White Board of Trustees, mostly General Conference officials, opposed his efforts to publish anything new from Ellen White's vast collection of manuscript materials.[90]

Catherine Booth and Alma White, whose authority in their movements was less powerful, were better able to pass it on to their sons than were Mary Baker Eddy and Ellen White, whose charisma derived, at least in part, from claims to direct divine inspiration. The Salvation Army was headed by Catherine's favorite, Bramwell Booth, after William's death. [91] Alma White passed the leadership of The Pillar of Fire to her son, Arthur K. White.[92] Thus the authority of divine inspiration, while giving its' recipient greater authority, proved more difficult to pass on in the case of these women.

The women who founded religious movements in the nineteenth century were iconoclastic in that they shattered the image of a wife and mother confined to the home. But men in their lives served as assistants, counselors, and defenders. The strong, loving relationships in the Booth family, especially between Catherine and William and between Catherine and Bramwell, were immensely valuable in meeting the challenges of founding the Salvation Army. The publishing and promotional skills of Ellen White's husband James and son Willie greatly expanded her influence within the movement. Alma White, bereft of the help of a husband, leaned heavily on her son, Arthur K. White. Even Mary Baker Eddy, who had to work without a husband or a son, drew on the dedication and skills of male assistants. While secular feminists drew their close supporters from the ranks of women, religious leaders who were women more conventionally sought help from men.

[1]Allen F. Davis, *American Heroine: The Life and Legend of Jane Addams* (London, 1973), 38, 53

[2]Ibid., 85, 90-91.

[3]Mary Earhart Dillon, *Francis Willard: From Prayer to Politics* (Chicago, 1944), 3; Ruth Bordin, *Frances Willard: A Biography*, (The University of North Carolina Press: Chapel Hill & London, 1986).

[4]Herbert A. Wisbey, Jr., *Pioneer Prophetess: Jemima Wilkinson, The Public Universal Friend* (Ithaca, New York, 1964), 63-64, 122-23, 125.

[5]Catherine Bramwell-Booth, *Catherine Booth* (London, 1970), 348.

[6]Ibid., 342.

[7]Ibid., 343.

[8]Ibid., 345.

[9]Ibid., 347.

[10]Ibid., 371.

[11]Ibid., 436.

[12]Robert Peel, *Mary Baker Eddy: The Years of Authority* (New York, 1977), 125.

[13]Robert Peel, *Mary Baker Eddy: The Years of Discovery* (New York, 1966), 278.

[14]Robert Peel, *Mary Baker Eddy: The Years of Trial* (New York, 1971), 22.

[15]Ibid., 136, 137.

[16]Ibid., 222.

[17]Ibid., 254; Robert Peel, *Mary Baker Eddy: The Years of Authority*, 127.

[18]Ibid., 78-83,113,114.

[19]Alma White, *The Story of My Life*, vol. 2, 264.

[20]Ibid., 299.

[21]Ibid., 313, 315.

[22]Ellen G. White, *Spiritual Gifts*, vol. 2 (Battle Creek, Mich., 1860), 89-90.

[23]Ellen G. White to Brother and Sister Howland, Aug. 15, 1850, Letter 12, 1850.

[24]Infra., 102-103.

[25]Ellen G. White to Willie White, Feb. 25, 1878, Letter 12, 1878.

[26]Ellen G. White to Brethren and Sisters, Dec. 16, 1854, Letter 5, 1854.

[27]James White to Edson White, Mar. 20, 1860.

[28]Ellen G. White to My Dear Sons, Mar. 25, 1861, Letter 21, 1861.

[29]Ellen G. White to Dear Willie, Mar. 3, 1860, Letter 2, 1860.

[30]Ellen G. White to My Dear Children, Aug., 1860, Letter 7, 1860

[31]Ellen G. White to Dear Children, Autumn, 1865, Letter 6a, 1865; Ellen G. White to Dear Son Edson, Oct. 19, 1865, Letter 7, 1865.

[32]Ellen G. White to Dear Son Edson, Sept. 22, 1866, Letter 4, 1866.

[33]Ellen G. White to Dear Son Edson, Feb. 13, 1867, Letter 4, 1867; Ellen G. White to Dear Son Edson, Feb. 11, 1868, Letter 3, 1868.

[34]Ellen G. White to Dear Children, Autumn, 1865, Letter 6a, 1865.

[35]Ellen G. White to Dear Children, Dec. 2, 1868, Letter 25, 1868.

[36]Ellen G. White to Dear Son Edson, June 10, 1869, Letter 6, 1869.

[37]Ellen G. White to Dear Son Edson, June 10, 1869, Letter 6, 1869; June 17, 1869, Letter 14, 1869; Jan. 14, 1872, Letter 2a, 1872.

[38]James White to Willie White, June 2, 1875.

[39]Ellen G. White to Sister Harriet, Jan. 30, 1857; Ellen G. White to Dear Edson, c. 1866, Letter 11, 1866; Ellen White to Edson and Emma, Aug. 21, 1874, Letter 47a, 1874.

[40]Ellen G. White to Henry and Edson, Mar. 14, 1860, Letter 1, 1860.

[41]Ellen G. White to Dear Son Edson, Jan. 19, 1867, Letter 2, 1867.

[42]Ellen G. White to Dear Son Edson, July 6, 1869, Letter 8, 1869.

[43]Ellen G. White to Dear Son Edson, May 25, 1869, Letter 5, 1869.

[44]Philip Greven, *The Protestant Temperament: Patterns of Child Rearing, Religious Experience, and Self in Early America* (New York, 1977), 52, 58-59.

[45]Ellen G. White, *Education* (Mountain View, Calif., 1903), 288-289.

[46]Ellen G. White to Dear Son Edson, Oct. 19, 1865, Letter 7, 1865.

[47]Ellen G; White to Dear Son Edson, June 10, 1869, Letter 5, 1869.

[48]Ellen G. White to Dear Son, June 17, 1869, Letter 14, 1869.

[49]Don F. Neufeld, ed., *Seventh-day Adventist Encyclopedia*, rev. ed. (Washington, D. C., 1976), s. v. "James Edson White."

[50]Ellen G. White to Edson White, c. Oct, 1892, Letter 57, 1892.

[51]Edson White to Ellen G. White, May 18, 1893.

[52]Ellen G. White to Edson, June 21, 1893, Letter 123, 1893.

[53]Ibid.

[54]Ibid.

[55]Ibid.

[56]Edson White to Ellen G. White, Aug. 10, 1893.

[57]Ron Graybill, *Mission to Black America: The True Story of James Edson White and the Riverboat Morning Star* (Mountain View, CA: 1971).

[58]At the time Edson went to Mississippi, the denomination had only one ordained Black minister. Ron Graybill, "Charles M. Kinny—Founder of Black Adventism," *Review and Herald*, vol. 154 (Jan. 13, 1977), 30-32.

[59]Ellen G. White to Willie White, Feb. 16, 1894, Letter 141, 1894.

[60]Ellen G. White to J. E. White, May 2, 1894, Letter 79, 1894.

[61]Ellen G. White to J. E. White, Jan. 5, 1903, Letter 11, 1903.

[62]Ellen G. White to Edson White, c. 1906, Letter 391, 1906.

[63]Ellen G. White to J. E. White, July 21, 1905, Letter 209, 1905.

[64]Ellen G. White to J. E. White, June 26, 1905, Letter 185, 1905.

[65]Ellen G. White to Dear Husband, July 15, 1874, Letter 43, 1874.

[66]Mary K. White to Willie White, Aug. 27, 1881.

[67]Ellen G. White to G. I. Butler, Oct. 30, 1906, Letter 348, 1906.

[68]Ellen G. White to F. M. Wilcox, Oct. 23, 1907, Letter 371, 1907.

[69]Ibid.

[70]Ellen G. White to O. A. Olson, Feb. 17, 1893, Letter 43, 1893.

[71]Ellen G. White to S. N. Haskell, Feb. 19, 1893; see also Ellen G. White to o. A.

Olson, July 19, 1893, Letter 63, 1893.

[72]Willie White to Ellen G. White, Dec. 15, 1881.

[73]Ellen G. White to Willie White, Nov. 9, 1881, Letter 11, 1881.

[74]Ellen G. White "Diary," Feb. 4, 1893, Ms. 76, 1893.

[75]Ellen G. White to J. Ings, Aug. 17, 1887, Letter 66, 1887.

[76]Ellen G. White to O. A. Olson, June 24, 1894, Letter 54a, 1894.

[77]Don F. Neufeld, ed., *Seventh-day Adventist Encyclopedia*, rev. ed., s.v. "William Clarence White."

[78]Ellen G. White to G. I. Butler, Aug. 1, 1888, Letter 59, 1888.

[79]Ellen G. White to Edson White, May 5, 1897, Letter 36, 1897.

[80]Ellen G. White to Willie White, Nov. 8, 1892, Letter 83, 1892.

[81]Willie White to Mary C. Mortensen, June 12, 1893.

[82]Ellen G. White to Brother Miller, June 4, 1891, Letter 18c, 1891.

[83]Ellen G. White to Willie White, Oct. 13, 1892, Letter 75, 1892.

[84]Willie White to Edson White, Sept. 30, 1895.

[85]Willie White to A.O. Tait, Sept. 2, 1894.

[86]Willie White to B. E. Nicola, June 2, 1902.

[87]Ellen G. White to Brethren Prescott and Daniells, May 20, 1904, Letter 173, 1904.

[88]Quoted in Arthur L. White, *Ellen G. White: The Early Elmshaven Years* (Washington, D.C., 1981), 335-336.

[89]Clarence Crisler to Willie White, Dec. 9, 1902.

[90]"Minutes of the Meeting of the White Book Trustees," Oct. 26, 1920, White Estate Document File #801; Paul McGraw, "Without a Living Prophet," *Ministry*, vol. 73 (Dec., 2000), 11-15.

[91]Frederick Coutts, *No Discharge in This War* (New York, 1974), 142, 175; Wiggins, Arch P., *The History of the Salvation Army* (London, 1968), 238.

[92]Bishop Arthur Kent White Memorial Issue," *Pillar of Fire*, vol. 82 (Nov. 1, 1981).

CHAPTER FOUR

Visions and Ecstasy

Ellen White's claim to divine revelations given in trance-like visions constituted an important basis of her authority and set her distinctly apart from the other women religious founders of her time. For Christian Scientists, Mary Baker Eddy's infrequent visions foreshadowed her triumph over various difficulties, but the revelation she claimed as the source of her teaching came to her while she was fully conscious.[1] Alma White received occasional revelations and symbolic dreams, but did not consider them unique to herself or use them to legitimate her authority. Catherine Booth laid no claim to immediate inspiration. She believed that what she experienced of the Spirit's power was accessible to all Christians.

In this chapter I will attempt to ascertain the role Ellen White's visions played in the establishment and perpetuation of her authority. Both the form and the content of the visions must be explored to discover why Adventists accepted them as genuine while others attributed them to mesmerism or hysteria. The ways in which her visions were explained and defended tells much about how Ellen White's influence was exercised.

Her first vision occurred in December of 1844 just after she had turned 17. She was attending a small women's prayer meeting when, as she put it, "the power of God came upon me as never before."[2] Thereafter, visions frequently accompanied periods of fervent prayer. White would appear initially to faint, then, while still unconscious of her surroundings, she recovered and would move about. She sometimes spoke short sentences and disconnected words and phrases. Later accounts made a good deal of the fact that she did not seem to breathe during her visions. Her eyes remained open and after coming out of vision, everything appeared dark. However, her sight was not damaged by this exposure. On some occasions her muscles became so fixed and rigid that efforts to move the fingers of her clasped hands failed. Feats of unusual strength were also reported. [3] These dramatic waking visions declined during the 1860's and died out entirely in the 1870's. After that, religious dreams, or "visions of the night," which White had experienced since adolescence, became her principal revelatory vehicle.

Psychologists and anthropologists have observed a wide range of trance, possession, and dissociative states in various cultures. In today's culture, similar states can be brought on by many stimuli: the hysteria of a rock concert, the sensory deprivation of solitary confinement, the monotony of long-distance driving, the "high" of hallucinogenic drugs, the rhythmic drumming, chanting, and dancing of religious rituals, hypnosis, and the euphoria of sexual orgasm.[4]

Religious ecstasy shares some characteristics with other altered states of consciousness, and psychologists suspect that common, if little understood, mental mechanisms are at work in all these phenomena.[5] Meanwhile, anthropologists affirm that many trance experiences and "possession" states are socially conditioned and socially relevant. They note that such experiences appeal to women who, being less powerful in most cultures, use them to transcend their otherwise marginal roles.[6]

In earlier American religious movements led by women, the leaders were not alone in receiving visions. We are told that "prophecies, visions, and revelations of God greatly abounded" in the Shaker community.[7] "Mother" Ann Lee shared her visions with many Shakers as a common gift; they did not imply a special calling to religious leadership. Visions were somewhat more important in establishing the authority of the black Shaker, Rebecca Jackson, who founded a small community in Philadelphia in the mid-nineteenth century. She, like other black women preachers, derived considerable power from her prophetic dreams, premonitions, inner, audible voices, and waking visions.[8] Like Ann Lee, Jemima Wilkinson, the "Public Universal Friend," also shared ecstatic gifts with her followers. Sarah Richards' visions were so prolific that Wilkinson dubbed her the "Prophet Daniel." Like Ellen White, Richards would swoon as she went into vision, lie "motionless and apparently lifeless" for some time, then arise to deliver her messages.[9]

More typical of the experience of devout men and women of Ellen White's own time, but still within the realm of dissociative religious experiences, were the reveries of the holiness leader, Phoebe Palmer. Her "visions" were of a private, mystical variety, occasions of profound unity with the divine which carried no specific messages or information:

My soul was wrapped in unutterable visions of glory....The holiness of God was presented to my ravished soul, yet it did not seem inapproachable, like the burning bush. No voice issued forth, but love,—infinite love. Such a joyous consciousness of oneness of spirit, such a consciousness of identity in this atmosphere of glory.... I never felt before in such blessed unity, the unity of the God-head.[10]

If the youthful Ellen White was aware of Ann Lee or Jemima Wilkinson, she probably believed they were both false prophets. She doubtless heard of Phoebe Palmer, but knew nothing of her inner experience.[11] However, the emerging Adventist community recognized a few genuine visionaries. A relative by marriage to Ellen White, Hazen Foss, is said to have had visions which he refused to relate.[12] William Foy, a Black, experienced visions in Boston in 1841 and 1842. For some time Foy travelled about New England, telling what he had seen during his trances. When he arrived in Portland, Maine, late in 1844, John and Charles Pearson, who were Millerites and friends of Ellen White and her family, persuaded Foy to publish his visions in a pamphlet.[13] White doubtless heard Foy relate his vision before her first one occurred in December of 1844. Foy published his pamphlet the next month (January, 1845) and when White printed hers a year later, it bore several striking parallels to Foy's work.[14] The differences were sufficient to demonstrate that White did not simply copy Foy's account, but Foy was a part of the essentially apocalyptic and ecstatic setting in which Ellen White's visions originated. The fact that Foy was Black reinforces the suggestion that persons of marginal status were sometimes able to use visions to improve their lot.

Significantly, after Ellen White's waking visions had died out in the 1870's, Adventists began to discount the validity of all other visionaries. Foy came to be known as a prophet who failed. It was said that he received a further vision which he did not understand and did not relate, and that he died soon afterwards. Actually, Foy lived until 1893, although he abandoned his Millerite affiliations and became a Free-will Baptist clergyman.[15]

Foss and Foy were not the only recognized visionaries during the period when Ellen White was experiencing trances.[16] In an attempt to show that other Christians also believed in the continuity of spiritual gifts, Adventist evangelist M. E. Cornell marshaled the evidence in a pamphlet called *Miraculous Powers*. He cited John Wesley's statement that God had favored several of his converts with "divine dreams, others with trances and visions," and quoted the early church fathers, Justin Martyr, Irenaeus, Origin, and Cyprian in favor of visions.[17] From American religious history, Cornell recounted the story of William Tennent's three days in a trance, and drew upon a Methodist layman's remarkable book, *Shouting in all Ages of the Church*—a protest against waning religious enthusiasm among Wesley's heirs.[18] James White's introduction to Cornell's pamphlet claimed that the examples were given only to "show the faith of the church," but Cornell was inclined to accept the genuineness of the examples he cited. He avoided all mention of visionaries such as Joseph Smith, Ann Lee, or Joanna Southcott.[19]

Cornell's tract, first published in 1862, was reprinted in 1875, and then disappeared. With it disappeared the tendency to argue that Ellen White's waking visions were legitimate because others had experienced or believed in similar visions. Yet Adventists continued to defend other special doctrines by showing their antiquity and acceptance by other Christians. J. N. Andrews work, *The History of the*

Sabbath, for instance, was only the beginning of a tradition in Adventist historiography which culminated in the twentieth century with Leroy Froom's massive works: *The Prophetic Faith of Our Fathers* and *The Conditionalist Faith of Our Fathers*.[20] So long as Ellen White had visions, Adventist writers granted other visionaries a certain validity. When they ceased, her visions came to be viewed in a more unique and magical light.

The trances Ellen White experienced related closely to other characterics of Adventist worship. She and the writers who recounted the visions stressed that they occurred in a calm, solemn manner. While it is likely that some did, it is quite clear that most of the waking visions were ecstatic phenomena, a part of the enthusiastic religious experience all early Adventists shared. The fact that her revelations came in visions did not make her experience alien to her fellow believers. Visions were merely a more exotic form of the religious excitement they all enjoyed. Believing themselves deeply moved by the Spirit of God, it was easier for them to believe the Spirit moved her. James White defended religious exuberance in the *Review*, calling those who criticized it "lukewarm, deceived," and "hardened."[21] Ellen White told how she had seen in vision that God's children should "unitedly get the victory over the powers of darkness and sing and shout to the glory of God."[22] Adventist emotionalism was restrained compared to the violent outbursts generally associated with frontier camp meetings, but many shouted, some swooned, and three or four spoke in tongues, although the latter practice was never encouraged.[23]

Many early Adventists were drawn from the ranks of the "shouting Methodists," so named because of the fervor and enthusiasm of their religious experience and worship services.[24] Visions were a rare but not unknown occurrence in American Methodism, where shouting and swooning were the most common manifestations of enthusiasm.[25] Shouting was not incoherent bellowing, although there were those also who "screeched" and "screamed."[26] Rather shouting, or "praising God" employed standard phrases such as "Hallelujah," "Glory to God!" or "Glory!" thrice repeated. These phrases crop up in the literature of Adventism, Methodism, and many other denominations through the 1850's. Aside from shouting, swooning was the most frequent result of religious enthusiasm among Methodists and early Adventists. The worshipper, "slain by the Spirit," would fall to the floor in unconsciousness so deep that the uninitiated sometimes feared for his or her life. As a teenager, Ellen Harmon swooned on several occasions while her Methodist mother assured concerned onlookers her daughter would safely recover.[27]

The early visions occurred during periods of intense religious excitement. They should be classified as ecstatic experiences, a part of the religious enthusiasm which characterized early Adventism. While Mrs. White is said to have experienced visions under varied circumstances, the following collection of contemporary accounts of specific visions place them amidst the "shouts" of the believers:

> Sister Durben knew what the power of the Lord was, for she had felt it many times; and a short time after I fell, she was struck down, and fell to the floor, crying to God to have mercy on her. When I came out of vision, my ears were saluted with Sister Durben's singing and shouting with a loud voice.[28]

> The spirit came and we had a powerful season. Brother and Sister Ralph were both laid prostrate and remained helpless for some time. I was taken off in vision and saw concerning

the state of some here.[29]
The power came down like a mighty, rushing wind, the room was filled with the glory of God, and I was swallowed up in the glory and taken off in vision.... While I was in vision, the doctor came, he heard the shouting in vision and would not come in.[30]

The power came down more and more, and we all shouted and praised the Lord as much as we were a mind to. In this state of feelings among us Ellen was taken off in vision.[31]

The brethren prayed over me and I was healed and taken off in vision. I had a deep plunge .in the glory, and the state of things in Washington [N.H.] was revealed to me.... Brother Baker was healed and he glorified God in a loud voice, he had a baptism of the Holy Ghost.[32]

I had a deep plunge in the ocean of God's love. In vision again....Sister Mead healed. A mighty shout. She slain by the spirit.[33]

When seated, Mrs. W. began to praise the Lord, and continued rising higher and higher in perfect triumph in the Lord, till her voice changed, and deep, clear shouts of Glory! Hallelujah! thrilled every heart. She was in vision.[34]

The frequency of such visions declined in direct proportion to the decline in all forms of emotional worship in Adventist circles. Both waned beginning in the late 1850's though both continued to flare up occasionally. Adventist historians have tended to ignore both the enthusiasm of early Adventist worship and the connection of its decline with the declining frequency of the visions during the 1860s and 1870s. Waking visions did not wholly cease until the late 1870's, but neither did enthusiastic worship. James White reports that during one of his wife's talks in late 1859, "the house rang from full shouts of praise from several in the congregation."[35] In November of 1860 James White wrote that he had "felt more of the power of God" than he had "at any time for three years:"

> Brethren Ingraham, Sanborn, and I were praying in another room, while a brother was anointing his wife. The room was filled with the power of God. I was standing, but with difficulty. I fell upon my face, and cried and groaned under the power of God. Brethren Sanborn and Ingraham felt about the same. We all lay on the floor under the power of God.[36]

Late in 1865, at the time when the believers in Rochester were praying so fervently for James White's recovery, "Shouts of victory and praise to God ascended to heaven for his tokens of love and acceptance."[37] In March of 1866, a pastor in Oswego, New York, reported that "Loud praises of God ascended from most, if not all the house; and continued until after midnight."[38]

James and Ellen White made a trip west to Waukon, Iowa, in December of 1856. The trip was designed to effect reconciliation between the Whites and several prominent believers in the Waukon area. Writing of the meeting immediately afterwards, James White reported that as church members began to confess their lack of consecration:

The Spirit of God filled the place. Some who had been almost silent for months, shouted the high praises of God. The
words, "Glory" and "Hallelujah," seemed to fall far short of ex-
pressing the exceeding joy which filled nearly every heart.[39]

Thirty years later, J. N. Loughborough remembered these same
meetings, adding that on that occasion Ellen White had three visions,
two of them in one evening. Loughborough says: "Light and glory
came in. Immediately Sr. White was in visions and .... several others
were greatly moved by the power of God."[40]

In the 1870's, feeling still ran high on some occasions:

The blessing and power of God rested upon your father and
mother. We both fell to the floor. Your father, as he rose upon
his feet to praise God, could not stand. The blessing of God
rested upon him with remarkable power. ... Elder Loughborough felt the power of God all through his body. The room
seemed holy . . . . We shouted the high praises of God . . . .
Streams of light seemed to come upon us from our heavenly
Father and the room seemed to be illuminated with the presence of the Lord.[41]

Pastor J. H. Waggoner and James White both "fell to the ground
twice under the special power of God" while praying together in
1874.[42] In 1877, at another session of prayer for the healing of James
White, Ellen White reports: "We wept and shouted for joy. Father's
face was lighted up with the glory of God. Sister Ings felt his power
as never before. We all shouted the praise of God. ... We praised our
Saviour nearly all night."[43]

In 1880, an aged believer, while dying, "shouted the praise of God while tears rolled from his sightless eyes."[44] Just as these last manifestations of ecstatic religious experience were passing from the Adventist scene in the 1870's, so too the ecstatic visions were drawing to a close. In 1868 James White estimated that his wife had experienced between 100 and 200 visions, but noted that they had "grown less frequent" in recent years.[45] Indeed they had. A careful search for specific visions reveals that Mrs. White experienced only about a dozen during the 1860's, only three in the 1870's, and none thereafter.[46] Comments she made during these decades concerning the length of time since her most recent vision coincide with the established dates to all but eliminate the possibility that other visions also occurred.[47] This distribution of visions matches well the declining frequency of other manifestations of religious excitement in Adventist circles. The two phenomena waxed and waned together.

As ecstasy began to wane in the 1860's and 1870's, detailed descriptions of Ellen White's trance states began to appear. The more uncommon ecstatic experiences became in the church, the more uncanny the visions seemed, and the more Adventist apologists made of what seemed in later years to have been supernatural aspects of the visionary trance itself. Earliest among these seemingly miraculous phenomena to be discussed was Ellen White's apparent lack of normal breathing during visions. In extant sources, the phenomenon is mentioned only twice prior to the mid-1860's. James White writes of a vision in 1848, saying: "She was in vision one and one half hours in which time she did not breathe at all."[48] The uncanny occurrence was not mentioned again until 1859, when another minister, Daniel T. Bourdeau, wrote that "while the Spirit of God rested upon those who were with her, she was breathless."49 Finally, in 1866, J. N. Loughborough added yet another feature, claiming that "while in this condition, audible words were spoken without breath."50 He was quite sure she did not breathe, for, he said, "Were there one particle of breath it would produce steam on a looking glass. But this test applied while she is in vision will detect no breath whatever." James White also mentioned the tests to which his wife was subjected: "During the entire period of her continuance in vision, which has at different times ranged from fifteen minutes to three hours, there is no breath, as has been repeatedly proved by pressing upon the chest, and by closing the mouth and nostrils."51

What is historically important here is not so much what happened physiologically, but the fact that as the visions decreased in frequency, Adventists came to accept their unusual features as one proof of their validity. In earlier times, it had sometimes been feared that those "slain by the Spirit" were literally dead. It seems likely this fear arose from the subject's failure to breathe normally. The Methodist Benjamin Abbott, seasoned veteran of many enthusiastic revivals, recalled one occasion when even he was afraid that a certain young man would not recover, observing that his body was growing cold and blue.52 When such subjects revived and arose "praising God," it was the praise, not the recovery, that Abbott used to prove the genuineness of his work. Here again, the physical phenomena itself did not seem uncanny to those familiar with it.

Even skeptical appraisals of the visions seem to have changed as enthusiastic worship became less widespread in American culture. In the early days, the visions were often attributed to mesmerism. While rejecting divine intervention, this explanation accepts the visions as in some sense "normal," and to some extent externally caused. Later, as ecstatic phenomena became more unusual, psychopathological explanations such as hysteria and epilepsy were advanced. Now the visions were thought to arise from Ellen White's own diseased state.[53] She paid no attention to the later charges, but the earlier suggestion that her visions were caused by mesmerism troubled her deeply. Both J. N. Loughborough and Joseph Bates, later staunch defenders of the visions, at first believed them to be caused by mesmerism.[54] "Grieved and desponding" because of these accusations, she "often went alone to some retired place" to pour out her soul, and there would be "taken off in vision."[55] The clear implication is that since she was alone, the visions could not have been caused by mesmeric influence. When one skeptic tried to mesmerize her by peeking through his spread fingers as she was speaking, she believed she had successfully resisted his influence by calling on "extra angels."[56]

While the common heritage of religious enthusiasm helped Adventists accept the visions as genuine divine revelations, that acceptance by no means insured that Ellen White would be seen as one who had been specifically called to the prophetic office, one whose visions had an authority both separate from and higher than the authority of their own inner experiences. That acceptance was won by the cogent, relevant content of the visions.

Anthony F. C. Wallace, in his seminal article on revitalization movements, observed that cultures in conflict are often brought back to equilibrium when elements which have already attained currency in the society come into coherent, usable form in a dramatic moment of insight, usually involving "one or several hallucinatory visions by a single individual." These visions, though essentially dream formations, are unlike ordinary night dreams in that they often occur while the subject is awake or in an ecstatic trance. Furthermore, they impress the dreamer immediately as being important, their content is in large part a rational and well-constructed intellectual argument, and the recollection of them is unusually rich in detail. Such visions may or may not arise from unconscious neurosis, in any case, they offer creative insights that resolve basic conflict and sometimes work startling cures in the recipient and his or her community.[57]

All of these characteristics are seen in Ellen White's experience. In almost every line, her first vision "fit" the needs of the confused, struggling Millerite community in Maine. These were a people torn by fanaticism and factionalism, ridiculed and persecuted by their neighbors and civic authorities. Into this discouraging situation, the youthful Ellen White came with a resonate "vision" of assurance and direction. She had seen the Advent people, she said, travelling on a path, high above the dark, wicked world. If they simply kept their eyes fixed on Jesus, they could safely journey to the holy city. Behind them, a bright light was shining, a light which her angel guide told her was the "Midnight Cry," a term derived from a Biblical parable which Millerites had used to describe their mission during the summer of 1844 when they gave the "midnight cry" that Jesus was going to return in October. The vision, then, assured them that God had been with them all along, even though they had not correctly understood his plan. The vision went on to describe the beauties and joys of paradise, and to depict a band of Adventists as they toured the heavenly land. They felt, Ellen said, that they had a "perfect right" to be there.

Actually, in her descriptions of heaven, Ellen was weaving together various Biblical passages, words of assurance and comfort from the epistles of Paul, apocalyptic spectacles from Daniel, and scenes of shimmering light and soaring joy from Revelation. For example, although the Bible does not name the "twelve manner of fruit" born by the "tree of life," Ellen identified some of those delicacies as "manna, almonds, grapes, figs, and pomegranates." The manna and almonds were from the Biblical tradition which said the Israelites' "ark of the covenant" contained a "golden pot of manna" and Aaron's rod which "budded, blossomed, and bore almonds." In vision, Ellen had seen the prototype of that ark in the heaven. The "grapes, figs, and pomegranates," were the three fruits the Israelite spies brought back from the land of Canaan. She had cast her vision in the form of a "good report" from the heavenly Canaan.[58] In content then, as well as in form, this vision, like many others, took common experiences and common beliefs, cast them in a new context, and derived from them a new basis for authority.

The symbiotic relationship between Ellen White's visions and her religious community was dramatically illustrated in the early 1850's when, because of heavy criticism from Sunday-keeping Adventist groups, James White determined he would no longer publish his wife's visions in the *Review and Herald*. He intended to reserve them for an "extra" which would go only to those who already believed in their authenticity. Although this "extra" was supposed to be published every two weeks, only one appeared, and for the next four years, Ellen got relatively little public exposure.[59] During this period her visions became less and less frequent until by 1855 she had concluded that her "work in God's cause was done," and that she had "no further duty to do" but to save her own soul and carefully attend to her "little family."[60] However, at this point church leaders decided that their neglect of the visions had led to a decline in spiritual life. They publicly confessed their fault, and almost immediately, Ellen began to have visions again.

To her, these circumstances showed that God would not continue to bestow a gift that was not appreciated and used. To Max Weber, they would prove that "it is recognition on the part of those subject to authority which is decisive for the validity of charisma."[61]

Confronted with the fact of the visions, and inclined to accept them for many reasons, Adventists interpreted the visions as something the Bible had promised and predicted. Opposing ministers argued that such spiritual gifts were intended for and limited to apostolic times. Adventists countered with Ephesians 4:11-14, where the apostle mentions various gifts and states that their purpose was to "edify" the church "till we all come in the unity of the faith, and of the knowledge of the Son of God, unto a perfect man." Since the church had not yet achieved this unity and perfection, spiritual gifts were still to be expected. A great deal was also made of the prophecy of Joel 2:28-32, which promised that in the "last days" God would pour out his Spirit, "and your sons and your daughters shall prophesy, and your young man shall see visions, and your old men dream dreams."[62] Finally, by linking the King James version's wording of Rev. 12:17 with that of Revelation 19:10, Adventists argued that in the last days the "remnant" or true church would be known for keeping the commandments of God and having "the testimony of Jesus," which was the "spirit of prophecy." This exegetical argument, introduced as early as 1855, not only helped convince Adventists that the gift of prophecy was to be expected in the church, but since they believed Ellen White possessed that gift, it uniquely identified their community as the true remnant of God's church.[63] Even as they argued for the legitimacy of Ellen White's gift, Adventists also took pains to assert that they accepted the Protestant principle of the Bible and the Bible only as their standard of faith and doctrine. They insisted that their doctrines were not "vision views," as their enemies had charged, but were based on Scripture. The Bible itself taught the doctrine of spiritual gifts, however, so they must accept its teaching and receive the testimony of the visions.

However valid this exegesis, it still had not demonstrated that Ellen White was herself the recipient of the gift of prophecy. From the very beginning, attempts to establish her prophetic credentials have been muted in Adventist literature, especially in the earliest period when Adventist periodicals were evangelistic as well as internal communication media. When public discussion did get down to Mrs. White's case, it contended that she was an "unassuming and humble person" and that the "fruits" of her visions were good, leading "to meekness and humility and holy living," and inciting "deep heart searching before God."[64] In an 1847 pamphlet, Joseph Bates defended her as a "self-sacrificing, honest, willing child of God," and said the visions had given him light on many conflicting and difficult texts of Scripture.[65]

Although early arguments for the visions made little of the trance phenomena itself, they did stress that the visions conveyed information which Ellen White could not otherwise have known. James White responded to a friend who believed the visions to be only religious reveries "in which her imagination runs without control upon themes in which she is most deeply interested."[66] The content of the visions, the friend thought, was "obtained from previous teaching, or study."[67] White denied that his wife's visions were influenced by her environment, pointing to one case where she reversed her own doctrinal position on the basis of a vision, and another which led her to advocate a position entirely new to her and to her companions. Finally, he mentioned a vision in Topsham, Maine, where she was guided to the planets, including two he identified as Jupiter and Saturn, and gave information about their moons, although, James claimed, she had previously known nothing about astronomy.

In 1847, a Dorchester, Massachusetts, engraver, Otis Nichols, tried to persuade William Miller that Ellen White had the true gift of prophecy, arguing she met Biblical tests of a true prophet.[68] While Nichols said nothing about the visions themselves being miraculous, he opined that her calling had been "most remarkable." Only 17, she had been sick with "dropsical consumption" and confined to the house for nearly five years. When called to deliver her first message, she was scarcely able to walk across the room or talk above a whisper, but "God fulfilled his word [and] gave her strength of body and a clear, loud, audible voice to talk nearly two hours with tremendous power." Her preaching "fed, comforted, strengthened the weak, and encouraged" the Millerite groups to "hold on to the faith." Nichols told how once when a sheriff had tried to arrest her, he and his men were unable to do so for over an hour and a half even though "they exerted all their bodily strength to move her while she or no one else made any resistance." He also claimed that the healing of the sick in response to her prayers was "as remarkable as any that are recorded in the New Testament."

Ellen White's 1860 autobiography, *Spiritual Gifts*, was a major document in establishing the validity of her experience. Here, as in Otis Nichols' letter, miracles of healing were stressed. More than two dozen healings are recorded in the book, several immediately preceding visions. In order to further demonstrate the authenticity of her gift, Mrs. White claimed numerous cases where the Lord had shown her "where to go... who to fear, and who to trust."[69] In several instances, she was shown persons in vision whom she had never met and who, according to her account, she was later able to identify when she encountered them for the first time. There are also a number of instances where she claimed to have seen some secret evil or duplicity on the part of a person whom the other church members trusted.[70]

The only story connecting a miracle to the circumstances of a specific vision involved an occasion when she is said to have taken a large, heavy Bible, held it outstretched on one hand in a position where she could not see the pages and proceeded to point to texts and quote them correctly.[71]

As the waking visions became rarer in the late 1870's, Ellen White commonly referred to her revelatory experiences as "dreams." Since the beginning of her career she had experienced dreams which she accepted as special revelations from God, but as years passed, virtually all of her revelations came under this label. "I had dreams in reference to the [publishing] office," she wrote once.[72] To her husband she confided: "I dreamed night before last that I was talking with two ladies who had been privileged to learn the truth."[73] To a minister: "In my dreams you are in peril, in danger of losing your soul through neglect."[74]

Occasionally during this transition period Mrs. White was not completely sure what she should call her revelations. On one occasion she mentioned "a dream or vision of the night—I cannot tell certainly which."[75] On another, she recalled an "important dream" in which she thought she was "taken off in vision and shown that an angel was addressing our ministers."[76]

From 1890 onward, Mrs. White used less specific terms in referring to her dreams, terms which de-emphasized their dream-like qualities and stressed their authority as divine revelations. "I was in earnest conversation with you in the night," she wrote one young woman.[77] To another person, she said: "I was deeply moved by the Spirit of the Lord to tell you many plain things."[78] And again: "The Lord has presented your case before me several times."[79] Phrases such as "Instruction was given me," "I have received light," and "a scene was clearly presented to me," tended to take the focus off the mode of a revelation and emphasize its source and content.

There were good reasons to de-emphasize the similarity between her dreams and the dreams of others. Although Adventists believed God communicated through dreams, they also believed Satan could inspire dreams or that they could arise from "the multitude of business" in a person's daily life. Ellen White acknowledged that the majority of dreams were in the latter category and were experiences with which the Spirit of God has nothing to do. "However," she said:

> Dreams from the Lord are classed in the word of God with visions, and are as truly the fruits of the spirit of prophecy as visions. Such dreams, taking into account the persons who have them, and the circumstances under which they are given, contain their own proofs of genuineness.[80]

Even though the Bible considered dreams and visions equally valid modes of divine revelation, Adventists had long recognized a difference between them. One minister wrote:

> Dreams and visions widely differ as a source of reliable communication. In visions the whole person, mental and physical, is under the entire control of a higher power; therefore what is then communicated is really from the being holding this control over the person. In dreams we are more liable to

be swayed by our thoughts through the day and the external circumstances and influences around us; therefore from their nature and varied sources we cannot rely upon them with that certainty that we can upon visions.[81]

This sort of reasoning may account for Mrs. White's reluctance to continue to classify her revelatory experiences as dreams. The fact that many other individuals thought they received revelations in dreams may also have motivated her to let the term "dream" fall into disuse, although even from her own point of view, what she experienced in a vision was scarcely distinguishable from a dream.[82] Willie White said he once quizzed her: "Mother, you often speak of matters being revealed to you in the night season. You speak of dreams in which light comes to you. We all have dreams. How do you know that God is speaking to you in the dreams of which you so frequently speak?"[83] "Because," Mrs. White replied, "the same angel messenger stands by my side instructing me in the visions of the night, as stands beside me instructing me in visions of the day."

She saw the presence of this "same angel" as very significant. She mentions him as "the young man who has often appeared to me and instructed me,"[84] or "A man of noble appearance (the same one that has often appeared to counsel and inform me of important matters)"[85] or "A young man ... whom I have frequently seen in my dreams and who has given counsel as one whose judgment was not to be questioned."[86] Angel guides often appeared in religious visions, being especially prominent in the apocalyptic visions of the Biblical prophets. It is a measure of Ellen White's conventionality that her angel guide was male. The black prophetess, Rebecca Jackson, acquired a female guide after she was exposed to the Shaker concept of androgynous deity.[87]

Gradually then, Ellen White's charisma was isolated from similar phenomena. The enthusiasm of early Adventist worship was ignored, along with the ecstatic character of the early visions. Other visionaries were ignored or discredited. The miraculous aspects of the visions were emphasized. Finally, her dreams were placed in a separate category from the dreams of others. None of this development was necessarily conscious or deliberate, but as it progressed, it gave the visions a special aura, and reinforced their authority as divine messages.

Ellen White's visions were clearly more important to her and her movement than were most of the mystical, revelatory, or visionary experiences of the other female religious leaders of her time. It is tempting to conclude that the claim to direct inspiration was in itself an enduring source of authority and influence. After all, the women who did claim direct divine inspiration for their writings—Ellen White and Mary Baker Eddy—are the same women whose writings are still revered and widely published by their churches. Catherine Booth's books of sermons can be had only in libraries and rare book stores. On the other hand, there were scores of would-be prophets who claimed immediate divine inspiration, Rebecca Jackson being one example. Obviously such a claim is not sufficient to insure continued authority. However, where other factors secured for the woman a recognized leadership role, and where a sufficiently large supporting community developed, the claim to inspiration tended to perpetuate the leader's influence further beyond her death.

---

[1]Gilbert C. Carpenter, Jr., *The Visions of Mary Baker Eddy: As Recorded by Her Secretary, Calvin A. Frye, From 1872-1894 with Interpretations Written by Her Sometimes Assistant Secretary* , Gilbert C. Carpenter (Rumford, R.I., 1935); Robert Peel, *Mary Baker Eddy: The Years of Discovery* (New York, 1966), 233, 279; Robert

Peel, *Mary Baker Eddy: The Years of Trial* (New York, 1971), 75, 97, 135, 250, 290.

[2]Ellen G. White, *Spiritual Gifts*, vol. 2, 30.

[3]James White, *Life Incidents*, 272,273; n.a., "Ellen G. White In Vision: the Testimony of Eye Witnesses," (duplicated, Washington, D.C., 1952); Nellie Sisley Starr, "Seeing Ellen G. White in Vision," (duplicated, Washington, D.C., 1928); J. N. Loughborough, *The Rise and Progress of the Seventh-day Adventists* (Battle Creek, MI: 1892), 103, 104.

[4]Arnold M. Ludwig, "Altered States of Consciousness," in Raymond Prince, ed., *Trance and Possession States* (Montreal, 1966), 69-95.

[5]William Sargant, *The Mind Possessed: A Physiology of Possession, Mysticism, and Faith Healing* (London, 1973), 4, 6, 8, 44.

[6]I. M. Lewis, *Ecstatic Religion: An Anthropological Study of Spirit Possession and Shamanism* (London, 1971), 30-32.

[7]n.a., *Testimonies of the Life, Character, Revelations and Doctrines of Mother Ann Lee, 2nd ed.,* (Albany, N.Y., 1888, reprint New York, 1975), 65.

[8]Jean McMahon Humez, ed., *Gifts of Power: The Writings of Rebecca Jackson: Black Visionary, Shaker Eldress* (n.p., 1981), 6.

[9]n. a., *Memoir of Jemima Wilkinson* (Bath, N.Y., 1844), 153-154; Herbert A. Wisbey, Jr., *Pioneer Prophetess, Jemima Wilkinson, The Public Universal Friend* (Ithaca, New York, 1964), 63. Wisbey conjectures that Richards suffered from epilepsy. However, but her symptoms are explicable without resort to psychopathology.

[10]Richard Wheatley, *The Life and Letters of Phoebe Palmer* (New York., 1876), 97.

[11]In an 1861 article in the Adventists' *Review and Herald*, Palmer's public speaking was cited as a justification for women speaking in public. J. A. Mowatt, "Women as Preachers and Lecturers," *Review and Herald*, XVIII (July 30, 1861), 65.

[12]J. N. Loughborough, *The Rise and Progress of the Seventh-day Adventists* (Battle Creek, Mich., 1892), 72, 73; Ellen G. White to Mary Foss, Dec. 22, 1890, Letter 37, 1890.

[13]William E. Foy, *The Christian Experience of William E. Foy Together with the Two Visions He Received in the Months of Jan. and Feb., 1842,* (Portland, Maine, 1845), 9, 21-23.

[14]Tim Poirier, "Black Forerunner to Ellen White: William E. Foy;" Spectrum, 17 (August, 1987), 23-25. Ellen G. White, "Interview with Mrs. E. G. White, Regarding Early Experiences," Aug. 13, 1906, White Estate Document File #733c.

[15]J. N. Loughborough, *Rise and Progress of the Seventh-day Adventists*, 73; Lelia A. Clark Johnson, *Sullivan and Sorrento Since 1760* (Ellsworth, Maine., 1953), 65-66. Johnson has mistakenly recorded Foy's death date as 1892. His gravestone and death certificate give 1893. For a biography of Foy that considers him faithful to his divine commission, see Delbert Baker, *The Unknown Prophet* (Hagerstown, MD: 1987).

[16]J. N. Loughborough, "A Remarkable Vision," *Review and Herald*, vol. 21 (May 19, 1863), 194-195.

[17]M. E. Cornell, *Miraculous Powers: The Scripture Testimony on the Perpetuity of Spiritual Gifts* (Battle Creek, Mich., 1862), 45, 50, 51, 52.

[18]Ibid., 75, 79, 123; G. W. Henry, *Shouting: Genuine and Spurious, in All Ages of the Church* (Oneida, N. V., 1859).

[19][This footnote is incorrect. Read this letter at EGW Center to see what it is about.] Ellen G. White to James White, Feb. 27, 1880, Letter 7, 1880.

[20]J. N. Andrews, *The History of the Sabbath*, (Battle Creek, Mich., 1859, 1862, 1873, 1887); Leroy Froom, *The Prophetic Faith of Our Fathers* (Washington, D.C., 1950-1954); *The Conditionalist Faith of Our Fathers* (Washington, D.C., 1965-1966).

[21][James White], "The Immediate Coming of Christ," *Review an Herald*, vol. 3 (Jan. 20, 1853), 141.

[22]Ellen G. White to "The Church in Brother Hastings' house," Nov. 7, 1850, Letter 28, 1850.

[23]Ellen G. White, *Testimonies for the Church*, vol. 1, 44, 45, first published 1860; Statement of Mrs. S. Howland, Mrs. Frances Howland Lunt, Mrs. Rebekah Howland Winslow, N. N. Lunt, (Battle Creek, Mich., n.d.); Hiram Edson, "Beloved Brethren," *Present Truth*, vol. 1 (Dec., 1849),35; F. M. Shrimper to *Review and Herald*, vol. 2 (Aug. 19, 1851), 15.

[24]Ann Taves, *Fits, Trances, & Visions: Experiencing Religion and Explaining Experience from Wesley to James* (Princeton: Princeton University Press, 1999), 76-108.

[25]See John Ffirth, *Experience and Gospel Labours of the Rev. Benjamin Abbott* (New York, 1833), 188, 234, 238, 274. Wesley himself had, on occasion, defended some visions on the basis of their results. He also discouraged reliance on them, pointing out that they "might be from God, but they might not." John Wesley, *The Works of John Wesley*, vol. 1 (London, 1872, Reprint, Grand Rapids, Mich., n.d.), 35-36; vol. 8, 284; vol. 12, 35-36.

[26]John Ffirth, *Experience... of the Rev. Benjamin Abbott*, 116.

[27]Ellen G. White, *Life Sketches* (Battle Creek, Mich., 1880), 160.

[28]Ellen G. White to Joseph Bates, July 13, 1847, Letter 3, 1847.

[29]Ellen G. White to Brother Hastings, Mar. 29, 1848, Letter 1, 1848.

[30]Ellen G. White to Brother Hastings, portion written June 1, 1848, Letter 1, 1848.

[31]James White to Brother Hastings, Jan. 10, 1850.

[32]Ellen G. White to Brother Howland, Nov. 12, 1851, Letter 8, 1851.

[33]James White to Brethren in Christ, Nov. 11, 1851.

[34]James White, "Eastern Tour," *Review and Herald*, vol. 15 (Dec. 1, 1859), 13.

[35]Ellen G. White to Brother Bates, Dec. 7, 1872, Letter 2, 1872.

[36]James White to Ellen G. White, Nov. 6, 1860.

[37]Ellen G. White, "Our Late Experience," Feb. 20, 21, 1866, Ms. 1, 1866.

[38]Elias Goodwin, "Monthly Meetings in New York," *Review and Herald*, vol. 27 (Mar. 6, 1866), 110.

[39]James White, "Western Tour," *Review and Herald*, vol. 9 (Jan. 15, 1857), 84.

[40]J. N. Loughborough, "Recollections of the Past—No. 16," *Review and Herald*, vol. 63 (Nov. 30, 1886), 745.

[41]Ellen G. White to Edson, Willie, Dec. 7, 1872, Letter 20, 1872.

[42]Ellen G. White to Brother Littlejohn, Nov. 4, 1974, Letter 58, 1874.

[43]Ellen G. White to Children, Aug. 31, 1877, Letter 11, 1877.

[44]Ellen G. White to S. N. Haskell, Nov. 17, 1880, Letter 3, 1880.

[45]James White, *Life Incidents*, 272.

[46]Loughborough's claim that she experienced a public vision at the Oregon Campmeeting in 1884 cannot be credited. Such an occurrence would have been very dramatic at that late date, and yet a full report of her activities at the meeting, published soon after, makes no mention of a public vision, nor does Mrs. White mention one in letters from that time. See J. H. Waggoner, "North Pacific Camp Meeting," *Signs of the Times*, vol. 10 (July 17, 1884), 424; J. N. Loughborough, "The Study of the Testimonies—No. 2," *General Conference Daily Bulletin*, vol. 5 (Jan. 29, 30, 1893), 20.

[47]James White, "Monterey and Battle Creek," *Review and Herald*, vol. 31 (June 16, 1868), 409.

[48]James White to Dear Brother and Sister, Aug. 26, 1848.

[49]D. T. Bourdeau to Editor, *Review and Herald*, vol. 13 (Feb. 24, 1859), 61.

[50]J. N. Loughborough, "Remarkable Fulfillments of the Visions," *Review and Herald*, vol. 29 (Dec. 25, 1866), 30.

[51]James White, *Life Incidents* (1868), 272.

[52]John Ffirth, *Experience... of the Rev. Benjamin Abbott*, 123.

[53]Ron Numbers, *Prophetess of Health: A Study of Ellen G. White* (New York, 1976), 91, 180-181, 252; D. M. Canright, *Seventh-day Adventism Renounced* (New York, 1889), 151-154.

[54]J. N. Loughborough, "Remarkable Fulfillments of the Visions," *Review and Herald*, vol. 29 (Dec. 25, 1966), 30; James White, *A Word to the "Little Flock"* (Brunswick, Maine, 1847), 21.

[55]Ellen G. White, *Spiritual Gifts*, vol. 2, 57. If this happened, it would have been one of those rare occasions when a vision occurred that was not surrounded by the shouts and enthusiasms of fellow believers. But no accounts of visions reported at the time of their occurrence describe them occurring when Ellen White was alone.

[56]Ibid., 63.

[57]Anthony F. C. Wallace, "Revitalization Movements," *America Anthropologist*, vol. 58 (Apr., 1956), 271.

[58]Ellen G. White, *Spiritual Gifts*, vol. 2, 30-35.

[59]*Review Extra*, vol. 2 (July 21, 1851), 4.

[60]Ellen G. White, "Communication from Sister White," *Review and Herald*, vol. 7 (Jan. 10, 1856), 118.

[61]S. N. Eisenstadt, ed., *Max Weber on Charisma and Institution Building* (Chicago, 1968), 49.

[62][Arthur L. White], ed., *Witness of the Pioneers Concerning the Spirit of Prophecy*

(Washington, D.C., 1961).

[63]James White, "Peter's Testimony" *Review and Herald*, vol. 7 (Oct. 16, 1855), 61.

[64]D. T. Bourdeau to Editor, *Review and Herald*, vol. 13 (Feb. 24, 1859), 61.

[65]Joseph Bates, J. H. Waggoner, and M. E. Cornell, "Address," *Review and Herald*, vol. 7 (Dec. 4, 1855), 79.

[66]James White, ed., *A Word To the "Little Flock"*, 21.

[67]Ibid., 22.

[68]Otis Nichols to William Miller, April 20, 1846.

[69]Ellen G. White, Spiritual Gifts, vol. 2, 45.

[70]Ibid., 48, 157, 170.

[71]Infra., 115.

[72]Ellen G. White to Willie, Mary, March 10, 1878, Letter 15, 1878.

[73]Ellen G. White to James White, Feb. 27, 1880, Letter 1, 1880.

[74]Ellen G. White to Brother Waggoner, Nov. 4, 1885, Letter 10, 1885.

[75]Ellen G. White to Drs. Caldwell and Gibbs, May 10, 1888, Letter 85, 1888, see also Ellen G. White to Uriah Smith, Feb. 19, 1884, Letter 11, 1884.

[76]Ellen G. White to James White, April 19, 1880, Letter 24, 1880.

[77]Ellen G. White to Carrie Gribble, Sept. 13, 1893, Letter 2, 1893.

[78]Ellen G. White to William Gage, Oct. 22, 1893, Letter 22, 1893.

[79]Ellen G. White to A. T. Jones, Sept., 1902, Letter 164, 1902.

[80]Ellen G. White, *Testimonies for the Church*, vol. 1, 569, 570, first published 1867.

[81]David Arnold, "Dreams and Visions," *Review and Herald*, vol. 7 (Feb. 28, 1856), 171; See also G. I. Butler, "Visions and Prophecy," *Review and Herald*, vol. 43 (May 12, 1874), 173.

[82]There were a few occasions during later years when Mrs. White did have revelatory experiences during her waking hours. However, no physical phenomena accompanied these reveries. See Ellen G. White to Edson White, Mar. 21, 1896, Letter 131, 1896; Ellen G. White, "Friday, Mar. 20, I rose early," Mar. 20, 1896, Ms. 12c, 1896.

[83]Arthur L. White, *Ellen G. White, Messenger to the Remnant* (Washington, D.C., 1969), 7.

[84]Ellen G. White to Willie White, Dec. 25, 1877, Letter 44, 1877.

[85]Ellen G. White to S. N. Haskell, Oct. 12, 1875, Letter 34, 1875.

[86]Ellen G. White, "Work in California," [1874], Ms. la, 1874.

[87]Jean McMahon Humez, ed., *Gifts of Power: The Writings of Rebecca Jackson, Black Visionary, Shaker Eldress*, 38.

CHAPTER FIVE

The Spirit and the Scriptures

The Bible was the brick of which much of nineteenth-century Anglo-American culture was built. The very fact that evolution and higher criticism triggered so much opposition is an indication how essential the Bible was to the Victorian framework of meaning.[1] Robert Ingersoll's career as a "professional infidel" depended as much on the Bible's importance as did Benjamin Warfield's reputation as a defender of scriptural inerrancy.[2] Since Timothy L. Smith found a rich infusion of Biblical themes in groups as diverse as Mormons and transcendentalists, it comes as no surprise that Biblical language and thought forms pervaded the work of the female founders of nineteenth century denominations.[3] Catherine Booth is said to have read the Bible eight times before she reached her teens.[4] Alma White's copy was so heavily underlined that the markings came to have little value.[5] The two leaders who claimed special revelations were also heavily indebted to the Bible. Although she knew much of it by memory, Ellen White had seventeen copies of the Bible in her personal library when she died.[6] Robert Peel has shown how Mary Baker Eddy also wove the phrases, terms, images, allusions, and even the rhythms of the King James Version into her published and unpublished writings.[7]

Ellen White's charismatic authority was reinforced by Scripture at every available opportunity. Even the physical phenomena which accompanied her early visions were shaped by what she and other Adventists understood to be the prophet Daniel's condition when experiencing a vision. Like him, she first lost strength, then regained it. Observers testified that, like him, she did not breathe or close her eyes.[8] Other Biblical passages also provided models. When, early in her experience, Ellen resisted what she believed to be God's call to share His message with others, she was, like John the Baptist's skeptical father Zachariah, struck dumb and compelled to write what she wished to say on a slate. What she wrote was fifty texts of Scripture she had just seen in a vision "written in letters of gold."[9]

Besides figuring prominently in the content of the visions, the Bible played rich symbolic roles in Ellen White's experience. During a meeting in the Thayer home in Randolph, Massachusetts in 1845, Ellen experienced a vision nearly four hours long. Thayer had heard that if a vision was of the Devil, it could be arrested by opening a Bible and placing it on the person experiencing it. According to an eyewitness account written fifteen years later, Thayer placed a large family Bible on Ellen's chest as she lay on a sofa in trance, whereupon she took the Bible, walked to the center of the room, held it as high as she could, and declared, "the inspired testimony from God." Then, although she could not see the pages, she pointed to various texts and quoted them. When the onlookers checked the passages, they acknowledged her accuracy.[10] The story captured the imagination of Adventists from its first telling and symbolized their understanding of Ellen's relationship to the Bible—a frail, sickly girl who exalted the Scriptures and, by virtue of her supernatural gift, was able to expound them without being able to see them with her natural eyes.

White's sermons were generally expository, commenting clause by clause on long passages of Scripture. When a Scripture index was created for forty-five of her books, the abbreviated references filled 150 printed pages.[11] Material from virtually every chapter and from the majority of all the verses of the Bible were either cited or commented upon somewhere in her writings.

Mary Baker Eddy's teachings have long been attacked by her theological opponents as discordant with the Bible.[12] But, as Timothy Smith has shown in the case of Joseph Smith, one need only change the angle of vision slightly to see that she too was deeply indebted to the Bible. Eddy's clerical opponents recognized and feared the Biblical appeal of Christian Science. One critic, Isaac Haldeman, said he would have paid no attention to it "if it did not come in the name of Christ, quote the Bible, [and] use Christian nomenclature."[13] Doubtless many converts felt the same. It was to the Bible that Eddy turned after her legendary "fall on the ice" in Lynn, Mass., in 1866.[14] Especially was she drawn to the miracles of Jesus, where she "discovered" the most perfect "demonstration" of divine "Science."[15] In accord with Eddy's instructions, the Bible, along with her textbook, *Science and Health*, are the only "pastors" in Christian Science churches, and passages from both are read in every service.[16] She wrote in the first of the "six tenets" of Christian Science, "As adherents of Truth, we take the inspired Word of the Bible as our sufficient guide to eternal Life"[17] Although she did not dwell at length on specific behavior, the things proscribed of Christian Scientists were the same things other Christians found condemned in the Bible. The "Christianization of daily life" was as much her goal as it was the goal of any "Bible-believing" Protestant. "It is chastity and purity, in contrast with the downward tendencies ... of sensualism and impurity, which really attests to the divine origin ... of Christian Science," Eddy wrote; "the emphatic purpose of Christian Science is the healing of sin."[18]

The debt Mrs. Eddy and Mrs. White owed to Scripture, can explain, in part, their success, and it can curb the temptation to see them as mystical ecstatics spinning cultic beliefs and practices out of their fertile imaginations. However, the movements they founded were not only distinct but competing and antagonistic to each other. Although they read a common Bible, sharp differences grew out of their variant interpretations. Examination of their hermeneutics— their methods of interpretation—is therefore crucial. From an outsider's point of view, it may be possible to consider religious founders such as Joseph Smith, Mary Baker Eddy, and Ellen White as a part of the American "mainstream" because of their heavy debt to the same Bible that most other Americans respected so highly. Yet their contemporaries judged them to be "outsiders."[19] One of the chief reasons for this was that to one degree or another, they claimed to offer an extra-canonical doctrinal authority. New converts to any Protestant denomination might say that the Bible became a "new book" to them, but for the thousands of converts to Christian Science and Seventh-day Adventism who said the same, new interpretations had indeed made it a new book.[20] In a Protestantism which theoretically insisted on the right of individual interpretation, in an America jealous of the rights of private citizens, and in a culture where authorities of all kinds were increasingly discredited, these leaders both defended the

Bible against the inroads of skepticism and provided an interpretation of it which they and their followers accepted as the product of revelations direct from the same God who had inspired the original authors of Scripture. Both because they did this and because those interpretations were in some sense "deviant," they and their followers were very much "outsiders."

Although the non-charismatic leaders, Catherine Booth and Alma White, used different interpretive methods, both arrived at fairly conventional doctrines. Catherine Booth's simple hermeneutics were typically Wesleyan: "I like to let one Scripture explain another,"[21] she said, "and surely we should take that which is plain and unmistakable as a key to unlock and interpret that which at first sight is difficult and contradictory."[22] Her early theological reading may account for the fact that she used her Bible in such a traditional way. She studied not only Methodist devotional literature, but also the theological works of Luther, Bunyan, Butler, Newton, Wesley, Fletcher, Henry, Clarke, Barnes, Finney, and many others.[23] Later, Phoebe Palmer became a favorite.[24] Initially, Booth found her reading confusing. She decided to reject all theories about God and religion which contradicted her "innate perceptions of right and wrong."[25] Could it have been her repeated reading of the Bible that gave her the self-confidence to trust those "innate" perceptions? In any event, her mentors' high regard for the Bible and similar ways of interpreting it insured that Booth's "innate perceptions" would not foment much doctrinal innovation.

Booth's published sermons were thoroughly and conventionally Biblical. She was a topical rather than expository preacher, but whether she spoke on "The Fruits of Union with Christ," the "Conditions of Effectual Prayer," "Saving Faith," or "Hindrances to Holiness," she laced the sermon with Biblical texts and allusions. In her role as the Salvation Army's "ambassador" to upper-class Britons, Booth helped deflect the criticisms and quiet the fears of those who disliked the boisterous enthusiasm of Army meetings.[26] Her ability to preach evangelical sermons based soundly on the Book they all knew and respected helped overcome prejudice and win respect for the Army. Booth generally assumed that her audience accepted the Bible's authority and her own hermeneutics, although she occasionally defended Scripture against "Christian free-thinkers" who thought its inspiration no higher than Shakespeare's.[27]

Booth laid no claim either to a unique message or to special divine guidance in interpreting the Bible's teaching. An unusual measure of the orthodoxy of her hermeneutics is the fact that she did not use Scripture to defend her vegetarian dietary preference.[28] By way of comparison, Ellen and Alma White, who also eschewed meat, made free use of Biblical arguments to defend their practice.[29] Booth's doctrinal orthodoxy may have provided her some license for her cultural deviance, both as an advocate for the lower classes and for women. Only her "deviant" piece of interpretation, her pamphlet on woman's rights, is kept in print by her church.

Alma White's allegorical interpretations exhibit a more idiosyncratic use of Scripture, yet her doctrine remained generally conventional. Her college-educated husband sometimes argued with her all night over her interpretations, but to no avail.[30] Interpretation of the typology embedded in Scripture itself had a long and respected history, but Alma went far beyond the Reformation and Puritan exegetes who reveled in types and ante-types. Typology rests on the assumption that a historical person or event prefigures a later person or event. The Bible often interprets its own types, but in allegory, as Perry Miller once explained, "there is a correspondence only between the thing and the association it happens to excite in the impression-able and treacherous senses of men."[31] Alma White's exegesis was clearly allegorical. In the early part of her career, she found the Wesleyan "second blessing" in every second text of Scripture. The Holy Place of the Israelite tabernacle was the first blessing, the Most Holy Place the second.[32] In the story of the Prodigal Son, the father's kiss was the first blessing, the "best robe" and the "fatted calf" the second.[33] As her denomination began to take shape, this theme receded and Scripture seemed to bespeak the contrast between the old and dying religions of the past and the fresh promise of a new movement. The "jawbone of an ass" which Sampson used to slay the Philistines became for Alma a symbol of her new church.[34]

It was this allegorical approach which enabled her to use the Bible to defend radical feminism on the one hand and the Ku Klux Klan on the other. When the Klan's anti-Catholicism made it an attractive ally against the allegedly Catholic-inspired persecution of her street preachers, she "discovered" that the Klan had been favorably prophesied in the Bible.[35]

Although Alma White's hermeneutics were unstable, the major doctrines she taught were thoroughly conventional. Her flirtation with the Klan did not last past the 1920's. Her main emphasis was on the Wesleyan second blessing and the Biblical validity of enthu-siasm in public worship. She felt she received "help and inspiration when writing on Bible subjects," but it was the guidance any Christian might claim.[36] If God "gave" her texts, He might do the same for others.

The Biblical interpretations of the charismatic leaders, Ellen White and Mary Baker Eddy, who used their own revelations as her-meneutic tools, deviated more widely from traditional Protestantism.

Eddy's Biblical interpretations were, to use one of her phrases out of its context, "hopelessly original."[37] Yet Christian Scientists insist on their validity as true explanations of the Bible. They draw an analogy to Einstein's discovery of the theory of relativity. Einstein did not make the theory true; he merely made a truth accessible which was inherent in nature all along. Eddy's teachings on the topic suggest that her "discovery" became the "key" which disclosed the meaning of all Scripture. Consequently, one finds a distinct tendency on her part always to link the study of Scripture to the study of *Science and Health*. Ellen White believed her writings also help clarify the meaning of Scripture, but she made the connection much less frequently and much less explicitly. In Christian Science services, before the reading of each lesson-sermon, the Reader quotes Eddy's statement: "The canonical writings, together with the word of our textbook [*Science and Health*], corroborating and explaining the Bible texts . . . constitute a sermon . . . uncontaminated by human hypotheses."[38] Within that textbook is the *Key to the Scriptures* consisting in part of a glossary of Biblical words with unique Christian Science definitions. This glossary, Eddy wrote, contains "the metaphysical interpretation of Bible terms, giving their spiritual sense, which is also their original meaning."[39] "Original," in this context, has nothing to do with Greek or Hebrew. It is rather the "spiritual sense" which Eddy believed to be the true intention of Biblical revelation. By supplying her own definition of Biblical terms together with her own vision of the nature of reality, Eddy assumed a role as interpreter of Scripture which neither Catherine Booth nor Alma White ever claimed. Eddy studied and respected the Bible a great deal more than many critics have imagined, but she considered her discovery as essential to its proper understanding. She claimed to have uncovered the true "spiritual sense" of

Scripture, and because God was "Spirit," the meaning of Scripture was "wholly spiritual." In order to discern this spiritual meaning, "the revelation, discovery, and presentation of Christian Science" was "requisite in the divine order." There was "no possibility of misinterpretation" when the Bible was thus read and practiced.[40] Mrs. Eddy offered a unique and uniquely authoritative interpretation.

Ellen White originated none of Seventh-day Adventism's cardinal tenets. These were worked out earlier by her husband and other former Millerites.[41] Still, her visions confirmed what they had agreed upon and occasionally selected among discordant interpretations which developed.[42] When this happened, Adventist pioneers felt that Ellen was placing heaven's approval on their work. During the years of doctrinal formulation, she claimed that she could not even understand the Bible except when God explained it to her during a vision.[43] This reinforced their impression that she merely relayed divine messages. Her early visions were not a source of religious teaching or unique Biblical interpretation. Still, their appearance as inspired confirmations of the group's consensus gave Mrs. White preeminence in the movement. Her assumption of this confirmatory role suggested that she had greater doctrinal authority than any other person or group in the church.

The interpretations Ellen White confirmed, and the hermeneutics she endorsed, were more conventional than those of Mary Baker Eddy. White intended to be in perfect accord with historic Protestant views of Scripture. The most important of her several dozen books, *The Great Controversy*, spent nearly half its pages reviewing Reformation history in order to trace the development and application of the *sola scriptura* (Scripture alone) principle.[44] She was intent on convincing her audience that the Reformers were right to insist that the Bible must interpret itself rather than be interpreted by the Fathers, tradition, or the teaching authority of the church. "The Bible is its own expositor," she wrote elsewhere. "Scripture is to be compared with Scripture."[45]

> God will have a people upon the earth to maintain the Bible, and the Bible only, as the standard of all doctrines and the basis of all reforms. The opinions of learned men, the deductions of science, the creeds or decisions of ecclesiastical councils, as numerous and discordant as are the churches which they represent, the voice of the majority—not one nor all of these should be regarded as evidence for or against any point of religious faith. Before accepting any doctrine or precept, we should demand a plain "Thus saith the Lord" in its support.[46]

Whatever tensions she may have felt between her standard of letting the Bible interpret itself and her expectation that Adventists would defer to her interpretations, Ellen White still urged believers to study the Bible alone with no preconceptions and no commentator's assistance.

Although theoretically clear, the practical reconciliation of her stated position with her own interpretive authority created ambiguity almost from the start. As early as 1860, one minister's wife wrote in her diary:

> There is some difference of views as to the place [the visions] should occupy in the church. Some hold them as equal authority with the Bible and are designed to correct and guide

the church.... Others believe the Bible does not sanction such use of them. Oh, that we might understand just the right position to take in regard to them.[47]

On several occasions, Ellen White refused to use her authority to settle interpretive disputes. In their effort to affirm the continuing force of the Ten Commandments, Adventists had gravitated by the late nineteenth century to a position which taught that the "law"" spoken of in the Epistle to the Galatians as having had no saving power except as a "schoolmaster" leading sinners to Christ was really the ceremonial law of Moses, not the Ten Commandments. They said it was the round of rituals and ceremonies prescribed by Moses that, like a schoolmaster, taught the Jewish nation about Christ. Thus Christ's life and death did not cancel the force of the Ten Commandments, as some opponents claimed, for these had a different function. A. T. Jones and E. J. Waggoner challenged this view at the General Conference Session of 1888.[48] They held that the "schoolmaster" law was indeed the Ten Commandments. Since all merely human efforts to keep them were doomed to fail, the Ten Commandments, like a schoolmaster, taught the sinner his need of Christ. General Conference President G. I. Butler feared this position would leave the church's belief in the seventh-day Sabbath of the fourth Commandment vulnerable to antinomian arguments which suggested that once the sinner came to Christ, he had no further need for the commandments. Mrs. White, however, refused to settle the exegetical dispute. She did not even discuss the meaning of the passages until nearly a decade had passed. She urged only that both sides study their Bibles with Christian charity.[49]

In 1905, however, when another Adventist preacher, Albion F. Ballenger, challenged the denomination's unique interpretation of the "heavenly sanctuary," Mrs. White's response changed dramatically.[50] "Elder Ballenger has mystified minds by his large array of texts," she said. The texts were true, but he had placed them where they did not belong.[51] Instead of offering an alternative exegesis, however, she appealed to the history and tradition of the Adventist church, pointing out that the sanctuary doctrine had "stood for the past fifty years."[52]

Though she claimed Biblical support for the doctrine, she also appealed to her authority as the medium through which the Spirit had long since confirmed Adventist interpretations. The church's doctrines had been vindicated by "God's word and the manifestation of the Holy Spirit," they had been "sought out by prayerful study, and testified to by the miracle working power of the Lord."[53] " I am thankful," she wrote, "that the instruction contained in my books establishes present truth for this time. These books were written under the demonstration of the Holy Spirit."[54] She seems not to have sensed that such arguments contradicted her own rule that no authority outside Scripture should have any weight in deciding what the Bible taught. Ballenger, undeterred, rejected her arguments. To accept them, he said, would

> place the thousands upon thousands of pages of your writings in books and periodicals between the child of God and God's Book. If this position be true, no noble Berean dare believe any truth, however clearly it may seem to be taught in the Scriptures, until he first consults your writings to see whether it harmonizes with your interpretation.[55]

Certainly Ellen White would not admit that she had changed

her position on the authority of the Bible, but in a moment of crisis, she had in fact claimed that her writings should conclude the argument. Yet a few years later, when a dispute over a passage in Daniel was causing widespread divisions among ministers and leaders in the church, she specifically requested both sides to refrain from using her writings to establish what the Bible taught.[56] She seems not to have regarded her interpretive authority as absolute, but clearly, it could not be ignored. Adventist evangelists might preach the church's Biblical understandings without any public reference to Ellen White, but in their private studies and in doctrinal discussions with fellow Adventists, they deferred constantly to her interpretations.

In retrospect, it is clear that the female founders who did claim direct divine inspiration—Mary Baker Eddy and Ellen White—exercised a more authoritative role as interpreter of the Bible than did those who made no such claim. Within their movements, they curbed deviant interpretations and thus functioned to solidify and unify their church's doctrinal positions.

Mrs. White reinforced Adventist beliefs in other ways as well. If a doctrinal system is to be based on a Bible which is understood to express God's thoughts directly, albeit in human words, then such a book must be held in very high regard. She taught her fellow Adventists such an attitude. She wrote and said more about the importance, value, and power of the Bible than did any other female founder. She discussed the nature of its inspiration and made suggestions as to how it ought to be studied.

Perhaps because she knew her own inspiration was not verbally conveyed, White took a moderate view of the topic. She drew on a moderate contemporary, Calvin Stowe, even to the extent of paraphrasing the language of his *Origin and History of the Books of the Bible* in one of her messages. "It is not the words of the Bible that are inspired," she wrote, "but the men. Inspiration acts not on the man's words or his expressions but on the man himself, who, under the influence of the Holy Ghost, is imbued with thoughts. But the words receive the impress of the individual mind."[57] Here she parted company with conservatives like Charles Hodge who said: "No man can have a wordless thought any more than there can be a formless flower."[58] Accordingly, she never insisted on the absolute inerrancy of the Bible.

Generally, however, her positions on these topics resembled the views George Marsden identifies with the forerunners of Fundamentalism. Like them, she spoke of the Scriptures and used them in such a way that it would have made little difference had she taught that they were actually dictated by God. She sometimes appeared to endorse verbal inspiration:

Momentous truth is conveyed to the mind through the reading of the Scriptures. Every word is a valuable pearl. No word is to lose its virtue and force. One word changed would injure the thought and destroy the lesson taught. By incorrect punctuation the meaning of the word of God may be greatly altered. The Holy Spirit directed and impressed the writers of the Bible. These men did not write words of human wisdom, but words given them by God.[59]

The context of this statement makes plain that she was not primarily concerned with whether the words of Scripture were dictated; rather, she was trying to impress her readers with the authority of what the Bible teaches. To her, as to the Fundamentalists, the practical application of the Bible in preaching, witnessing, and spiritual growth mattered most. If a literal reading was to reveal its teaching, the Bible had to be a book in which the limitations of human bias, error, language, and culture were, in large measure, overridden by God's revelations. Ellen White did not deny that the personalities of the individual authors were reflected in the Bible, but she said far more about the divine origins of the book than she did about the human medium which brought it into being. Adapting the words of Henry Melvill, an Anglican preacher of mid-century London, Ellen White declared: "The word of the living God is not merely written, but spoken. The Bible is God's voice speaking to us, just as surely as though we could hear it with our ears."[60] Ellen White also insisted on the unity of the Bible. It taught one harmonious message from Genesis to Revelation rather than an assortment of "theologies" derived from its various authors and reflecting their cultural settings. The unity of the Old and New Testaments had been emphasized also in the writings John Wesley, the Beecher family and the early Puritan divines.[61] This legacy of appreciation for the Old Testament made it all the easier for Ellen White to accept and stress the centrality of the seventh-day Sabbath once she saw it expounded in tracts written by another former Millerite, Joseph Bates. Those who set aside the Old Testament err, she argued:

> In rejecting the Old, they virtually reject the New; for both are parts of an inseparable whole. No man can rightly present the law of God without the gospel, or the gospel without the law. The law is the gospel embodied, and the gospel is the law unfolded. . . . The Old Testament sheds light upon the New, and the New upon the Old. Each is a revelation of the glory

of God in Christ.[62]

White's writings abound in Old Testament lore, and her private correspondence alluded frequently to David, Moses, and Elijah. She wrote two major narratives of Old Testament history, *Patriarchs and Prophets*, and *Prophets and Kings*.

Finally, along with Wesley and the forerunners of Fundamentalism at Princeton, White insisted on the perspicuity of Scripture. "The Bible is a plain book," Charles Hodge had argued, and Ellen White contended that

> The interpretation by the common people, when aided by the Holy Spirit, accords best with the truth as it is in Jesus. The great truths necessary for salvation are made clear as noonday, and none will mistake or lose their way except those who follow their own judgment instead of the plainly revealed will of God.[63]

As early as 1864, White condemned those who "eagerly" received the "suppositions of geologists which dispute the Mosaic record."[64] Scientific research had become a "curse" to many she said, because even the greatest minds "if not guided by the word of God in their research, become bewildered."[65] Rightly understood, science and the Bible agreed. "Together they lead us to God."[66] But the Bible was "not to be tested by men's ideas of science;" rather, science was to be "brought to the test of the unerring standard."[67] Later in the century she warned of higher critics who "put themselves in the place of God."[68] "The work of higher criticism, in dissecting, conjecturing, reconstructing, is destroying faith in the Bible as a divine revelation," she said. This criticism was "robbing God's word of power to control, uplift, and inspire human lives."[69]

This was her main concern: the power of the Bible to control, uplift, and inspire. She believed the Bible had tremendous power. In Adventist schools it stood as "the highest, the most important textbook.[70] Nothing, she said, helped to cultivate a retentive memory like studying the Scriptures, because this brought the mind in contact with the "deep, broad principles of eternal truth."[71]

> The searching of all the books of philosophy and science cannot do for the mind and morals what the Bible can do, if it is studied and practiced.... If all would make the Bible their study, we should see a people further developed, capable of thinking more deeply, and showing a greater degree of intelligence, than the most earnest efforts in studying merely the sciences and histories of the world could make them.[72]

This much-praised Bible was used by Ellen White and her fellow Adventists to support a number of deviant doctrines. Belief in the continued relevance of the seventh-day Sabbath was accompanied by an expectation that the Sabbath would become the focal issue in the eschatological conflict between good and evil. God would test the loyalty of all humankind on whether they acknowledged his right to set aside the seventh day as sacred time. In one sense, Adventists merely rescued the Puritan Sabbath which was sinking under waves of European immigrants for whom Sunday was a day for recreation as well as worship. By shifting to a different day and infusing it with eschatological significance, Adventists preserved a day of worship wholly dedicated to religious activities. More truly unique was the Adventist reinterpretation of the significance of 1844. With Ellen

White's support, they declared that Daniel's prophecy of a "cleansing of the sanctuary" referred not to Christ's second coming as Miller had taught, but to a special work of "investigative judgment" which was initiated in 1844. For these and other deviant doctrines, Adventists believed Ellen White provided divine confirmation.

Thus while Ellen White and Mary Baker Eddy both honored and supported the Bible, claiming they were only making clear what the Bible actually taught, their authority lent support to deviant interpretations. By interweaving their doctrinal authority with that of the Bible they not only preserved their church's unique teachings, they also maintained their own influence in their churches. Their interpretations were bound up with the very definitions of Seventh-day Adventism and Christian Science. Today, while the non-charismatic founders, Catherine Booth and Alma White are nostalgic memories, the charismatic founders, Ellen White and Mary Baker Eddy, are non-negotiable authorities whose writings are studied in Talmudic detail.

---

[1]Paul Carter, The Spiritual Crisis of the Gilded Age (DeKalb, Ill., 1971), 34-42, 137-138, 188; James Moore, The Post-Darwinian Controversies (New York, 1979); Paul C. Gutjahr, An American Bible: A History of the Good Book in the United States, 1777-1880 (Palo Alto, CA: Stanford University Press, 2002); David Daniell, The Bible in English: Its History and Influence (New Haven, CT: Yale University Press, 2003).

[2]Robert Ingersoll, About the Bible (New York, 1894); David D. Anderson, Robert Ingersoll (New York, 1972), 92,100-102; Sidney Warren, American Freethought, 1860-1914 (New York, 1943), 89-95; Susan Jacoby, The Great Agnostic: Robert Ingersoll and American Freethought (New Haven, CT: Yale University Press, 2012).

[3]Timothy L. Smith, "The Book of Mormon in a Biblical Culture," Journal of Mormon History, vol. 7 (1980), 3-21, and "Transcendental Grace: Biblical Themes in the New England Renaissance," (unpublished manuscript, presented to the American Historical Association, Dec., 1981).

[4]Frederick L. Booth-Tucker, *The Life of Catherine Booth*, vol. 1 (New York, 1892), 18. Roger Joseph Green, *Catherine Booth: A Biography of the Cofounder of the Salvation Army* (Ada, MI: 1996); Roy Hattersley, Blood and Fire: The Story of William and Catherine Booth and the Salvation Army (New York: Doubleday, 1999).

[5]Alma White, *The Story of My Life*, vol. 3, 230; Susie Cunningham Stanley, *Feminist Pillar of Fire: the life of Alma White* (Cleveland, Ohio: Pilgrim Press, 1993).

[6]Ron Graybill and Warren H. Johns, "An Inventory of Ellen G. White's Private Library" (duplicated, Washington, D.C., 1981), 6,27.

[7]Robert Peel, *Mary Baker Eddy: The Years of Authority* (New York: Holt, Rinehart and Winston, 1977), 106-107.

[8]James White, *Life Incidents*, 272; J. N. Loughborough, *The Great Second Advent Movement* (Washington, D.C., 1905), 204-211; S. N. Haskell, *Bible Handbook* (Washington, D.C., 1919), 138, cites Daniel 10:8-16.

[9]Ellen G. White, *Early Writings* (Washington, D.C., 1945), 22-23.

[10]Ellen G. White, *Spiritual Gifts*, vol. 2, 77-79.

[11]Ellen G. White Estate, *Comprehensive Index to the Writings of Ellen G. White*, vol. 1 (Mountain View, Calif., 1962), 21-176.

[12]Allen W. Johnson, *The Bible and Christian Science* (New York, 1924); Isaac M. Haldeman, *Christian Science in the Light of Holy Scripture* (New York, 1909); Lyman Powell, *Christian Science, The Faith and its Founder* (New York, 1917); Louise C. Benedict, *The Bible vs. Christian Science* (Los Angeles, 1927).

[13]Isaac Haldeman, *Christian Science in the Light of Holy Scripture*, 5.

[14]Steven Gottschalk, *The Emergence of Christian Science in American Religious Life* (Berkeley, Calif., 1973), 31; Robert Peel, *Mary Baker Eddy: The Years of Discovery* (New York, 1966), 197.

[15]Gottschalk, *The Emergence of Christian Science*, 19-20, 23, 32.

[16]Mary Baker Eddy, *Manual of the Mother Church* (Boston, 1936), 32; Steven Gottschalk, *The Emergence of Christian Science*, 192.

[17]Mary Baker Eddy, *Science and Health with Key to the Scripture* (Boston, 1934), 497.

[18]Mary Baker Eddy, *Science and Health*, 272; *Rudimental Divine Science* (Boston, 1919), 2; see also Gottschalk, *The Emergence of Christian Science*, 241.

[19]R. Laurence Moore, "Insiders and Outsiders in American Historical Narrative and American History," *American Historical Review*, vol. 87 (April, 1982), 390-412.

[20]Steven Gottschalk, *Emergence of Christian Science*, 238.

[21]Catherine Booth, *Life and Death* (London, 1883), 67.

[22]Ibid., 17.

[23]Catherine Bramwell-Booth, *The Life of Catherine Booth* (London, 1970), 27-28; Catherine Booth, *Papers on Practical Religion* (London, 1891), 62.

[24]Catherine Bramwell-Booth, *The Life of Catherine Booth*, 102.

[25]Catherine Booth, *Life and Death*, 30.

[26]Bramwell-Booth, *Catherine Booth*, 234, Catherine Booth, *Popular Christianity*

(London, [1887]), 52, 64, refers to the "genteel, refined, religiously trained" persons making up her audience.

[27]Catherine Booth, *Popular Christianity*, 70.

[28]Catherine Bramwell-Booth, *Catherine Booth*, 131, 151-2, 348; William Booth, *Orders and Regulations for Field Officers of the Salvation Army* (London, 1891), 70.

[29]Alma White, *Why I Do Not Eat Meat* (Zarephath, N.J., 1915); Ellen G. White, *Counsels on Diet and Foods* (Washington, D.C. 1946), 373-378, 380, 392.

[30]Alma White, The Story of My Life, vol. 2, 34, 35, 124,147.

[31]Perry Miller, "Introduction" for *Jonathan Edwards' Images or Shadows of Divine Things* (New Haven, Conn., 1948), 4, cited in Mason I. Lowance, Jr., *The Language of Canaan: Metaphor and Symbol in New England from the Puritans to the Transcendentalists* (Cambridge, Mass., 1980), 5.

[32]Alma White, "The Holy Place and the Most Holy Place," *Pentecostal Union Herald*, vol. 3 (Aug. 1902), 8.

[33]Alma White, *The Story of My Life*, vol. 2, 64.

[34]Ibid., vol. 3, 41.

[35]Alma White, *The Story of My Life*, vol. 5 (Zarephath, N.J., 1943), 168,174, 264; *Klansmen: Guardians of Liberty* (Zarephath, N.J., 1926); *Heroes of the Fiery Cross* (Zarephath, N.J., 1928); *The Ku Klux Klan in Prophecy* (Zarephath, N.J., 1925).

[36]Alma White, *Looking Back from Beulah*, 168; *The Story of My Life*, vol. 2, 211, 212; vol. 5, 5.

[37]Mary Baker Eddy, *Retrospection and Introspection* (Boston, 1920), 35.

[38]*Christian Science Quarterly*, (all editions).

[39]Mary Baker Eddy, *Science and Health* (Boston, 1934), 579-599.

[40]Ibid., 238.

[41]LeRoy Froom, *Movement of Destiny* (Washington, D.C., 1971), 107.

[42]Ellen G. White, Spiritual Gifts, vol. 2, 98-99.

[43]Ellen G. White, *Selected Messages*, Book 1 (Washington, D.C. 1958), 207.

[44]William Johnsson, "An Evaluation of The Shaking of Adventism," *Andrews University Focus*, vol. 15 (Spring, 1979), 31.

[45]Ellen G. White, *Counsels to Parents, Teachers, and Students* (Mountain View, Calif., 1943), 462.

[46]Ellen G. White, *The Great Controversy* (Mountain View, Calif., 1939),595.

[47]Angeline Andrews, diary entry for July 28, 1860, Loma Linda University Library, Loma Linda, Calif.

[48]Infra, 148.

[49]Woodrow W. Whidden II, *E. J. Waggoner: From the Physician of Good News to Agent of Division* (Hagerstown, MD: 2008) 99-103; Ronald Graybill, "Ellen White's Role in Doctrine Formation," *Ministry*, vol. 54, (October 1981), 7-11.

[50]Graybill, "Ellen White's Role," 8-12.

[51]Ellen G. White, "Diary," Oct. 31, 1905, Ms. 145, 1905.

[52]Ellen G. White, "A Warning Against False Theories," May 24, 1905, Ms. 62,

1905.

[53]Ellen G. White, "The Sabbath Truth in the Sentinel," May 20, 1905, Ms. 59, 1905; Ellen G. White, "An Appeal for Faithful Stewardship," Mar. 29, 1905, Ms. 44, 1905.

[54]Ellen G. White to W. W. Simpson, Jan. 30, 1906, Letter 50, 1906.

[55]Albion F. Ballenger, *Cast Out for the Cross of Christ* (Tropico, Calif., 1909),110.

[56]Bert Haloviak, "In the Shadow of the 'Daily:' Background and Aftermath of the 1919 Bible and History Teacher's Conference," (unpublished manuscript, Washington, D.C., 1979); Bert Haloviak and Gary Land, "Ellen G. White and Doctrinal Conflict: Context of the 1919 Bible Conference," *Spectrum*, vol. 12 (June, 1982), 19-34.

[57]Ellen G. White, *Selected Messages*, Book 1 (Washington, D.C., 1958), 21; cf. Calvin Stowe, *Origin and History of the Books of the Bible* (Hartford, Conn., 1867), 19.

[58]George Marsden, *Fundamentalism and American Culture* (New York, 1980), 112.

[59]Ellen G. White, "A Work to be Done for God," June 16, 1900, Ms. 40, 1900; *Christ's Object Lessons*, 132; *Testimonies for the Church*, vol. 4 (Mountain View, Calif., 1948), 9, first published 1876.

[60]Ellen G. White, *Testimonies for the Church*, vol. 6, 393, first published 1900; Graybill, Warren H. Johns, and Tim Poirier, "Henry Melvill and Ellen G. White: A Study in Literary and Theological Relationships," (duplicated, Washington, D.C., April, 1982), 36. This document can also be found online; see Henry Melvill, *Sermons*, Vol. 1 (New York, 1850), 159.

[61]Marie Caskey, *Chariot of Fire: Religion and the Beecher* Family (New Haven, Conn., 1978),374,375; Mason I. Lowance, Jr., *The Language of Canaan*, 35.

[62]Ellen G. White, *Christ's Object Lessons*, 128.

[63]Charles Hodge, *Systematic Theology*, vol. 1 (New York, 1873), 183; Ellen G. White, *Testimonies for the Church*, vol. 5, 331, first published 1885.

[64]Ellen G. White, *Spiritual Gifts*, vol. 2, 95.

[65]Ellen G. White, *The Great Controversy*, 522.

[66]Ellen G. White, *Counsels to Parents, Teachers, and Students*, 426.

[67]Ibid., 425.

[68]Ellen G. White to A. G. Daniells and Brother Salisbury, Jan. 21, 1897, Letter 48, 1897.

[69]Ellen G. White, *Acts of the Apostles* (Mountain View, Calif., 1911), 474.

[70]Ellen G. White, *Fundamentals of Christian Education* (Nashville, Tenn., 1921), 231.

[71]Ellen G. White, *Counsels to Parents, Teachers, and Students*, 483; Ellen G. White, *Selected Messages*, Book 1, 244; cf. Henry Melvill, *Sermons*, edited by C. P. McIlvaine, 3rd edition (New York, 1844), 72.

[72]Ellen G. White, *Fundamentals of Christian Education*, 130.

CHAPTER SIX

Charisma and Order

Max Weber saw the prophet not merely as a charismatic challenge to established order and routine, but as a creator of "a unified view of the world derived from a consciously integrated and meaningful attitude toward life."[1] The careers of the "prophets" among the female founders of nineteenth century religious movements indicate that their "integrated attitude toward life" expressed itself in the building of institutions. Significantly, it was Ellen White and Mary Baker Eddy, not Catherine Booth and Alma White, who were most concerned with the orderly development and internal harmony of their churches. Thus, the two women in this quartet who were most possessed of visions and enthusiasms were also the keenest, most methodical institution builders.

The organizational contributions of Catherine Booth and Alma White can be covered in a few words. Alma White launched a journal, established missions, appointed subordinates, built churches and founded schools. But neither in her lengthy autobiography nor in her church paper did she dwell on organizational problems as such. Rather, each advance was a miracle, each difficulty a conflict between sanctified and unsanctified personalities, each new building a triumph of God's leading, not a part of an emerging structure. Catherine Booth counseled William on the organizational development of the Salvation Army and did much to shape Salvationist doctrine, but she does not stand out as an architect of church order.[2]

Weber spoke of a "charismatic structure" which knew nothing of an "ordered procedure of appointment and dismissal," but Mrs. White and Mrs. Eddy, once convinced they were appointed by God or self, certainly knew much about order.[3] Charisma, that sense of special gifts which set leaders apart, may not be "an institutional and permanent structure," but it can create, and in the cases of White and Eddy, did create institutional structures.[4] After these structures were in place, the women founders used their charisma either to facilitate innovation or strengthen existing institutions—whichever seemed necessary. This ability both to establish order and to introduce new measures was the genius of their leadership. Theirs was the power both to make and to break the rules.

Ellen White began creating order at age seventeen. Her first vision helped orient the disappointed Millerites by assigning them a new position on the path to heaven that they thought had ended. From the confusion of the moment, she pointed them to the redeemed saints, 144,000 in number, "perfectly united," standing in a "perfect square" on the heavenly sea of glass.[5] A similar ability to extract order out of confusion and contention marked her role in the developing church. Unlike Mary Baker Eddy, the "Mother" who gave birth to a church, Ellen White was midwife, nursemaid, and governess. Her husband James has been deemed the Adventists' "father of church order,"[6] but his innovations succeeded best when Ellen provided a divine endorsement for them.

As Sabbath-keeping Adventists developed into a distinct group with more or less unified beliefs, James and Ellen White encountered a major barrier to the needed institutional stability: The "come-outer" spirit that early Adventists shared with antislavery and other reformers of their time. In the early 1840s, many abolitionists decided that the established churches were too formal and too fettered to slavery to justify their continued affiliation with them.[7] Among the abolitionists as among the Millerites, the apocalyptic call was sounded: "Come out of her my people."[8] In some cases, the Millerites *were* abolitionists, or at least former abolitionists. George Storrs, Joseph Bates, Joshua V. Himes, Josiah Litch, and Charles Fitch are examples.[9] Even Angelina Grimke Weld proclaimed herself an "intellectual believer" in Miller's arguments. When disappointed that Christ did not return to earth literally, she reinterpreted the anticipated arrival as a spiritual reign, and decided that the judgment the Bible predicted was already underway in that truth was sitting in judgment on "all human organizations—Political, Ecclesiastical, and Social. . . . I have no doubt," she said, "that the Babylon of Revelation is the whole professing Church including every sect, hence the command, 'Come out of her my people.'" Grimke rejoiced that so many were testifying against the Church's "corruption and at the same time refusing to form another sect."[10] Millerites damned organized religion for its attitude toward millenarianism just as abolitionists damned it for its attitude toward slaves and slave-holders. Railing against the suppression of Adventist sentiments, George Storrs asked:

Which of [the churches] will suffer a soul to remain among them in peace, that openly and fearlessly avows his faith in the Advent at the door? Are not the terms of remaining among them undisturbed, that you "wholly refrain" from public expressions of faith in the coming of the Lord this year?[11]

Storrs' disillusionment, like that of many abolitionists, expressed itself in a strong anti-organizational stance. A church, as he viewed it, meant coming together "with one accord in one place." Love alone bound its members. This was the visible church, "and no organization of human invention can make it more visible, or more really the Church of God."[12] Indeed, the true church was oppressed primarily by those who were "manufacturing" creeds and organizing "parties." Storrs doubtless meant these words to associate the old-line churches with economics and politics, two enterprises he probably considered even more corrupt. For him and many other Adventists through the 1850's, churches formed by "man's invention" became "Babylon" the moment they were organized. "The Lord organizes his own church by strong bonds of love," Storrs said; "stronger bonds than that cannot be made."

The Whites credited Storrs for their belief in the sleep of the dead, but on organizational matters they took a more pragmatic view.[13] Their role in establishing the first periodical for Sabbath-keeping Adventists illustrates that view. From 1849 until the church was organized in 1863 the *Review and Herald* was its most important institution. The paper contained doctrinal articles and sermons, recorded meetings and listed ministers' itineraries, kept tabs on contributions, advertised tracts and books, and provided a forum where laypersons could express their views and record their conversion experiences.

Movements may exist with little formal structure, but they cannot exist without a communication network; and studies of leadership dynamics show that persons at the crossroads of communications networks tend to emerge as leaders.[14] Thus when Ellen came out of vision in 1849 and said to James, "I saw that you must begin to publish a little paper," she in effect launched the organization of the Seventh-day Adventist Church.

Here and there Mrs. White's early visions addressed other organizational problems as well. When travelling preachers needed money to "speed on their way, and feed the flock with present truth," Ellen White claimed to have been "shown that those who had means, were required to help speed those messengers."[15] When some volunteer preachers proved incompetent, Mrs. White curtailed them: "I saw that the cause of God had been hindered and dishonored by some travelling who had no message from God."[16] She also sought to control the proliferation of new theological ideas by elevating the authority of preachers who had been in the movement from the beginning:

> I also saw that the shepherds should consult those in whom they have reason to have confidence, those who have been in all the messages [the messages of the three angels of Rev. 14, interpreted by Adventists to embrace the announcement of Christ's coming, the call to separate from the fallen churches and the seventh-day Sabbath], and are firm in all the present truth, before they advocate any new point of importance, which they may think the Bible sustains. Then the shepherds will be perfectly united, and the union of the shepherds will be felt by the church. Such a course I saw would prevent unhappy divisions, and then there would be no danger of the

precious flock being divided, and the sheep scattered, without a shepherd. [17]

By establishing the authority of those who had been longest in the movement, she insured continuity. These were also the men who had the deepest respect for her gifts, the men who were most willing to follow her innovative suggestions. With some notable exceptions, she would maintain this ordering principle throughout her life, requiring that new ideas be submitted to the "brethren of experience," and urging deference and respect for the pioneers of the movement.[18]

The visions continued to call on heavenly models to reinforce the fledgling church's organization: "I saw that everything in heaven was in perfect order. Said the angel, 'look ye, Christ is the head, move in order, move in order. Have a meaning to everything.' Said the angel, 'Behold ye, and know how perfect, how beautiful, the order in heaven; follow it.'"[19]

In December, 1853, James White launched a major organizing effort among Sabbath-keeping Adventists. For him, it seemed the "wildest fanaticism" to assume that a church was free from restraint and discipline. He noted how "many of our Advent brethren who made a timely escape from the bondage of the different churches ... have since been in a more perfect Babylon than ever before."[20] White expounded on the "calling, qualifications, and duties of the gospel minister." They should be ordained, and they alone should teach and administer the sacraments of communion and baptism. As James completed a series of articles on the subject, Ellen issued an endorsement of his position: "the church of God must flee to God's word, and become established upon gospel order," she said.

Brethren of experience, and of sound mind, should assemble, and follow the word of God, and with fervent prayer, and by the sanction of the Spirit of God, should lay hands upon those who have given full proof that they have received their commission of God, and set them apart to devote themselves entirely to the work. And by this act show the approving voice of the church, in their going forth as messengers to carry the most solemn message ever given to men.[21]

She also endorsed a suggestion that the church paper appear weekly instead of by-weekly as before.[22] With her sanction, local churches began to ordain local deacons.[23]

As the church grew, financial and legal requirements pressed it toward fuller organization. The economic panic of 1857 taught church leaders that the continuance of the work required more than haphazard donations of members. A plan called "systematic benevolence" was adopted that urged both fixed and graduated contributions based on property. Eventually a straight ten percent "tithe" for the support of the ministry replaced the earlier approach. As with other innovations, James introduced the new giving plan, then Ellen added prophetic endorsement:

The plan of systematic benevolence is pleasing to God. . . . I saw that there would be order in the church of God, and that system is needed in carrying forward successfully the last great message of mercy to the world. God is leading His people in the plan of systematic benevolence.[24]

Once systematic giving started, other organizational moves followed quickly. The church formed a legal association in 1860 to conduct publishing operations. The next year a conference in Battle Creek chose a denominational name and organized the first state-wide conference in Michigan. Other states followed suit, and in 1863 delegates from the local conferences met to form the General Conference of Seventh-day Adventists.[25] The structure thus established served virtually unchanged for the remainder of the nineteenth century.

Since Ellen White came from a Methodist background, and since the Methodist church also organized itself by "conferences" of local congregations which in turn formed a "General" conference, one might assume this influenced Adventism. James White and Joseph Bates, the other two major founders, came from the Christian Connection, a New England denomination which favored independent local congregations and eschewed any name but "Christian" and any creed but the Bible. There is no evidence, however, that Ellen White urged any particular system of organization. The Methodist system was probably adopted because it best met Adventist needs. Church members were widely scattered in rural areas; no settled ministers served individual congregations. Instead, itinerant Adventist preachers, first called "messengers," moved from place to place like Methodist circuit riders, preaching to believers who gathered in for "conference" meetings. These meetings naturally evolved into formal administrative sessions attended by elected representatives of local congregations.

Was Mrs. White's role in Adventist organization any different from that of other women founders? Mrs. Eddy was, in a much more explicit sense, the "Founder" of her church. She specified virtually every detail of how it was to function and, so long as she lived, reserved for herself the ultimate organizational authority. Initially, the only Christian Scientists were those who had sat through Mrs. Eddy's classes on healing. These formed a loose organization in 1875, then became the Christian Science Association in 1877.[26] In 1879, Mrs. Eddy organized and chartered the Church of Christ, Scientist.[27] Since most of the members lived in the Boston area, this congregational structure sufficed to meet their needs. Unlike Mrs. White, who held no formal office, Mrs. Eddy became president of her church. In 1881, after the traumatic defection of some, the remaining members ordained her as their pastor, declaring:

> We ... do herein express to our beloved teacher, and acknowledged leader, Mary B. Glover Eddy, our sincere and heartfelt thanks and gratitude. ... We do understand her to be the chosen messenger of God to bear his truth to the nations, and unless we hear "Her Voice," we do not hear "His Voice." ... We look with admiration and reverence upon her Christ-like example of meekness and charity, and will, in future, more faithfully follow and obey her divine instructions, knowing that in so doing we offer the highest testimonial of our appreciation of her Christian leadership.[28]

Mrs. Eddy's power, heretofore based on charisma alone, thus acquired a constitutional base.

In 1889, after another defection took out nearly a third of the members, Mrs. Eddy sensed some weaknesses in her organization. Now she was able to use the innovative power of her charisma to lift her above the structures she had formed. Dramatically, she closed and dissolved her Massachusetts Metaphysical College, terminated the Christian Scientist Association, resigned her pastorate of the Mother Church, disorganized it, and withdrew from Boston to the isolation of Concord, New Hampshire. There, step by step, she reconstructed her church on a more secure basis.[29] Mrs. Eddy's power to do all this, both legally and in terms of her church members' willingness to comply, illustrates the powerful combination of formal and charismatic authority she exercised.

In her reconstructed communion, Mrs. Eddy's constitutional authority was even more distinct. In 1895, she published the first edition of the *Manual of the Mother Church*.[30] From the beginning this was theoretically the ultimate authority for all church actions. However, as long as Mrs. Eddy lived, her own authority transcended the *Manual*. She had written it, and she could add or delete by-laws. What is more, the *Manual*, granted Mrs. Eddy many special privileges and powers. In its final form, some thirty-five by-laws contained "consent" clauses which granted Mrs. Eddy veto power over all important appointments.[31] If she decreed that a member had treated her "disrespectfully or cruelly" the member would be excommunicated upon her "complaint." The *Manual* concluded with a rule that it could not be revised "without the written consent of its author," a provision which has prevented any changes since her death.[32]

The contrasts between Mrs. White's and Mrs. Eddy's authority should not be overdrawn. Mrs. Eddy's formal authority would have been worth nothing if the profound respect she commanded had withered away. And if Mrs. White's authority lacked constitutional legitimacy, it could still challenge constitutional power, as she amply demonstrated in a confrontation with George I. Butler. In 1888, Butler was finishing an eight-year term as president of the General Conference. Added to his previous term of three years, he had held the office as long as James White himself. Alarmed by the new ideas of two young theology professors at Healdsburg College in California, A. T. Jones and E. J. Waggoner, he had pushed a resolution through the 1886 General Conference forbidding Adventist colleges to teach any doctrinal views "not held by a fair majority of our people," unless they could be examined by the "leading brethren of experience."[33] On the face of it, this resolution supported Ellen White's position on such matters. But she knew its only purpose was to stifle Jones's and Waggoner's views. "Was this conscientiousness inspired by the Spirit of God?" she asked rhetorically. Turning the tables on Butler, she attacked him for a series of articles in which he suggested varying degrees of inspiration in different portions of Scripture. These ideas, Mrs. White said, "should never have seen the light of day."[34] When Butler attempted to prevent the teachers from presenting their views to the 1888 General Conference in Minneapolis, Mrs. White intervened.[35] Butler's attitude had convinced her he had been in office "three years too long" and that "all humility and lowliness had left him."[36] When the nominating committee consulted her on candidates for president, she apparently shared her view. A new president was elected, and Butler retired to Florida in disgrace.[37] Meanwhile, A. T. Jones toured Adventist camp meetings with Ellen White, taught classes for ministers in Battle Creek, and sparked a denomination-wide revival in 1892.[38] Later, with Mrs. White's support, he became editor of the *Review and Herald* when Uriah Smith, a Butler supporter who had held the chair for many years, was demoted to assistant editor.[39]

Had Mrs. White been bound by her own principle of submitting new ideas to the "brethren of experience," the denomination would have been cut off from theological growth and revival. Her authority was independent of and superior to the General Conference President. If she chose to, she could topple him.

Even though Ellen White could remove the denomination's president, she did not flaunt her power. At times, she even submitted to the authority of the General Conference. In 1891 the church's leaders asked her to go to Australia to assist in developing the Adventist work there. Suspecting, probably correctly, that some officials merely wanted to be rid of her for a while, and having "not one ray of light" that it was God's will she go to Australia, she nevertheless went "in submission to the voice of the General Conference, which I have ever maintained to be authority."[40] Intending to stay only a year or two, she stayed nine.

This apparent withdrawal from the center of action may actually have strengthened Ellen White's hand even as Mary Baker Eddy's withdrawal from Boston enhanced her authority. From their distant headquarters they dispatched directives to church leaders and articles for church periodicals. Neither Christian Science nor Adventist church leaders questioned the right of these women to publish whatever they pleased in church papers. But without face to face contact, it was difficult for those leaders to plead for modifications in the directives they received or to explain extenuating circumstances when rebuked.

At a distance, both women grew larger in the popular view. Mrs. Eddy finally had to forbid Christian Scientists from coming to Concord to "haunt" her daily carriage rides, trying to get a glimpse of her.[41] Mrs. White was not so adulated, but nearly every month accounts of her pioneering exploits appeared in the *Review and Herald*. She took other steps also to see that her role in founding the American church was not forgotten either. She persuaded the new General Conference President, O. A. Olson, to authorize her old friend and fellow pioneer, J. N. Loughborough, to tour the numerous Michigan churches, relating stories from pioneer times.[42] Despite the church's growth in California, Michigan remained the "great heart of the work," and Ellen White knew that little could be accomplished without the support of Michigan believers. Loughborough had "stood firmly" for her "testimonies," and the people needed to hear his "vindication" of them.

This modest suggestion profoundly influenced Ellen White's image in her church. By this time, Ellen White's dramatic public visions had ceased. The healings which seemed so common in the early days of the church were rarely seen. A new generation of Adventists was growing up unfamiliar with the church's pioneer saga. Loughborough not only told stories; he also collected anecdotes from aged believers and wove them into his book, *The Rise and Progress of the Seventh-day Adventists*, published in 1892. Although his scholarship left much to be desired, his stories of miracles in Ellen White's early career and his accounts of the fulfillments of her predictions became a part of Adventist folklore.[43] By recreating the miracles of the early days, Loughborough helped keep Ellen White's charisma alive.

Meanwhile in Australia, church workers were learning that although their prophet had no official authority, she expected certain patterns of deference to prevail. In 1897 Ellen White and others established Avondale College. The board called H. Camden Lacey, a Tasmanian educated in America, to head the school, but failed to consult Ellen White about the appointment. For this oversight she labeled the board "incapable."[44] When Lacey ignored her during the early months of his tenure, she became even more disturbed:

I feel troubled because Brother Herbert Lacey ... would feel perfectly competent to manage everything. ... He has not been to me—who have been through that experience given me of God—to ask advice or counsel as to any light given me of the Lord, that I could suggest safe methods of planning and executing....

If I am considered a cipher after carrying the load I have carried, if it is considered that everything can run just as well as if I were elsewhere, then it is time for me to turn my face toward America.[45]

Lacey quickly learned that if he wanted to succeed in a project that Mrs. White valued, he needed her cooperation.

In Australia, Mrs. White thrived. She enjoyed pioneer work in new territory more than tending the troubles of established institutions. But she was not happy with developments in America. She found it difficult to persuade the General Conference to send the workers she felt were needed in that new field. The world-wide depression of the 1890's hit Australia even harder than it did America, but the Seventh-day Adventist Church, like other Protestant denominations of the period, was without centralized fiscal planning.[46] A plethora of overlapping and competing agencies thwarted efforts to distribute funds evenly. This tangle of boards and agencies left the General Conference increasingly impotent. The Review and Herald Publishing Association and the Battle Creek Sanitarium both employed more workers and handled more money than the General Conference. The publishing house even served as a banking institution for individual Adventists.[47] Dr. John Harvey Kellogg's "non-denominational" social and medical work in Chicago consumed major resources while Australia begged for funds for church buildings and ministers' salaries.[48] Mrs.

White helped raise $11,000 for her son's educational and evangelistic work among blacks in Mississippi only to see the entire amount misappropriated to other projects.[49] In this case, the funds had been collected by the International Sabbath School Association, an agency which was already overcommitted to mission projects in the South Seas. The money went to the Polynesians and Blacks went without.

Mrs. White saw these problems in moral terms. Signs of "worldliness" at the Review alarmed her. The publishing house managers demanded wages higher than most other denominational workers. They carried on commercial printing, even publishing Wild West stories and books tinged with spiritualism.[50] She complained they had no more respect for her "testimonies" than for any other literary production.[51] She also resented their failure to promote the latest edition of her book, *The Great Controversy* because colporteurs could make more money selling other volumes.[52]

Meanwhile, the new General Conference President, O. A. Olson, attempted some organizational changes.[53] He did not address the problem of independent agencies, but he did try to coordinate the work of the conferences. He divided the United States into districts and appointed an assistant to supervise each. He intended these districts to become "Union Conferences," a level of administration between the state conferences and the General Conference. He felt these "Unions" could better manage local conferences, and better evaluate local problems for the General Conference. Whereas in the United States Olson was never able to bring these Union Conferences into being, when he visited Australia in 1894, he succeeded. There, with a less entrenched church structure, and with the support of Ellen and Willie White, Olson set up the first "Union Conference" in January, 1894.

A. G. Daniells, an able young minister from Iowa and a close confederate of the Whites, headed the new conference. Willie White took the vice-presidency. Daniells and White immediately began to subsume the church in Australia under the jurisdiction of the Union Conference. For instance, they took over responsibility for the local periodical, *The Bible Echo*, from the Signs Publishing Company in Melbourne. Activities in behalf of religious liberty were similarly brought under their control.[54]

Mrs. White, her son Willie, and A. G. Daniells returned to America in September, 1900. At an historic General Conference session the next April, Mrs. White called for a reorganization of the church, and Daniells, her erstwhile Australian cohort, was promptly appointed chairman of the large "committee of council" to affect the reorganization. This large committee broke into smaller groups, the most important of which was a Committee on Organization, chaired by Willie White. Despite rumors to the contrary, none of this had been plotted in advance. Daniells and the Willie White simply knew what needed to be done, and their link with the founder gave them the power to do it. In spite of a ten-year absence, they were able to walk with Mrs. White into the center of the denomination's organization.[55] Whereas Olson had struggled for a decade to organize union conferences, now, with Ellen White's active support, they came into being in two weeks. The General Conference Executive Committee was enlarged from 13 to 25, and most of the independent agencies were made departments of the General Conference.

The Presidency of the General Conference was soon to fall in line with the bureaucratizing trend. At the 1901 Session, the delegates had tried to avoid this by electing no president. Instead, they wanted the General Conference Committee to elect its own chairman, who might serve as briefly as one year. Since earlier presidents had some-times exercised what little power they had in an arbitrary manner, an effort was made to curb the power of anyone man. A. G. Daniells was elected "chairman," but felt he could not function without the title and office of president. At the 1903 Session, the presidency was restored, and, as it turned out, professionalized. Whereas earlier presidents had moved in and out of the office, holding lesser posts or working as evangelists between terms, Daniells stayed in office for twenty years. The presidency had become a full-time career position.[56]

One obstacle remained to the achievement of complete control of the denomination's machinery: Dr. John Harvey Kellogg. By 1901, Kellogg's Medical Missionary and Benevolent Association employed 2,000 workers at the Battle Creek Sanitarium and its satellite hospi-tals around the country, while the ministers and evangelists in the en-tire church numbered only 1,500.[57] Kellogg had his own publishing house, colporteurs, periodicals, and medical school. He resisted all efforts to bring these under General Conference control. Disdaining the church's ministers because of their lack of education and their persistent disregard for strict health principles, he also grew increas-ingly skeptical of Ellen White's leadership.[58]

Kellogg's power began to erode soon after Ellen White returned to America. She had long questioned the concentration of Adven-tist institutions in Battle Creek. The Adventist metaphor for church growth was agricultural. Members, like seed, should be scattered. In order to disperse them, Ellen White had been urging leaders to de-velop smaller institutions in many locations.[59] First to heed her call were Percy T. Magan and E. A. Sutherland who, in 1901, moved Bat-tle Creek College to rural Berrien County in south-western Michigan and named it Emmanuel Missionary College (now Andrews University).[60] Kellogg had relied on his proximity to the college to legitimate his nursing and medical schools. In the face of Ellen White's opposition, he reopened Battle Creek College on its old site across from his Sanitarium. Mrs. White warned Adventist parents not to send their students to Battle Creek, and by 1910, both the new Battle Creek College and Kellogg's medical school had failed.[61]

The Battle Creek Sanitarium itself burned to the ground in February, 1902. As Mrs. White hesitated in giving specific directions about the rebuilding of the Sanitarium, Kellogg moved rapidly to construct a huge new building in Battle Creek, ignoring counsels which called for smaller sanitariums in numerous places. In less than three months, the cornerstone was in place.[62] In the absence of specific instructions, the General Conference leaders were swept along in Kellogg's wake and approved his rebuilding plans, believing that with the help of the community, a new, modest-sized building could be erected free of debt.[63] Never again would Daniells be so easily persuaded by Kellogg.

The fire that destroyed the Review and Herald Publishing House in December of the same year dealt a further blow to Kellogg's position.[64] Mrs. White had been warning the publishers for years that unless they operated a more representative Christian establishment, the judgments of God would fall on them. Fourteen months before the disaster, she had written the board chairman: "I have been almost afraid to open the *Review*, fearing to see that God has cleansed the publishing house by fire."[65] The sequence was so uncanny that some even suspected an over-zealous supporter of Ellen White of setting the fire.[66] The event, following so soon after the Sanitarium fire, was naturally seen as a divine judgment on the whole denomination for failing to heed Mrs. White's counsels to break up the modern "Jerusalem" which Adventists had established in Battle Creek. Daniells saw an opportunity to move both the General Conference and the Review out of Battle Creek. If he could do so, the denomination would no longer look to Battle Creek for leadership, and Kellogg would no longer stand at the heart of Adventist power.

The General Conference Session of March, 1903, voted to move the church headquarters to some point in the East. J. S. Washburn, pastor of the church in Washington, D.C. and an old friend of Ellen White's, urged the delegates to consider the nation's capital as a location. As the search committee explored various options, Mrs. White grew to favor Washington more and more, finally indicating that she had been instructed by God that Washington was the appropriate place.[67]

Despite the publishing house fire, Daniells had trouble pulling the denomination's center away from Battle Creek. Relocating the Review and Herald became even more difficult when some stockholders instituted legal action to prevent its leaving. The rest of the denomination might favor a move, but Battle Creek Adventists had homes, property, and investments to consider. Developing cereal companies were turning Battle Creek into an "Adventist mining camp." But Daniells prevailed when he stood up in the local Tabernacle to read Ellen White's ringing endorsement of the move to Washington.[68] The General Conference and the Review arrived at their new home late in 1903. In May of 1904, Mrs. White came to Takoma Park, the Washington suburb in which the new offices had located. Residing there for several months, she reported to the church in glowing terms on the idyllic setting of the new headquarters. This overcame the remaining opposition to the move.[69] Thus in a key and controversial administrative innovation, Ellen White provided charismatic support.

Kellogg's undoing came when he published a book to help fi-
nance his new Sanitarium. In it, he struggled to reconcile an increasingly secular science with his traditional religious values. The result
was a quizi-pantheistic volume, *The Living Temple*. After futile efforts
to reconcile Kellogg to the denomination, Mrs. White condemned the
book as an "alpha of apostasy" that depersonalized God and deified
man.[70] Kellogg and his associates reacted with a spate of criticisms
designed to show Mrs. White's inconsistencies and failures, and in
1907 Kellogg was disfellowshipped from the Seventh-day Adventist
Church.[71]

Kellogg, of course, had charisma of his own. His colorful personality, ready speech, and medical mystique all suggested he too was
gifted—but not like Ellen White. Kellogg had "talents," Ellen White
had "revelations." In 1903, Kellogg had wanted the General Conference to underwrite his efforts to start a new sanitarium in England.
But Daniells, working under strict new financial policies, refused the
request.[72] Meanwhile, Mrs. White seemed oblivious of financial re-
straints. At the denomination's new headquarters, the Washington,
D.C. Sanitarium Association was founded in 1904 in order to operate
a local sanitarium.[73] Unlike most Adventist sanitariums, this one, on
Mrs. White's orders, had no ties whatever to Kellogg's institutions.[74]
Next, she learned of an inactive sanitarium in Paradise Valley, near
San Diego. Knowing that the Southern California Conference could
not afford to purchase it, she borrowed half the $4,000 price and per-
suaded a wealthy Adventist woman, Josephine Gotzian, to donate the
rest. Six years later, at Ellen White's urging, the conference took control. A second sanitarium, in the Los Angeles suburb of Glendale, was
established by the same process.[75] With Southern California Conference officials looking on fearfully, Mrs. White pushed for a third Sani-

tarium in their territory. During the General Conference Session of 1905, when she and the conference leaders were all in Washington, the opportunity arose up to purchase a spacious but defunct hotel in Loma Linda, near San Bernardino and Riverside.[76] Ellen White encouraged J. A. Burden, an Adventist pastor who was pushing the project, to secure the property "by all means." But the conference officials, already struggling with two new sanitariums and deep indebtedness, told Burden to wait until they could get back to California. Clearly, if Kellogg had been asking to start the new Sanitarium, the church's new pay-as-you-go policy would have made it impossible. But Burden, acting on Ellen White's authority, borrowed the money for the down payment in spite of the lack of support from the Southern California Conference.

In starting so many institutions, Mrs. White, because of her charisma, was able to ignore established financial policies and do what she felt needed to be done. She visited Loma Linda in June, 1905. As she walked over the grounds, she claimed to recognize the place from a vision four years before, and decided that Loma Linda should become the church's medical training school on the West Coast.[77] A week later, at a hastily called meeting of the Southern California Conference constituency, Mrs. White gave a stirring address. G. A. Irwin, a vice-president of the General Conference, told the story of Ellen White's recent role in founding Avondale College in Australia. Then the delegates voted to take on the additional responsibility of financing the new Sanitarium.[78] Thus as Kellogg moved out of the church, Loma Linda assumed the work of educating the church's medical personnel. Eventually it became Loma Linda University.

In the church's early days, Ellen White established order and curbed deviant ideas by demanding they pass muster with senior ministers. Midway through her career she championed the younger ministers, Waggoner and Jones, against the church's hierarchy. Later, she helped reorganize the denomination and move its headquarters. Working hand in hand with the church's president, she reestablished the authority of the General Conference over the publishing and medical work which had grown disproportionately powerful. At the same time, oblivious to the church's strict fiscal policies, she established three sanitariums in one debt-ridden conference. By and large, both her ordering and innovating initiatives succeeded. This was doubtless in large part because Adventists believed in her charismatic gifts, believed that God, in effect, told her when to make rules and when to break them. It cannot be shown that her chosen course was always the best, but it cannot be doubted that her power both to establish order and to introduce innovation profoundly influenced the development and organizational structure of her church.

S. N. Eisenstadt has contended that charisma is related to institution building, but primarily in the sense that the quest for ultimate meaning which characterizes charisma becomes imbedded in institutions and thus serves as a source of renewal.[79] He did not explore the possibility that the prophet himself (or in this case, herself) might be both an iconoclast and an institution builder. Weber's charismatic leader has generally been interpreted as oblivious, even hostile to formal structure, but few such leaders will be found—even in Biblical times. Since the prophetic claims of Ellen White and Mary Baker Eddy so clearly qualify them as charismatic, they teach us that charisma is a form of authority which can both bring order out of chaos and inject new life into rigid institutions.

---

[1]S. N. Eisenstadt, ed., *Max Weber: On Charisma and Institution Building*, 266.

[2]Salvation Army, *The Salvation Army: Its Origin and Development* (London, 1945), 15; Catherine Bramwell-Booth, *Catherine-Booth* (London, 1970), 260, 272.

[3]S. N. Eisenstadt, ed., *Max Weber*, 20.

[4]Ibid., 21.

[5]Supra, 101-102.

[6]Leroy E. Froom, *The Prophetic Faith of our Fathers*, vol. 4 (Washington, D.C., 195?), 1059.

[7]Lewis Perry, *Radical Abolitionism: Anarchy and the Government of God in Anti-Slavery Thought* (Ithaca, New York, 1973), 92-96.

[8]Revelation 18:4.

[9]LeRoy Froom, *The Prophetic Faith of Our Fathers, vol.* 4, 529, 533, 551; Jonathan Butler, "Adventism and the American Experience," Edwin Gaustad, ed., *The Rise of Adventism* (New York, 1974), 175-176; Joseph Bates, *The Autobiography of Elder Joseph Bates* (Battle Creek, Mich., 1868), 235-238; F. D. Nichol, *The Midnight Cry* (Washington, D.C., 1944), 187-218.

[10]Angelina Grimke Weld to Sarah Grimke, Jan. 1845. Theodore Dwight Weld Papers, Library of Congress. Gerda Lerner, in *The Grimke Sisters from South Carolina* (New York, 1971), 306-308, sees Angelina's Millerism as an irrational reaction to a miscarriage. Since many Millerites were former abolitionists, no such explanation seems necessary. The lengthy letter cited here shows a woman as adept at handling the prophecies of Daniel and Revelation as any Millerite, and just as skillful at adapting them to fit with everything else she believed about the church and the world.

[11]George Storrs, "Come Out of Her My People," *The Midnight Cry*, vol. 6 (Feb. 15, 1844).

[12]Ibid.

[13]Don F. Neufeld, ed., *Seventh-day Adventist Encyclopedia*, rev. ed. (Washington, D.C., 1976), s.v. "Storrs, George"

[14]Fred E. Fielder and Martin M. Chemers, *Leadership and Effective Management* (Glenview, Ill., 1974), 28-29.

[15]Ellen White, "Dear Brethren and Sisters," *Present Truth*, vol. 1 (Sept., 1849), 32.

[16]Ellen G. White "To the 'Little Flock'" *Present Truth*, vol. 1 (Apr., 1850),72.

[17]Ellen G. White, "Dear Brethren and Sisters," Present Truth, vol. 1 (Nov., 1850),86.

[18]Ellen G. White, *Testimonies for the Church*, vol. 5, 293, first published, 1885.

[19]Ellen G. White, "Vision at Paris, Maine," Dec. 25, 1850, Ms. 11, 1850.

[20]James White, "Gospel Order," *Review and Herald*, vol. 4 (Dec 6, 1863), 173.

[21]Ellen G. White, *Supplement to Christian Experience and Views*, (Rochester, N.Y., 1854), 18,19.

[22]Ibid, 14.

[23]H.S. Gurney to Dear Brother White, *Review and Herald*, vol. 4 (Dec. 17, 1853),

199; M. E. Cornell to Dear Brother White, *Review and Herald*, vol. 5 (Jan. 24, 1854), 7.

[24]Ellen G. White, *Testimonies for the Church*, vol. 1 (Mountain View, Calif., 1948), 190-191; see also Arthur L. White, "Mrs. Ellen G. White and the Tithe," (duplicated, Washington, D. C., 1959).

[25]Don F. Neufeld, ed., *Seventh-day Adventist Encyclopedia*, rev. ed., s.v. "Organization."

[26]Robert Peel, *Mary Baker Eddy: The Years of Trial* (New York, 1971),62.

[27]Ibid., 63.

[28]Robert Peel, *Mary Baker Eddy: The Years of Trial*, 99.

[29]Ibid., 252-259; Robert Peel, "The Background of the Mother Church," *The Christian Science Journal*, vol. 100 (June, 1982), 338-340.

[30]Robert Peel, *Mary Baker Eddy, The Years of Authority* (New York, 1977), 90.

[31] Robert Peel, "The Future of the Mother Church," *The Christian Science Journal*, vol. 100 (Aug., 1982), 529.

[32]Mary Baker Eddy, *Manual of the Mother Church* (Boston, 1936), 104.

[33]G. I. Butler, "General Conference Proceedings," *Review and Herald*, vol. 63 (Dec. 14, 1886), 779.

[34]Ellen G. White, "The Discerning of Truth," c. Jan. 1889, Ms. 16, 1889, reports her earlier reaction to the resolution.

[35]A. V. Olson, *Thirteen Crisis Years, 1888-1901*, rev. ed. (Washington, D.C., 1981), 91.

[36]Ellen G. White to Brother Fargo, May 2, 1889, Letter 50, 1889; Ellen G. White to Mary White, Nov. 4, 1888, Letter 82, 1888.

[37]G. I. Butler to Ellen G. White, Sept. 24, 1892.

[38]Ron Graybill, "A.D. 1892: Revival Comes to Michigan," *Insight*, vol. 2 (March 30, 1971), 3-6.

[39]Eugene Durand, *Yours in the Blessed Hope, Uriah Smith* (Washington, D.C., 1980), 40, 266.

[40]W. P. Bradley, "When God Overrules," *Review and Herald*, vol. 159 (April 1, 1982),7-9; Ellen G. White to A. G. Daniells, et. al., Sept. 20, 1896, Letter 27, 1896; Ellen G. White to J. E. White, Aug. 9, 1896, Letter 124, 1896.

[41]Mary Baker Eddy, *Manual of the Mother Church*, 48; Robert Peel, *Mary Baker Eddy: The Years of Authority*, 258.

[42]Ellen G. White to O. A. Olson, Oct. 7, 1890, Letter 20, 1890.

[43]The book was revised and reprinted in 1905 as *The Great Second Advent Movement*. On Loughborough's faults as a historian, see Ron Graybill, "J. N. Loughborough, Historian?" (Unpublished, 2013).

[44]Ellen G. White to Willie White, June 6, 1897, Letter 140, 1897.

[45]Ellen G. White to Willie White, May 6, 1897, Letter 182, 1897.

[46]Ben Primer, *Protestants and American Business Methods* (Ann Arbor, MI: 1979).

[47]Arthur L. White, *Ellen G. White: The Early Elmshaven Years* (Washington, D.C., 1981), 70-71; A. V. Olson, *Thirteen Crisis Years, 1888-1901*, rev. ed., 179.

[48]Jonathan Butler, "Ellen G. White and the Chicago Mission," *Spectrum*, vol. 2 (Winter, 1970),41-51; Arthur L. White, "Adventist Responsibility to the Inner City," *Review and Herald*, vol. 147 (Nov. 5, 1970),1-5; "A Shift in Emphasis," Ibid., (Nov. 12,1970),7-10, "Strategy of Diversion," Ibid., (Nov. 19, 1970), 8-11, "A Work Others Will Not Do," Ibid., (Nov. 26, 1970),4-6.

[49]Ron Graybill, *Mission to Black America* (Mountain View, Calif., 1971), 106.

[50]Arthur L. White, *Ellen G. White: The Early Elmshaven Years*, 227-229.

[51]Ellen G. White to J. Edson White, Aug. 9, 1896, Letter 124 1896.

[52]Ellen G. White to Brethren, May 14, 1890, Letter 1, 1890.

[53]Terry W. Carlisle, "O. A. Olsen's Contribution to the Seventh-day Adventist Church's Organizational Structure," (unpublished manuscript, Andrews University, Berrien Springs, Mich., 1974).

[54]O. A. Olson, "Proceedings of the Australian Union Conference of Seventh-day Adventists," *Bible Echo*, vol. 9 (Feb. 26, 1894), 62-63.

[55]Arthur L. White, *Ellen G. White: The Early Elmshaven Years*, 70-96.

[56]Ibid.; Don F. Neufeld, *Seventh-day Adventist Encyclopedia*, rev. ed., s.v. "A. G. Daniells." Mrs. White did urge Daniells into some evangelistic campaigns around 1910, but did not ask him to give up the presidency to conduct them.

[57]A. V. Olson, *Thirteen Crisis Years, 1888-1901*, 184.

[58]Richard W. Schwarz, *John Harvey Kellogg, M.D.*, (Nashville, Tenn., 1970), 175, 177; John Harvey Kellogg, et. al, "Interview at Dr. J. H. Kellogg's House, Oct. 7, 1907," White Estate Document File #45k.

[59]Arthur L. White, *Ellen G. White: The Early Elmshaven Years*, 151.

[60]Emmett K. Vande Vere, *The Wisdom Seekers* (Nashville, Tenn., 1972), 95-118.

[61]Dores Robinson, *The Story of Our* Health Message (Nashville, Tenn., 1943), 329-332; Richard Schwarz, John Harvey Kellogg, M.D., 104-107, 183.

[62]Schwartz, *John Harvey Kellogg, M.D.*, 70-71.

[63]Arthur L. White, *Ellen G. White: The Early Elmshaven Years*, 153.

[64]Milton Hook, Flames Over Battle Creek (Washington, D.C., 1977), 99-107.

[65]Ellen G. White, Testimonies for the Church, vol. 8, 91; Ellen G. White, "To the Managers of the Review and Herald Office," Oct. 16, 1901, Letter 138, 1901; W. C. White to E. G. Fulton, Oct. 17, 1901; I. H. Evans to Ellen G. White, Nov. 20, 1901

[66]Gerald Carson, *Cornflake Crusade* (New York, 1977), 134.

[67]Kit Watts, "Seventh-day Adventists Headquarters: From Battle Creek to Takoma Park," *Adventist Heritage*, vol. 3 (Winter, 1976), 42-50.

[68]Arthur L. White, *Ellen White: The Early Elmshaven Years*, 275.

[69]Ibid., 318-328.

[70]Arthur L. White, *Ellen G. White: The Early Elmshaven Years*, 279-306; Ellen G. White to J. H. Kellogg, Aug. 7, Letter 277, 1904.

[71]Richard Schwarz, "The Kellogg Schism: The Hidden Issues," *Spectrum*, vol. 4, (Autumn, 1972), 23-29.

[72]Arthur L White, Ellen G. White: *The Early Elmshaven Years*, 201-208.

[73]"Records of the Washington (D.C.) Sanitarium Association, Incorporated Feb-

ruary 1, 1904," White Estate Document File #13.

[74]Ellen G. White to Brother Hayward, Jan. 24, 1904, Letter 267, 1924.

[75]Dores Robinson, *The Story of Our Health Message*, 335,346.

[76]Ibid., 348.

[77]Ibid., 350.

[78]Ibid., 353.

[79]S. N. Eisenstadt, *Max Weber on Charisma and Institution Building*, xxxvii-lvi.

CHAPTER SEVEN

Feminism and Prophecy

Nineteenth century American women were expected to be religious, but not religious leaders who exercised authority over men. Many women considered even voting too public a role, and an invasion of male prerogatives. In 1871, a committee of "One Thousand Ladies" petitioned the U. S. Senate not to consider female suffrage, arguing that the Bible taught "a different and, for us, higher sphere apart from public life."[1] Elizabeth Cady Stanton agreed that the Bible forbade a public role for women and concluded that its "over-riding spirit" was unfriendly to her sex. Her *Woman's Bible* declared the Scriptures to be merely human documents, and none too elevating ones at that.[2]

The women who founded and headed religious organizations followed neither of these opposing examples. Alma White and Catherine Booth not only respected the Bible, they used it to defend their thoroughgoing feminism. On the other hand, Mary Baker Eddy and Ellen

White showed little interest in liberating womankind. Two things in particular separated the non-feminists from the others. Both bore a burden of doctrinal innovation which may have inhibited their advocacy of cultural deviance; and both exercised charismatic leadership in the true Weberian sense, leadership based on what their followers believed were unique divine gifts. Their achievements proved the value of their prophetic gifts but said nothing about the potential of other women. Earlier, the Amana Inspirationists had exhibited a similar pattern; they honored Barbara Heinemann as a "vehicle of the Spirit" while consigning women to distinctly inferior roles. Prophecy and feminism seem in these cases to have been negatively related.[3]

Alma White claimed no direct revelations. Her feminism may have been a psychic defense for one who in childhood felt rejected and emotionally abused, whose marriage was unhappy, and whose main avenue of adult fulfillment was her ability to preach. Yet when she began to exercise that talent, she encountered sharp resistance from Methodist church leaders.[4] Church officials probably found her abrasive style and aggressive personality a greater problem than her sex. Nevertheless, in the ensuing struggle for her right to preach, she found feminism a useful weapon. When it became clear that she would not win that right within Methodism, she left to found her own denomination.

The fact that Alma White worked primarily in the early decades of the twentieth century may have made a feminist posture more comfortable for her than it would have been for earlier founders. But she went far beyond comfortable positions, even for her time. In 1924, she launched a paper, *Woman's Chains*, specifically devoted to securing women's rights. In it she printed extracts from leading feminist journals and reported regularly on the fortunes of the wider movement. She invited speakers such as Mary DuBrow of Alice Paul's radical National Woman's Party to speak at her college in Zarephath, New Jersey.[5] She advocated women politicians, police officers, chauffeurs, and inventors. She insisted women had the right to be ordained preachers, and secured that right for them in her denomination. Her church remains today the only one of the four discussed here is led by a woman—Alma's granddaughter, Arlene White Lawrence. [2019 note: Her middle name was "Hart," not "White." She only led the church from 1981-1984]

Catherine Booth came to feminism by a different route. In an early pamphlet she reeled off a list of nearly two dozen distinguished women who were leaders in their churches, indicating that she had done considerable reading on the subject during her adolescent years when inactivity, enforced by a curvature of the spine, left her free to read voraciously.[6] She devoured the staples of Methodist devotional literature, especially the lives and writings of the saintly Hester Ann Rogers and Mary Bosanquet Fletcher.[7] She also read, understood, and enjoyed theological discourse. To this brilliant young woman, such reading suggested that she too might succeed in church work.

Booth was also inspired by a living example of female achievement, the American holiness preacher, Phoebe Palmer. When Mrs. Palmer visited Newcastle-upon-Tyne during a revival tour of England, a local cleric issued a pamphlet attacking women's right to preach.[8] Booth, who had already declared she would stand on Scripture "against the whole world" to defend women's "perfect" equality with men, fired off a tract of her own, *Female Ministry*. It became the basis of Salvation Army teaching on women's religious roles and rights.[9] In her treatise, Booth answered the major arguments advanced against women in the pulpit—that such behavior was unfeminine and unnatural, forbidden by Scripture, and unnecessary.[10] In her Scriptural arguments, Booth found evidence in 1 Cor. 11:1-15 that women did pray and prophesy in primitive Christian churches—otherwise, she asked, why would Paul have dictated "the proprieties of their appearance while so engaged?"[11] It followed then, that the prohibition against women speaking in church found in 1 Cor. 14:34-35 referred to another sort of speaking: "the inconvenient asking of questions, and imprudent or ignorant talking." Booth even called on Greek scholars to testify that the word in question, *lalein*, meant "to chatter, to babble," not to talk sensibly.[12] As for 1 Tim. 2:12-13, Booth argued that Paul's prohibition on women teaching or exerting authority over men dealt only with their personal behavior at home, and forbade only such teaching as is "domineering," or "involves the usurpation of authority over the man."[13]

In her analysis of the women preachers in mid-Victorian Britain, Olive Anderson concludes that even though Catherine Booth and her contemporaries did encourage a "modicum of practical emancipation" within the church, their ideas owed little or nothing to the women's rights movement, and contributed little if anything to its spread. Anderson grants that Mrs. Booth was exceptionally radical in her views, but claims she remained "a firm believer in the subordination of women so far as their domestic and social position was concerned."[14] Actually, Catherine Booth taught that in Christ, a woman's subjection to her husband was all but eliminated. The Christian couple realized "as blissful and perfect a oneness" as though the curse had never been pronounced on Eve's sin. Even for non-Christians (a status which Booth never thought normative) this subjection was not because of any natural inferiority, but was only a punishment for sin; moreover, it involved only the woman's relationship to her own husband. Booth maintained that she did not wish to alter women's domestic or social position from that laid down in the Bible, but her interpretation of the Bible made it a pro-feminist book.[15]

Booth had a keen sense of the oppression of women and a strong desire to improve their educational opportunities. A woman's training from babyhood, she said, was "calculated to crush and wither her aspirations after mental greatness rather than excite and stimulate them." She lamented that until very recently, the typical woman had been educated to be merely a "serf, a toy, a plaything."[16] Although she was reluctant to push her own daughters into public life, Catherine did so nonetheless. Evangeline founded the Salvation Army in America. Booth saw to it that spouses of Salvation Army officers received the same training as their husbands or wives, and although the number of female leaders in the top echelons of the Salvation Army has declined in recent years, the Army remains committed to the principle of equality for women within its ranks.[17]

Mary Baker Eddy has sometimes been depicted as a feminist, in part because her theology had a feminist flavor.[18] She believed that only the first chapter of Genesis presented a true account of God's creative acts. She saw the variant creation narrative in Genesis 2, which portrayed Eve's creation from Adam's rib, as sensual, contradictory, and totally false.[19] Mrs. Eddy argued that God is both Father and Mother. The latter metaphor, she said, conveyed "His tender relationship to His spiritual creation."[20] In one early printing of *Science and Health*, she went so far as to speak of God as "She," but reverted to the masculine pronoun in the next edition.[21] However, she seems always to have believed that "in divine Science we have not as much authority for considering God masculine, as we have for considering Him feminine, for Love imparts the clearest idea of Deity."[22] There is some possibility that Eddy had been exposed to the Shaker belief that Ann Lee, as the female equivalent of Jesus Christ, embodied the female principle of the Godhead.[23]

In spite of her theology, Mrs. Eddy did little to encourage women's deviation from traditional roles. True, her movement had a special appeal for women, and they have always made up a disproportionate number of Christian Science Practitioners.[24] Also, in most Christian Science congregations, a man and a woman serve together as "Readers," one of the more prominent local positions. But when asked in 1901 whether her successor would be a man or a woman, Mrs. Eddy replied: "I can answer that. It will be a man."[25] She frankly admitted that although she had "uniformly associated man and woman" in her endeavors, she had given "the preponderance to the masculine element" in her organization. In 1900, all the Directors and Trustees were men, and men outnumbered women three to one on the Board of Education. There were eleven men and two women on the Board of Lectureship.[26] In secular affairs, Mrs. Eddy believed women had an inalienable right to fill the "highest places in government," but she gave only mild encouragement to voting rights for women, saying that "if the elective franchise for women will remedy the evil without encouraging difficulties of greater magnitude, let us hope it will be granted."[27]

The divergence between the non-charismatic feminist religious leaders, Alma White and Catherine Booth, and the charismatic non-feminist leaders, Mrs. Eddy and Ellen White, is not as apparent in their theology as in the practical consequences of their leadership. The Pillar of Fire and the Salvation Army opened opportunities for female leadership; Christian Science and Seventh-day Adventism did not.

Among the founders, Ellen White was the least interested in feminist issues. Unlike Catherine Booth, she read very little during her formative years.[28] Unlike Alma White, her womanhood provoked surprisingly little opposition to her leadership. Ellen started her ministry in a new movement free of tradition and established doctrines. She willingly shared the leadership with men; and until her own authority was well established, she rarely interjected herself into the political process which legitimated the elected male leaders of the denomination. Even the non-Adventist public gave her little difficulty. She observed that people came to her meetings in Santa Rosa, California, in 1874, for the "rare fun" of hearing a "woman preacher," but by the end of the meeting they had "sobered down."[29] Occasionally, the Biblical texts which seemed to discourage women from preaching were raised against her, but compared to the constant opposition Alma White faced on that issue, the Adventist leader encountered little resistance.[30]

Moreover, Mrs. White's theology lacked feminist relevance, even though some of her comments on the creation and fall of humankind had a feminist tinge. She affirmed that in creation God had taken Eve from Adam's rib to signify that "she was not to control him as the head, nor to be trampled under his feet as an inferior, but to stand by his side as an equal ... his second self."[31] Yet even in this unfallen state, Eve was "not quite as tall as Adam" and needed somehow to be "protected" by him.[32] Once the Fall occurred, "their union could only be maintained and harmony preserved ... by submission on the part of the one or the other.... [Eve] was now placed in subjection to her husband." Ellen White conceded that man's abuse of this arrangement had "rendered the lot of woman very bitter," but observed that in hoping to enter "a higher sphere than that which God had assigned her," Eve, "like restless modern Eves," had fallen below it.[33]

Strangely, Ellen White never mentioned the passage in which Paul tells women to keep silent in church or the one where he declares he will not permit a woman to teach or have authority over a man.[34] When detractors used these texts to challenge her right to preach, male associates answered them.[35] This left would-be preachers among Adventist women without a response from Ellen White to Paul's strictures. And neither could they use her career, which depended on charismatic gifts, as a model. While the achievements of a woman like Catherine Booth showed what any woman could do, Ellen White merely demonstrated that God possessed the power to accomplish his ends by granting visions even to an uneducated person. Her womanhood as such had nothing to do with her leadership.

In the early years, Mrs. White cited the Scripture requiring wives to be subordinate. As she grew older, however, she advocated more independent roles for them, a shift probably born of long experience as a wife, career woman, and counselor who heard many tales of torment from women whose husbands took advantage of them. In 1862, she wrote: "It is the duty of the wife to yield her wishes and will to her husband. Both should be yielding, but the word of God gives preference to the judgment of the husband."[36] Never again would she advocate such submission. By 1870 she was chiding a man who had "been exalted", and "taken a position above" his wife.[37] A woman, she wrote, had "just as much right to her opinion" as her husband.[38] That same year she counseled wives not to "feel bound to yield implicitly to the demands" of husbands controlled by "base passion."[39] She did not, however, advocate sexual continence, believing that "instead of increasing moral purity" it would "hasten and strengthen moral pollution."[40]

In 1891, she took an even stronger position, remarking that if

Paul's injunction, "wives, submit yourselves to your own husbands" had ended with those words, many women would be better off not to marry.[41] She pointed out Paul's qualifying phrase, "as is fit in the Lord." She took this to mean that there was both a fitting and an unfitting sort of submission. "Entire submission" was unfitting as it should be made only to Jesus Christ.[42] God had given woman a conscience, and her individuality could not be merged with that of her husband.[43] Husbands who required complete subjection of their wives and allowed them no voice or will in the family were acting contrary to Scripture.[44] For them to "dwell constantly" on their position "as head of the family" was evidence not of manliness, but of weakness.[45] Indeed, if a husband was not himself subjected to Christ, then God did not design that he should have control. "If he is course, rough, boisterous, egotistical, harsh, and overbearing, let his lips never utter the word that the husband is the head of the wife for . . .he is not the husband in the true significance of the term.[46]

Mrs. White never denied that a woman should be subject to her husband, but she placed so much stress on the husband's responsibilities as to make that subjection pleasant enough. "When the spirit of Christ controls the husband the wife's subjection will only result in rest and benefit; for he will require from her only that which will result in good, and in the same way that Christ requires the submission of the church.[47] Christ, she pointed out, called his followers friends, not servants. Another decade passed, and White, by then 75 and a widow for twenty years, counseled a newly married couple: "Each is to minister to the happiness of the other . . . . but while you are to blend as one, neither of you is to lose his or her individuality in the other."[48] Neither husband nor wife should "make a plea for rulership," she advised; "do not try to compel each other to do as you wish. You cannot do this and retain each other's love."[49] She quoted the Pauline passages, but without comment on what many believed was their contradiction of her stress on complete mutuality in marriage. Mrs. White offered women little encouragement to pursue non-traditional vocations, although here again she moved from a conservative to a slightly more liberal position. She always affirmed that a woman's basic mission was to educate her children and run a well-ordered household. She elevated motherhood above every other role. The world, she wrote,

> needs women who are mothers not merely in name, but in every sense of the word. We may safely say that the distinctive duties of woman are more sacred, more holy, than those of man. Let woman realize the sacredness of her work and, in the strength and fear of God, take up her life mission. Let her educate her children for usefulness in this world and for fitness for the better world.[50]

The duties of such women were as important as any man's, even if he was "the chief magistrate of the nation."[51] Ellen White raised the pedestal as high as she could:

> The king upon his throne has no higher work than has the mother. The mother is queen of her household. She has in her power the molding of her children's characters, that they may be fitted for the higher, immortal life. An angel could not ask for a higher mission.[52]

In general, she subscribed to the stereotype which saw ambition, industriousness, and honesty as "manly traits," and amiability and self-denial as "womanly."[53] In commenting on the Biblical story of Jezebel, she suggested that Satan turned to women because he could use them more successfully than men.[54] In the 1870's Mrs. White quoted with approval Daniel Wise's classic statement of the doctrine of separate "spheres" for men and women. Wise, a Methodist clergyman, journalist, and implacable opponent of the women's rights movement, had asked:

> What is the sphere of women? Home, the social circle. What is her mission? To mold character, to fashion herself and others after the model character of Christ. Her place is not on life's great battle fields. Man belongs there. Woman must abide in the peaceful sanctuaries of home, and walk in the noiseless vales of private life. There she must dwell, beside the secret springs of public virtue. There she must smile upon the father, the brother, the husband, when, returning like warriors from the fight, exhausted and covered with the dust of strife, they need to be refreshed ... and cheered to renewed struggles by the music of her voice. There she must rear the Christian patriot and statesman, the self-denying philanthropist and obedient citizen. There, in a word, she must form the character of the world, and determine the destiny of her race.[55]

On another occasion, she wrote that every woman who was "at the head of a family" should study "the art of healthful cookery," if need be with the help of the best cook she could find, until she was "mistress of the art, an intelligent, skillful cook."[56]

Despite such advice to wives and mothers, Mrs. White did not glorify domestic chores as such. In Australia she urged that the kitchen help at the Adventist school be given periods of rest so that they would not have to "drudge, drudge, drudge, drudge" day after day.[57] She wanted her two adopted grand-nieces to learn a trade that would make use of "their mental ability to do good work and command good wages." If she died, she did not want them to have to hire themselves out to the "slavery" of doing housework. At the same time she saw to it that they learned how to cook so that they could "stand at the head of a household without embarrassment when that time should come."[58]

Mrs. White's ideal of womanhood excluded those "listless, useless girls who consider it unladylike to engage in active labor":

> They simper and giggle, and are all affectation. They appear as though they could not speak their words fairly and squarely, but torture all they say with lisping and simpering. Are these ladies? They were not born fools, but were educated such. It does not require a frail, helpless, over dressed, simpering thing to make a lady.[59]

In these fashionable young ladies, she wrote, "the soul of womanhood is dwarfed and belittled." She told how two gentlemen passed such a woman on the street, and when one inquired of the other about her, the second replied: "She makes a pretty ornament in her father's house, but otherwise she is of no use."[60] Thus Ellen White joined Catherine Beecher in lamenting the passing of the "strong, hardy, cheerful girls that used to grow up in country places." She reprinted a passage from Beecher's *The American Woman's Home*, fondly remembering those practical girls who could "wash, iron, bake, harness a horse and drive him, no less than braid straw, embroider, draw, paint, and read innumerable books."[61]

In spite of this admiration for the hardy, self-sufficient woman, Mrs. White told Adventists who felt called to "join the movement in favor of woman's rights" that they might as well sever their connection with the church. "The Scriptures are plain upon the relations and rights of men and women," she said.[62] The desire to preserve the stature of her own gifts may also have fired her opposition. She felt many people associated the women's rights movement with spiritualism, and that some of these confused Adventists with spiritualists because Adventists believed Mrs. White's visions to be the "restoration of spiritual gifts." If this continued, she warned, "The people would place them on the level with spiritualists and would refuse to listen to them."[63] Here again, prophecy and feminism proved incompatible.

Mrs. White's opposition to women's suffrage can be instructively contrasted with Catherine Beecher's, whose writings she appreciated and quoted. Both White and Beecher glorified the domestic role of women. Beecher opposed their voting because she feared the exercise of the franchise by the crude and ignorant women in the social classes below her.[64] White opposed it because she thought the flighty and fashionable women in the social classes above her would not use it wisely: "Women who might develop good intellects and have true moral worth are now mere slaves to fashion," she wrote. "They have not breadth of thought nor cultivated intellect. They can talk understandingly of the latest fashion, the styles of dress, this or that party or delightful ball," but they "are not prepared to intelligently take a prominent position in political matters."[65]

After James White died in 1881, Ellen grew to appreciate the role of the independent woman, at least in church work. During the

1890's, she said Adventists were not to belittle the gospel labors of women. She declared that if a woman "puts her housework in the hands of a faithful, prudent helper, and leaves her children in good care" while she pursues a religious calling, she should get wages from the church just as men did.[66] She insisted that minister's wives who helped their husbands in their work should be paid.[67] When childless ministers' wives inquired of her whether they should adopt children, she urged them not to do it.[68] They should either help their husbands as secretaries or "labor in the gospel ministry" themselves.[69] Although she never pushed this latter thought to the point of urging women's ordination, at least the "queen" of the pastor's household was no longer to be wholly tied to her children.

One reason why her influence never led Adventists to ordain women as ministers was that Ellen White always assigned them sex-specific roles. She thought women were particularly well adapted to giving "Bible readings" in homes, where they would be a great blessing in "reaching mothers and their daughters."[70] Some women could also act as "messengers of mercy" to visit "mothers and children in their homes and help them in the everyday household duties, if need be, before beginning to talk to them about the truth for this time."[71] Others could be church clerks, write letters, distribute tracts, and "read and explain the word to families, praying with them, caring for the sick, relieving their temporal necessities."[72] She never opposed Adventist women who spoke and preached in public, but she rarely mentioned this as a ministry for which women were fitted.

Nevertheless, Ellen White left one legacy of benefit to women: her religiously validated insistence on good health. Women were disproportionately affected by the pervasive ill-health of nineteenth century America. Frequently the victims of disease, they were also the family's nurses, and, as often as not, its widows and grieving mothers.[73] The women religious founders were no exception. Ellen White and Mary Baker Eddy both suffered severe illness during childhood and continued throughout their lives to experience cycles of ill health and recovery. Catherine Booth could scarcely remember a day when she was free from one kind of pain or another.[74] Yet Alma White, who seems to have been physically sturdy, declared healthful living to be a religious duty just as did Catherine Booth and Ellen White. All four women urged teetotal abstinence. All but Mrs. Eddy abstained from meats, and urged vegetarianism on their followers.[75] They were all skeptical if not downright hostile to regular physicians, and all except Alma White had strong ties to sectarian medicine, notably hydropathy.[76] Mary Baker Eddy's sectarian approach to healing was her own, despite the evidence of its tenuous ties to Phineas Parkhurst Quimby and other pioneers of mental healing; but even she tried the Graham diet and, on one occasion, Vail's Water Cure in Hill, New Hampshire.[77] Catherine and William Booth regularly worked themselves to exhaustion and retired to Smedley's Hydro in Matlock to recover.[78] Alma White did not embrace any form of sectarian medicine, but she much preferred faith healing to the ministrations of regular physicians.

Of all these women, Ellen White fixed healthful living most firmly in the doctrine of her church.[79] Joseph Bates, another founder of the Seventh-day Adventist Church, was a health reformer before Ellen White's earliest visions on health, but her vision of June 1863 convinced her that health was an urgent religious duty.[80] Then, in December, 1865, another vision led her to call for the first Adventist health-care institution, the Western Health Reform Institute in Battle Creek. White did not recognize the extent to which her ideas on particular diets were influenced by contemporary health reformers, but the "vision" that led Adventists to stress healthful living was clearly her own.

Given the massive commitment of Adventists to medical and health work, White naturally saw a place for women in this field, but again the preferred assignments were sex-specific. She urged both men and women to become nurses, but recognized the need for female physicians in only one specialty—obstetrics and gynecology. In 1908 she wrote:

> It is not in harmony with the instruction given at Sinai that gentlemen physicians should do the work of midwives. The Bible speaks of women at childbirth being attended by women, and thus it ought always to be. Women should be educated and trained to act skillfully as midwives and physicians to their sex. This is the Lord's plan.[81]

Such medical practice included, of course, the treatment of the "delicate diseases" which afflict women. Women's "secret parts," she wrote, should never be exposed to men, and women physicians should "utterly refuse to look upon the secret parts of men."[82] In the early years after Ellen White's death Adventist hospitals maintained these standards, and the percentage of female physicians on their staffs was substantial. But with the scope of their practice thus restricted, Adventist women physicians constantly lost ground in numbers and prestige against their male counterparts. Only in the 1970s did women graduates from the church's medical school at Loma Linda regain the approximately 1 in 5 ratio to males they enjoyed in the first decade of the school's history, from 1914-1924. In the intervening decades, they made up less than 10 percent of graduates.[83]

Ellen White, then, lacked the educational background, the personality, and the experiences which prompted other female religious leaders to develop a feminist theology or encourage a female ministry within their movements. Although her teachings during the later years allowed for relatively greater independence for women, her sex-specific recommendations concerning women's work outside the home set limits on their ambitions. Her church has not ordained women to the ministry, developed a significant force of female physicians, or encouraged female leadership in other areas. Her example was even less relevant since her role was based on a special divine calling and did not illustrate the potential of ordinary women. Nevertheless, she took seriously the needs of women within the home. She insisted on the wife's spiritual and physical freedom from husbandly domination. She urged health principles which improved the family's well-being. And she insisted that if women worked outside the home, they be paid equitable wages for doing so. Her influence on the women of her church was not negligible, even if she did not open the ministry to them.

---

[1]Quoted in Barbara Welter, "Introduction," to Elizabeth Cady Stanton, *The (Original) Feminist Attack on the Bible: The Woman's Bible* (N. Y., 1974), xv.

[2]Ibid., xxiv.

[3]Rosemary Radford Reuther and Rosemary Skinner Keller, eds., *Women and Religion in America*, vol. 1 (San Francisco, Calif., 1981),50,76.

[4]Alma White, *The Story of My Life*, vol. 2, 79, 80, 133.

[5]Alma White, "Representative of National Woman's Party Speaks at Zarephath," *Woman's Chains*, vol. 1 (March-April, 1924), 14; Carl Degler, *At Odds*, 402-404.

[6]Catherine Booth, *Papers on Practical Religion* (London, 1891), 135, 162-165; See also Lucille Sider Dayton and Donald W. Dayton, "'Your Daughters Shall

Prophecy,': Feminism in the Holiness Movement," *Methodist History*, vol. 14 (Jan. 1976), 74-77; Catherine Bramwell Booth, *Catherine Booth* (London, 1970),27,359.

[7]See, for example, H[ester] A[nn] Rogers, *A Short Account of the Experiences of Mrs. H. A. Rogers ... with Brief Extracts from Her Diary* (Dublin: 1803); Henry Moore, *The Life of Mrs. Mary Fletcher, Consort and Relict of the Rev. John Fletcher ... Compiled from Her Journal and Other Authentic Documents*, 3rd ed. (London, 1818).

[8]The Palmers mention the visit but not the opposition they encountered in Walter and Phoebe Palmer, *Four Years in the Old World* (New York, 1866), 93-120.

[9]F. L. Booth-Tucker, *The Life of Catherine Booth*, vol. 1 (New York, 1892), 118, 343-349, Catherine-Bramwell-Booth, Catherine Booth, 181-183.

[10]Catherine Booth, *Female Ministry; or, Woman's Right to Preach the Gospel* (first published, 1859, reprinted, London, 1975).

[11]Catherine Booth, *Papers on Practical Religion*, 137.

[12]Ibid., 142.

[13]Ibid., 150.

[14]Olive Andersen, "Women Preachers in Mid-Victorian Britain: Some Reflections on Feminism, Popular Religion, and Social Change," *The Historical Journal*, vol. 12 (1969), 467-484.

[15]F. L. Booth-Tucker, *The Life of Catherine Booth*, vol. 1, 116, 121.

[16]Ibid., 119

[17]Flora Larsson, *My Best Men are Women* (New York, 1974).

[18]Penny Hansen, in her dissertation, "Woman's Hour: Feminist Implications of Mary Baker Eddy's Christian Science Movement, 18851910, (Ph.D., University of California, Irvine, Calif., 1981), also stresses Eddy's health teachings as a "feminist" interest.

[19]Mary Baker Eddy, *Science and Health* (Boston, 1934), 521-528.

[20]Mary Baker Eddy, *Science and Health*, 332.

[21]Steven Gottshchalk, *The Emergence of Christian Science* (Berkeley, 1973), 53.

[22]Ibid., 517.

[23]Edward Deming Andrews, *The People Called Shakers* (New York, 1963), 56, 97, 158; n.a. *Testimonies of the Life, Character, Revelations and Doctrines of Mother Ann Lee*, second edition (Albany, New York, 1888, Reprinted New York, 1975), 2, 6; Robert Peel, *Mary Baker Eddy: The Years of Discovery* (New York, 1966), 53.

[24]Gage William Chapel, "Christian Science and the Nineteenth Century Woman's Movement," *Central States Speech Journal*, vol. 26 (Summer, 1975), 148.

[25]Robert Peel, *Mary Baker Eddy: The Years of Authority* (New York, 1977), 173.

[26]Ibid., 162.

[27]Mary Baker Eddy, *Science and Health*, 63; Mary Baker Eddy, *No and Yes*, (Boston, 1919), 45.

[28]Ellen G. White, *Spiritual Gifts*, vol. 2, 7-12.

[29]Ellen G. White to Dear Children, c. Feb., 1874, Letter 2a, 1874.

[30]Ellen G. White to James White, April 1, 1880, Letter 17a, 1880.

[31]Ellen G. White, *Patriarchs and Prophets* (Mountain View, Calif., 1958), 46.

[32]Ibid.; Ellen G. White, *Spiritual Gifts*, vol. 3 (Battle Creek, Mich., 1864), 34.

[33]Ellen G. White, *Patriarchs and Prophets*, 59; *Testimonies for the Church*, vol. 3,484, first published, 1875.

[34]1 Corinthians 14:34; 1 Timothy 1:11-15.

[35]Ellen G. White to James White, April 1, 1880, Letter 17a, 1880.

[36]Ellen G. White, *Testimonies for the Church*, vol. 1, 307, first published, 1862.

[37]Ellen G. White, *Testimonies for the Church*, vol. 2, 415, first published 1870. In 1889, she did urge one troublesome woman to acknowledge "the position God has given the husband as head of the household," but this was an individual case; Ellen G. White to Brother and Sister Craig, April 2, 1889, Letter 10, 1889.

[38]Ibid., 418.

[39]Ibid., 475.

[40]Ellen G. White, "I Was Shown," Dec. 27, 1858, Ms. 2, 1858.

[41]Ellen G. White to Brother Kynett, Feb. 15, 1891, Letter 18, 1891, see Colossians 3:18.

[42]Ellen G. White, The Adventist Home, 116.

[43]Ibid.

[44]Ibid.

[45]Ellen G. White, *The Adventist Home*, 215.

[46]Ellen G. White to Brother Kynett, Feb. 15, 1891, Letter 18, 1891.

[47]Ibid.

[48]Ellen G. White, *Testimonies for the Church*, vol. 7, 440, first published 1902.

[49]Ibid., 476.

[50]Ellen G. White, *Testimonies for the Church*, vol. 3, 565, first published 1875.

[51]Ellen G. White, "The Importance of Early Education," *Pacific Health Journal*, vol. 5 (June, 1890), 169.

[52]Ellen G. White, "Words for Mothers," *Signs of the Times*, vol. 17 (March 16, 1891), 85.

[53]Ellen G. White to Brother and Sister Craig, April 2, 1889, Letter 10, 1889.

[54]Ellen G. White, "Fragments of Old Testament History," Nov. 17, 1911, Ms. 29, 1911.

[55]Daniel Wise, *The Young Lady's Counselor* (Boston, 1852), 88-89, quoted in Ellen G. White, "Proper Education," *Health Reformer*, vol. 8, (July, 1873), 221.

[56]Ellen G. White, *Ministry of Healing*, (Mountain View, Calif., 1905, 1942), 303; Ellen G. White, *Testimonies for the Church*, vol. 2, 370, first published 1872.

[57]Ellen G. White to Willie White, June 7, 1893, Letter 130, 1893.

[58]Ellen G. White to Walling, April 13, 1888, Letter 2, 1888.

[59]Ellen G. White, *Testimonies for the Church*, vol. 3, 152, first published 1872.

[60]Ellen G. White, *Testimonies for the Church*, vol. 4, 644, first published 1881.

[61]Ellen G. White, "Proper Education," *Health Reformer*, vol. 8, (June, 1873), 190.

[62]Ellen G. White, *Testimonies for the Church*, vol. 1, 421, first published 1864.

[63]Ibid. On spiritualism and feminism, R. Laurence Moore, *In Search of White Crows: Spiritualism, Parapsychology, and American Culture* (New York, 1977), 83-

84; 117; Barbara Chesser, "Sex Roles and the Spirit World in Nineteenth Century America," (unpublished manuscript, Univ. of Calif., Los Angeles, 1976).

[64]Katherine Kish Sklar, *Catherine Beecher: A Study in American Domesticity* (New York, 1973), 266, 267.

[65]Ellen G. White, *Testimonies for the Church*, vol. 3, 565, first published 1865.

[66]Ellen G. White, *Gospel Workers*, (Washington, D.C., 1915, 1948), 453.

[67]Ellen G. White to Brother Mountain, Oct. 25, 1899, Letter 168, 1899.

[68]Ellen G. White, "The Laborer is Worthy of His Hire," Mar. 22, 1898, Ms. 43a, 1898; see also Ellen G. White, "The Echo Office and Commercial Work," Mar. 31, 1898, Ms. 47, 1898.

[69]Ellen G. White, "The Laborer is Worthy of His Hire," Mar. 22, 1898, Ms. 43a, 1898.

[70]Ellen G. White to A. G Daniells, Sept. 1, 1910, Letter 10, 1910.

[71]Ellen G. White, *Welfare Ministry*, (Washington, D.C., 1952) 146.

[72]Ellen G. White, *Testimonies for the Church*, vol. 6, 118, first published *1900*.

[73]Penny Hansen, "Woman's Hour: Feminist Implications of Mary Baker Eddy's Christian Science Movement, 1885-1910," 20-22.

[74]Bramwell Booth, *These Fifty Years* (London, 1929), 15.

[75]Catherine Bramwell-Booth, *Catherine Booth*, 151, 262, 348; *Why I Do Not Eat Meat* (Zarephath, N.J., 1915); Ellen G. White, *Counsels on Diet and Foods* (Washington, D. C., 1946),420-430; *Ministry of Healing*, 327-330.

[76]Catherine Bramwell Booth, *Catherine Booth*, 153, 164, 189, 290; Ronald L. Numbers, Ellen G. White: Prophetess of Health (New York, 1976).

[77]Robert Peel, *Mary Baker Eddy: The Years of Discovery*, 137, 145.

[78]Catherine Bramwell-Booth, *Catherine Booth*, 252, 258, 400; Lawrence Peach, *John Smedley of Matlock and his Hydro* (London, 1954)

[79]Mrs. Eddy, of course, focused even more directly on health, but sought to achieve it through spiritual healing, believing disease to have no reality except that which false belief gave it.

[80]George Knight, *Joseph Bates: The Real Founder of Seventh-day Adventism* (Hagerstown, MD: 2004), 49, 52, 199-202, 205.

[81]Ellen G. White, *Testimonies for the Church*, vol. 9, 176, first published 1909; Catherine Booth also opposed "male midwifery." See Catherine Bramwell-Booth, *Catherine Booth*, 197.

[82]Ellen G. White, *Counsels on Health*, (Mountain View, Calif. 1951), 364.

[83]Walter Clark, comp., "Women Graduates from Lorna Linda University School of Medicine," (unpublished manuscript, Loma Linda, Calif., 1982).

CHAPTER EIGHT

The Written Word

According to Ernest Sandeen, modern millenarian movements, particularly in America, develop differently from preindustrial millenarianism because of their symbiotic relationship to a different, modernizing culture. These movements, Sandeen thought, were distinguished in part by their quest for widespread acceptance through the manipulation of written sources and media.[1] The Millerites offer a prime example. Once Joshua V. Himes applied his promotional skills to Miller's ideas, the message was spread by a host of periodicals, books, tracts, and hymnals. In a giant movable tent evangelists even used pictorial charts to translate the beasts and dragons of Revelation into "staring Yankee realities."[2] Ellen White sprang from this heavily (if not highly) literate tradition. She and her husband started two publishing houses, launched three periodicals, and published scores of books, tracts, and pamphlets. When their son Edson founded the denomination's third American printing establishment in Nashville, the Whites were said to have printer's ink in their blood.[3]

Sandeen's observation does not help distinguish millenarian movements from other modern religious sects, however. Mary Baker Eddy was no millenarian, but her writings were even more essential to Christian Scientists than were Ellen White's to Seventh-day Adventists. Mrs. Eddy's books, like the Bible itself, were divided into numbered paragraphs for easy memorization and reference. Mrs. Eddy considered herself first and foremost a writer, but she was also a journalistic entrepreneur who amassed a modest fortune with her pen. *The Christian Science Monitor*, which she founded in 1908, attests to her appreciation of the power of the press.[4]

Both White and Eddy made astonishing claims for their writings. Mrs. Eddy proudly called *Science and Health*, her "babe . . . . the newborn Truth" that would "forever testify of itself, and its mother."[5] She said she would blush to praise *Science and Health* as she had, "were it of human origin, and were I, apart from God, its author."[6] In the same vein, the Adventist prophet said: "Sister White is not the originator of these books. They contain the instruction that during her lifework God has been giving her."[7] Her writings were "the voice of God speaking."[8] Whereas anciently God had used prophets and apostles to address his people, now, White said, he spoke to them "by the testimonies of His Spirit. There never was a time when God instructed his people more earnestly than He instructs them now."[9] Those who lost confidence in her testimonies would "drift away from Bible truth" and start a "downward march to perdition."[10]

But bold claims do not make a leader. In no small measure, these women gained the power and influence they enjoyed by communicating their ideas widely and effectively.

It is difficult to judge the amount of writing Ellen White published during her life time. A fair estimate, discounting for repetition, would be 20,000 printed pages of books and articles.[11] That a woman with only the briefest grammar school education should publish so much is truly remarkable. She was only nine when a classmate, "angry at some trifle," hit her in the face with a stone.[12] When she regained consciousness three weeks later, her health was "completely shattered," her nervous system "prostrated." She tried to return to school, but her hand trembled so that she could make "no progress in writing, and could get no farther than the first examples, which are called coarse hand." When she attempted to read, she remembered, "the letters on the page would run together, great drops of perspiration would stand upon my brow, and a faintness and giddiness would seize me."[13]

Still, Ellen may have learned more during the few years of schooling ascribed to her.[14] Since she consistently dates events of her childhood too early, she may have been older than nine at the time of her accident. Then too, children of her time and place sometimes started school as early as four or five.[15] A good enough reader to be called "downstairs to the primary room" to read lessons for the "little" children, Ellen clearly had moved beyond the primary grades herself.[16] When she attempted unsuccessfully to resume her education, she was enrolled in a "female seminary" rather than a grammar school.[17] Her disappointment was keen when she could not continue her schooling, for her "ambition to be a scholar had been very great."[18] Average students rarely have such ambitions.

Nevertheless, her education was so meager that James White thought only her divine inspiration could account for her achievements. "I now see why the Lord chose one in feebleness, and without a mind strengthened and disciplined to reason by study," he said.[19] Interestingly, John Bunyan's disciples had used the same argument two centuries earlier to foster their mentor's reputation for gifted ignorance and thereby enhance his stature as an inspired writer.[20]

While Mrs. White's literary success need not be minimized, she could never have achieved it without editorial secretaries. Her simple, vigorous style suited her direct way of saying things, but she never mastered the technical aspects of writing. "I am not a grammarian," she lamented, "I cannot prepare my own writings for the press."[21] Up until the 1870's, she relied on her husband to polish her prose. When illness limited his usefulness, she turned to secretaries—usually devoted spinsters who could interpret her "modern hieroglyphics."[22]

With effort, Mrs. White could write neatly and compose clear sentences. Early in her career, most of her letters went out in her own hand. But with editors to rely on, she devoted less and less attention to style, grammar and penmanship. She usually wrote in great haste and deep conviction. The result was a torrent of thoughts uninhibited by the conventions of complete sentences and compact paragraphs. Robert Peel said of Mrs. Eddy that "Some of the writing seems to be a rush and tumble of words, as though the writer's thoughts were flooding ahead of her pen. Sentences are chaotic, punctuation erratic, quotations inexact, meanings obscure."[23] The words might be applied to Ellen White as well.

Mrs. White wanted secretaries—copyists, she called them—who were not merely "mechanical."[24] She wanted "brain workers" who could "enter into the spirit of the work, and do it intelligently, grasping the ideas."[25] They had to remove the crudities of her style, leaving only the polished thought; but she urged them to preserve her words, and feared lest they take too many liberties with her language. They were to correct spelling and grammar, insert punctuation, reword sentences and frame paragraphs. Passages were to be assembled from different letters to form articles, and repetitious and extraneous material was to be eliminated.[26]

When she could find enough skilled help, Mrs. White had one secretary to handle her correspondence, another to transcribe sermons and prepare articles, and still another to prepare her books. From 1879 onward, Marian Davis was her "bookmaker." "She does her work in this way," Mrs. White explained:

> She takes my articles which are published in the papers, and pastes them in blank books. She also has a copy of all the letters I write. In preparing a chapter for a book, Marian re- members that I have written something on that special point, and if she finds it, and sees that it will make the chapter more clear, she adds it.[27]

Although Mrs. White wrote all the material her secretaries used, they relieved her of the laborious task of rewriting as well as the creative work of condensing and arranging material for publication. They greatly expanded the volume of her published writing and enabled her to present her views in clear, correct prose.

Remarkably, only one secretary rebelled against her anonymous role. Fannie Bolton, who worked with Mrs. White in Australia, took offence at hearing Adventist evangelist G. B. Starr laud the literary beauty of Ellen White's work. She asked whether it was right for Mrs. White to get credit for such beauty, when her writings had to be "almost entirely changed" from their original form.[28] Starr was shocked, and reported the incident to Mrs. White. Bolton apologized, admitting that sometimes the manuscripts needed "but slight editing." Temporarily she accepted the argument that once an article was passed back into Ellen White's hands it became, "when approved, the chosen expression of the Spirit of God."[29] Similar incidents continued, however, and several times Mrs. White had to fire and rehire the mercurial secretary. Finally, Bolton left Mrs. White's employment and returned to America.

Mrs. White's personal correspondence represented more than mere fodder for her articles and books. The many letters received from church leaders, members, and family friends kept her abreast of events and attitudes in the church. She also had access to Willie White's considerable correspondence. Every day she spent some time writing letters. In November of 1886, she was writing ten pages a day, much of it in correspondence.[30] While in Australia in 1894, she was sending 160 to 200 typewritten pages of letters each month to America, in addition to those mailed locally.[31] Added to her travelling, preaching, and counseling, it is no wonder Mrs. White found letter writing a "heavy tax" on her time, often requiring her to arise at three or four in the morning.[32]

Mrs. White discovered that the shrewd presentation of a letter could expand its influence. As conflicts with John Harvey Kellogg heated up in 1903, she wrote to him, but entrusted the letter to their mutual friend, A. T. Jones. Since the letter contained "very many plain admonitions" that might be "difficult for the doctor to understand," she wanted Jones to talk and pray with him, then read the letter to him when the moment seemed right.[33] This procedure made her missives harder to ignore. A similar effect was achieved by addressing a letter to one church leader, but sending copies to several of his colleagues at the same time.

Technological advances also increased the impact of Mrs. White's writings. In America, increases in the speed and reliability of postal service, together with significant reductions in postage costs, made letter-writing an important communications medium.[34] Improvements in the printing and distribution of books also aided her. The power press Isaac Adams invented in 1830 had captured the American market by the time the Review and Herald acquired one in 1857. Soon it was turning out eighteen copies of the *Review* per minute.[35] Having published very little prior to this time, Mrs. White now issued a *Testimony for the Church* nearly every year, and began to write lengthier books as well. As typewriters came into common use in the 1880's, Mrs. White's secretaries acquired them, and thereafter preserved her correspondence in letter books and carbon copies.[36] As she wrote, she expanded on religious themes, and once typed, these documents were not only sent out as letters, they were cut and pasted into articles and books. It is no accident that Mrs. White's literary output increased markedly after the introduction of the typewriter.[37]

By mid-century, commercial publishers, using improved distribution and advertising, often sold 50,000 copies of a popular novel, with a few titles topping the 100,000 mark.[38] For a small religious publisher like the Review and Herald, however, such sales were unheard of until and unsuccessful preacher, George A. King, peddled 1,000 copies of Uriah Smith's book on prophecy door-to-door.[39] Soon the Review marshaled a small army of colporteurs. In 1885, the 1884 revision of Mrs. White's book, *The Great Controversy Between Christ and Satan*, was given to the church's book salesmen. During the next three years it went through ten printings and sold 50,000 copies.[40] From that point onward, the demand for Mrs. White's books was strong, and she was constantly planning and preparing new volumes.

The evolution of *The Great Controversy*, Mrs. White's most important book, illustrates many facets of her writing. H. L. Hastings, an

Advent Christian writer, doubtless provided a catalyst for the book when he published *The Great Controversy Between God and Man* (1858).[41] Hastings' book, like Ellen White's, traversed history and prophecy from "Paradise Lost" to "Paradise Regained." John Milton's epics stand somewhere in the background of both.[42] On March 14, 1858, Mrs. White experienced a vision in Lovett's Grove, Ohio, during which she grasped the potential of the "controversy" theme as a framework for distinctive Adventist doctrines.[43] Shortly thereafter, she published her own version of the cosmic conflict, *The Great Controversy between God and His Angels and Satan and His Angels*.[44] The similar title is not the only link to Hastings' work. In the *Review and Herald* of March 18, 1858, James White had published a glowing review of Hastings' volume.[45]

Ellen White opened her book with Lucifer's rebellion in heaven, discussed the fall of man, and traced the "controversy" through Biblical times. She briefly described events from the fall of Jerusalem to William Miller's day. The remainder of the book offered interpretations of as-yet unfulfilled prophecies and described the triumph of the saints at the end of time. Between 1870 and 1884, four new volumes appeared under the general title, *The Spirit of Prophecy*. In these books, Mrs. White greatly expanded her "controversy" theme. The first three handled pre-history and Biblical times. In the last volume—*The Great Controversy* which, as noted earlier, the Review's colporteurs had sold so successfully—she added 100 pages on the Protestant Reformation.[46] In the latter part of the book, she described the ominous portents of the Spiritualist and sabbath reform movements, predicting that they would converge with Catholicism to persecute Seventh-day Adventists in the last days.[47]

Mrs. White regarded *The Great Controversy* as her most important work. She thought it "above silver or gold" because while writing it she had been "often conscious of the presence of angels of God."[48] The book was "not the product of any human mind," she wrote, but "God's direct appeal to the people."[49] It should be widely circulated because in it "the last message of warning to the world" was given "more distinctly" than in any of her other books. "It contains the story of the past, the present, and the future," and "in its outline of the closing scenes of this earth's history, bears a powerful testimony in behalf of the truth."[50]

Writing *The Great Controversy* had taken her beyond the simple homilies of her early years. Now she was describing the customs and cultures of Biblical times, writing lengthy historical narratives, and interpreting contemporary events. As she did so, she sometimes used the language and ideas of other authors without credit. Although the practice raised some controversy during her lifetime, it is significant here because it weighs so heavily on the question of her relationship to the intellectual currents of her time. It is also important because in recent years, scholarly and popular interest in Ellen White's literary sources has accelerated. Modern studies began in the early 1970's in *Spectrum*, an independent journal published for Adventist intellectuals.[51] In 1976, medical historian Ronald L. Numbers brought to topic to a wider academic community in his book *Ellen G. White: Prophetess of Health*.[52] Church officials' strong negative reaction to Numbers attracted some notice in the news media, but within the church, his work was little known except around Adventist colleges and administrative headquarters.[53] That situation changed when Long Beach, California, pastor Walter Rea, began to popularize and sensationalize the issue, finally publishing *The White Lie*. Rea was defrocked for his "negative influence," and this ouster, coming on the heels of the expulsion of Australian theologian Desmond Ford for heresy, attracted widespread media attention.[54]

The similarities between Mrs. White's writings and those of others were first noticed in the early 1860's in connection with her first health writings. Like other health reformers, she claimed more independence than the evidence would seem to allow.[55] Under the pressure of skeptical questioning, either she did not realize, or could not bring herself to acknowledge, how much was borrowed from her reading and conversation.[56] She did admit, however, that after her initial writing on health she had perused some health reform literature and noted with "surprised" how nearly it agreed with what the Lord had "shown" her.[57]

The habit of literary "borrowing" developed all too easily. For years, James and Ellen White had examined other periodicals and newspapers for selections to use in the *Review*. Often these were credited, but the search helped form the habit of selecting usable material. Mrs. White also kept scrapbooks of the children's stories she had clipped, adapting these in the telling and retelling and republishing some in a series called *Sabbath Readings* in 1881.[58] Adventists preachers and writers commonly borrowed from one another. Even someone as clearly conscious of plagiarism as Uriah Smith incorporated unacknowledged passages from Josiah Litch and George Storrs in his prophetic works.[59]

Then, in 1871, Ellen White got wider exposure to non-Adventist literature when she and her husband took over the *Health Reformer*, an Adventist paper addressed to a secular audience. Dr. Russell Trall edited the paper, but had alienated most of the subscribers with an absolute ban on salt and milk. The Whites took a more moderate view. In an effort to rescue the journal, James assumed the editor's chair and Ellen agreed to supply a monthly column and a "department" of selections.[60] The next three years she constantly scanned newspapers, magazines, and books for appropriate material on health, education, and temperance. Her column, in which she eschewed "religious" writing and made no claim to inspiration, incorporated long passages from other authors, all with attribution. In this role as a secular columnist, Mrs. White freely acknowledged and praised sources that extended from Harriet Beecher Stowe to Florence Nightingale.[61] But moving from such a role to that of an inspired "messenger," Mrs. White faced a dilemma. She still needed literary sources, but, unlike other writers, she was expected to function without them. The very fact that during her visions she was "entirely lost to earthly things" reinforced the belief that to speak for God, she must be free of human influence and virtually devoid of human knowledge.[62]

The hazards of claiming this type of inspiration become apparent in this context. During an 1882 controversy at Battle Creek College, Uriah Smith wrote her that he had "always supposed that a testimony was based on a vision," and since she had had no recent visions, he did not see how there could be any "testimony."[63] As an experienced church leader, Smith expected his own counsels to have weight in the church, but Ellen White was different: if she could not claim direct, unadulterated word from heaven, her "testimony" was only the opinion of an impressionable woman. In fact, the most common retort of people she reproved was the charge that "Someone has influenced Sr. White. ... someone has told her these things."[64]

Theoretically, Mrs. White rejected the idea that unless she was reporting a vision, her counsel should not be considered as inspired. Had not the Apostle Paul written his inspired epistle to the Corinthians in response to news he had received from the "household of

Chloe"?[65] Should not her own judgment bear some weight after she had spent years in the "school of Christ" being "trained and disciplined" for her special work?[66] But in the end, she tried to meet Smith's expectations:

> In these letters which I write, in the testimonies I bear, I am presenting to you that which the Lord has presented to me. I do not write one article in the paper expressing merely my own ideas. They are what God has opened before me in vision—the precious rays of light shining from the throne.[67]

Mrs. White insisted she was not in the habit of reading doctrinal articles even in the *Review and Herald*. She wanted to assure her readers that she did not have "any understanding of anyone' ideas and views, and that not a mold of any man's theories should have any connection with that which I write."[68] She did not think she could afford to recognize that she had been influenced by human opinions and at the same time claim she should exercise influence for God.

But the visions simply did not provide all the information and ideas necessary for books spanning Christian history, outlining health principles, advising on child rearing and education, and handling the myriad individual and organizational problems of a growing church. Willie White once described Mrs. White's historical visions as "flashlight views," in which the darkened landscape was suddenly illuminated by a flash of lightning.[69] But the story of Luther, to take a case in point, needed the names of villages, princes, and popes. Sequences had to be established, speeches recorded. Mrs. White and her editorial secretaries masterfully wove the sources into a unique Adventist pattern, but the historical facts they used came from books Mrs.

White had read—for example, histories of the Reformation by Merle D'Aubigne and James Wylie.[70] For New Testament backgrounds, she used Daniel March, Alfred Edersheim, William Hanna, and several others.[71] Half a dozen health reformers contributed medical insights. Where she followed a source in *The Great Controversy*, she included only the facts found in the source. She quoted some passages and paraphrased many others. Yet in the 1884 edition, she withheld credit even to her quotations.

In *The Great Controversy* (1884, 1888) Mrs. White borrowed heavily from other authors. Her *Sketches from the Life of Paul* (1883), *Patriarchs and Prophets* (1890), and *The Desire of Ages* (1898), made lesser use of unacknowledged sources. From the late 1870s onward, the *Testimonies for the Church* disclosed some dependence on her library.[72]

By contrast, Mary Baker Eddy borrowed far less.[73] She was a better writer than Ellen White in part because she had more schooling and spent more time with literature. As a child, she loved big words and wrote passable verse at the young age of 12. Her brother Albert, a Dartmouth graduate, supplemented her sporadic formal education with informal tutoring that exposed her, via his own essays, to rationalistic philosophy. In her youth Mrs. Eddy studied Milton, Shakespeare, Byron, and Wordsworth. She got a smattering of Jonathan Edwards and, via Lindley Murray's *Readers*, sampled many weighty passages of English prose and poetry.[74] Mrs. Eddy also kept her borrowing to a minimum by writing less, spending most of her time on one book, *Science and Health*, which she revised continually, publishing literally hundreds of editions.[75]

Helena Petrovna Blavatsky, the founder of the Theosophical Society, may be more comparable with Ellen White. "Somebody who knows all dictates to me," Blavatsky said, but both her contemporary critics and modern scholars have found considerable dependence on literary sources.[76]

When the scope of her writing expanded, first into health topics, and later into history, Mrs. White found herself in a position where plagiarism was hard to avoid. Her limited education did not equip her for the broad range of topics she tried to cover. Nevertheless, she felt "mightily wrought upon" to write. "Should I resist these impressions to write, when I am so burdened?" she asked. "I must obey the movings of the Spirit of God or withdraw myself from having any connection with the work."[77] "I take no credit of ability in myself to write the articles in the paper or to write the books which I publish," she said. "Certainly I could not originate them. I have been receiving light for the last forty-five years and I have been communicating the light given me of Heaven to our people."[78] This strong self-image as an inspired writer may have inhibited her ability to realize how much her writings depended on other authors. She could scarcely have sensed the degree to which her visions and dreams were shaped by her reading, and thus she came to believe that her revelations were the original sources of what she wrote. Perhaps she practiced some of the "pious deception" that scholars attribute to John Bunyan's attempts to deny obvious literary influences.[79] Until Mrs. White's letters and diaries are open to a broader company of qualified scholars, it will be difficult to answer these psycho-historical questions. [2019 Note: The polished, edited versions of all her writings were made available online in 2015, but access to her original handwritten documents is limited by the necessity of gaining approval for a visit and bearing the costs to travel to her Estate headquarters in Silver Spring, Maryland.] What is certain is that her use of literary sources, like her use of literary assistants, helped extend the scope and influence of her writing. By enriching her Adventist perspective with "gems of truth" from many conservative Protestant writers of her time, she added depth and interest to her books.

To dismiss her own contribution by suggesting that Ellen White's works were nothing more than borrowed materials, however, is unreasonable. There are still wide stretches of her writings where no literary dependence has been demonstrated. Source criticism of her work remains in its early stages, focusing more on the collection of apparent parallels than on analysis of how the borrowed materials was used in its new setting. And no student has yet analyzed or interpreted what was unique in the great body of her work.

Adventists of her own time were not wholly ignorant of Mrs. White's borrowing, but they expressed little concern about it. Although she never acknowledged the scope of her dependence, she made no special effort to hide her sources. In fact, she promoted some of the very books she had mined most heavily. In 1883, when the *Signs of the Times* offered *The Life and Epistles of the Apostle* Paul by W. J. Conybeare and J. S. Howsen as a premium to encourage new subscriptions, Mrs. White added her endorsement, saying she regarded the volume as one of "great merit" and "rare usefulness."[80] Her *Sketches from the Life of Paul*, published later that same year, made extensive use of Conybeare and Howson, as persons who read both books must have noticed. The previous December she had recommended Merle *D'Aubigne's History of the Reformation* as a Christmas gift—something "both interesting and profitable" to be read on "long winter evenings."[81] She could scarcely have believed that hundreds of readers of her 1884 edition of *The Great Controversy* would not observe the parallel passages.

D. M. Canright, an Adventist evangelist who broke with the

church in 1887, was the first to accuse Mrs. White publicly of plagiarism.[82] The Protestant Pastor's Union of Healdsburg, California,
invited him to give a series of lectures on "Seventh-day Adventism
Renounced" in the local theater. Although Ellen White was living near
the Adventist college in Healdsburg at the time, she was travelling
during Canright's visit. Canright attacked all the distinctive Adventist doctrines, then challenged the church's local pastor to a public debate.[83] In the latter, Canright discounted Ellen White's claims to prophetic inspiration. He declared she was a false prophet who worked
no miracles, made no accurate predictions, and allowed literary assistants to change the wording of her messages. He said the church
had suppressed her early writings, claimed she had lifted "seven solid
pages" from J. N. Andrews' *History of the Sabbath* for her book *The
Great Controversy*, and cited other examples of alleged plagiarism,
including some from D'Aubigne and Conybeare and Howsen.[84]

Canright created quite a stir in Healdsburg. The local newspaper
devoted long columns to his lectures and gave Adventists room to re-
spond with the countercharge that Canright himself had plagiarized
in one of his earlier pamphlets. And so he had, Canright admitted,
but only because the previous author had left the Adventist church
and only with the agreement of James White. Furthermore, Canright
pointed out that he did not claim his writings were divine messages.
Willie White's wife, Mary, clipped two copies of each story, pasting
one in a scrapbook and sending the other to her husband, who was
travelling with Mrs. White in the East. But Canright's allegations had
little apparent impact on the Adventists in the town. Some of his
charges against their prophet were overdrawn. It was easy to show
that although Mrs. White had used other authors, she had not lifted
"seven solid pages."[85]

His claim that she was profiteering increased the carriage traffic past her humble home but did nothing for his credibility. Shortly after Canright's lectures, the 1888 edition of *The Great Controversy* began to circulate. In it, Mrs. White pointed out that the "matters of history" which she covered in the book were "well known and universally acknowledged." This history, she had "presented briefly," condensing as much as "seemed consistent with a proper understanding" of its relevance. She explained that "in some cases where a historian has . . . summarized details in a convenient manner," his words had been quoted, but no specific credit was given since the quotations were not used "for the purpose of citing that writer as authority," but because his statement afforded "a ready and forcible presentation of the subject." She said she had made similar use of "those carrying forward the work of reform in our own time," by which she meant Adventist writers.[86]

Years later, John Harvey Kellogg claimed that he had privately protested Mrs. White's borrowing as early as 1884.[87] If he did, his public statements furthered her reputation as a unique writer. For example, when he collected her health writings for the book *Christian Temperance* in 1890, he either did not notice or did not care that some passages were taken from Larkin B. Coles.[88] In the preface to the book, he said that the material first appeared when the few who were advocating healthful living mixed their advice with the "most patent and in some instances disgusting errors." Kellogg claimed that except in Mrs. White's health writings, "Nowhere, and by no one, was there presented a systematic and harmonious body of hygienic truths, free from patent errors, and consistent with the Bible and the principles of the Christian religion."[89]

The plagiarism charge surfaced again in 1907, this time in a pamphlet published anonymously by Dr. Charles E. Stewart, a staff physician at Kellogg's Battle Creek Sanitarium. [2019 note: Further research revealed that Stewart was not the one who published the pamphlet. His was a letter of inquiry to Willie White which others published. He and his wife did withdraw their membership from the Adventist Church, but remained practicing Adventists all their lives and reared their family in the faith.] Stewart's pamphlet pointed to the same sources Canright had used—D'Aubigne, Wylie, and Conybeare and Howsen—adding only one brief snippet from health reformer Larkin B. Coles.[90] As with Canright's challenge, this one came from a partisan in an acrimonious debate and had little impact on the Adventist community.

Such debate as occurred among loyal church members centered on those historical statements of Ellen White which affected the church's prophetic interpretations, but here Adventist teachers and clergy were more concerned with accuracy than with sources. When she revised *The Great Controversy* in 1911, she instructed her editorial secretaries to cite the sources of all the quoted passages and to investigate a number of disputed historical points.[91] A few passages were reworded, but Clarence Crisler, the secretary who carried out the project, explained in private that this was not because Mrs. White had made any errors. Rather, since it was "quite impossible to prove" some points, they were removed to avoid disputes. In the course of identifying quotations, Crisler noticed paraphrased parallels and marked them, but his work only served to convince him that without divine aid "no mortal man could have done the work" Mrs. White did in "shaping up" the chapters of *The Great Controversy*.[92] When Willie White explained the revisions and to some extent the borrowing to the church, he conceded that his mother "never claimed to be authority on history."[93] The next year he said Ellen White did not want her writings used as authority "regarding the details of history or historical dates."[94] But aged ministers like S. N. Haskell would not allow any such diminution of the prophet's authority. One statement from Ellen White meant more to him, he said, than all the history books one could stack "between here and Calcutta."[95]

In the years after Ellen White's death, Willie White discussed her borrowing occasionally, but his comments did not spark a great deal of interest. In 1935 he lectured at a Bible School at Pacific Union College near St. Helena, California. His class enrolled some 30 secondary and college teachers, as well as several evangelists and missionaries. White circulated a questionnaire which asked, among other things: "If carefully prepared answers to the following points of criticism were made available to our workers, which points would especially interest and help you." Nearly all the students were concerned with the charge that Mrs. White's earliest writings were being suppressed. They also wanted an explanation for her prediction in 1856 that some then living would see Christ return to earth. Only half of them felt information on the charge of plagiarism would be helpful; nearly as many wanted to know how to explain the fact that Mrs. White had died owing money when she had urged church members to shun debt.[96] Nevertheless, Willie White explained carefully his view that her borrowing was merely a matter of convenience in describing what she had already been shown in vision.[97] The assurance that the concepts were from God even if the language was borrowed was apparently sufficient for most Adventists.

If early attitudes are any indication, Adventist laypersons read Ellen White primarily for spiritual benefit, not for historical information or literary beauty. "Your views are an encouragement and comfort to me," one woman wrote Mrs. White. "The first time I read them, I was very much animated, and said I could not believe Satan would ever give such views; for no one that read them could help feeling a greater desire to live righteously."[98] A Michigan believer said he "never realized more fully the importance of being devoted to God" than since he had read one of Ellen White's early *Testimonies for the Church*.[99] These testimonies, another thought, would surely lead him into a "closer walk with God."[100] Reading the first edition of *The Great Controversy*, another felt "greatly strengthened and encouraged," thankful that God was "mindful of his people in these last days of great peril, in giving us new and glorious light."[101]

As Mrs. White neared the end of her life, she and her staff were anxious to publish as many books as possible while she could still supervise and approve the work. *Ministry of Healing*, her mature statement on health, appeared in 1905. Four years later, her last volume of *Testimonies for the Church* was issued. *Acts of the Apostles* (1911), *Counsels to Teachers* (1913), *Gospel Workers* (1915), and *Life Sketches* (1915), completed her literary work. Before she died, she had nearly completed *Prophets and Kings*, a narrative commentary on the latter part of the Old Testament. This was published in 1917.[102]

"Whether or not "my life is spared," she said, "my writings will constantly speak, and their work will go forward as long as time shall last. . . . though I should not live, these words that have been given to me by the Lord will still have life and will speak to the people."[103] Mrs. White took steps to fulfill her own prophecy. In her will, she appointed a Board of Trustees to administer her Estate, charging them to attend to the "improvement of the books and manuscripts held in trust by them," to provide for the "printing of new translations thereof," and for the printing of "compilations from my manuscripts."[104]

It was in this Board of Trustees that her charisma was at last routinized. Although at first they did little beyond settling her debts, they eventually began dipping into her unpublished writings to construct new compilations. By organizing, packaging, and promoting her books in various ways, they have kept her charisma alive. Since her death, dozens of collections of her writings on various topics have appeared. Since there are more Spanish-speaking than English-speaking Adventists, most of her books have been translated into Spanish and her more important volumes are found in many other languages as well. Her little book on Christian conversion, *Steps to Christ*, is currently in print in 117 languages and has been translated into more than 200 languages. [105] The publication of a massive *Comprehensive Index to the Writings of Ellen G. White* in 1963 made their systematic and topical study much easier. [2019 note: Of course, the online publication of all her writings at egwwritings.org completely replaces the 1963 index. It is now possible to search for any word, phrase, or combination of words in any of her writings, or to isolate one's search to only those writings created during her lifetime or to search any specific work or combination of works.] Her authority and influence thus continue to be felt even as members of her church continue to ponder the impact of earthly influences on her.

---

[1]Ernest R. Sandeen, "The 'Little Tradition' and the Form of Modern Millenarianism," *The Annual Review of the Social Sciences of Religion*, vol. 4 (1980), 165-181.

[2]John Greenleaf Whittier, *The Writings of John Greenleaf Whittier*, Riverside ed., vol. 5: *Prose Works*, (Boston, 1889), 427.

[3]Don F. Neufeld, ed., *The Seventh-day Adventist Encyclopedia*, rev. ed. (Washington, D.C., 1976), s.v., "Review and Herald," "Review and Herald Publishing

Association," "Pacific Press Publishing Association," "Southern Publishing Association," "Signs of the Times," and "The Youth's Instructor"; Carol Hetzell, *The Undaunted: The Story of the Publishing Work of Seventh-day Adventists* (Mountain View, CA: 1967).

⁴Robert Peel, *Mary Baker Eddy: The Years of Authority* (New York, 1977), 88, 309-312.

⁵Robert Peel, *Mary Baker Eddy: The Years of Discovery* (New York, 1966), 291.

⁶Robert Peel, *Mary Baker Eddy: The Years of Trial* (New York, 1971), 279.

⁷Ellen G. White, "An Open Letter," *Review and Herald*, vol. 10 (Jan. 20, 1903), 15, in *Colporteur Ministry* (Mountain View, Calif., 1953), 125; see also Ellen G. White to Brother Colcord, Mar. 10, 1890, Letter 60, 1890.

⁸Ellen G. White, "Diary," Jan. 10, 1890, Ms. 23, 1890.

⁹Ellen G. White, *Testimonies for the Church*, vol. 4, 144, first published 1876.

¹⁰Ibid., 211; vol. 5,674.

¹¹Ellen G. White Estate, *Comprehensive Index to the Writings of Ellen G. White*, vol. 3 (Mountain View, Calif., 1962) 3193-3205.

¹²Ellen G. White, *Spiritual Gifts*, vol. 2, 7.

¹³Ibid., 8,11; James White and Ellen G. White, *Life Sketches* (1880), 134.

¹⁴It has been common for many years to say she had a "third grade education." Lina Mainero, *American women writers : a critical reference guide from colonial times to the present*, vol. 4, S-Z (New York, NY: Unger, 1981) p. 390; Vance Ferrell, *Prophet of the End* (Altamont, TN: Pilgrim's Books, 1984), 30; Rene Noorbergen, *Ellen G. White, Prophet of Destiny* (New Canaan, CT: Keats Pub., 1972), viii; Melissa and Greg Howell, *Fusion: Where You and God Connect* (Hagerstown, MD.: Review & Herald Publishing 2010), 218.

¹⁵Oliver Gerrish, et. al., "Report of the School Committee for 1837-38," *Eastern Argus* [Portland, Maine] (March 28, 1838), 2.

¹⁶Ellen G. White, [Interview] "Historical Jottings, White Estate Document File #733c.

¹⁷Ellen G. White, *Spiritual Gifts*, vol. 2, 14.

¹⁸Ellen G. White, *Testimonies for the Church*, vol. 1, 13, first published 1860.

¹⁹James White to Ellen G. White, March 20, 1880.

²⁰William York Tindall, *John Bunyan: Mechanick Preacher* (New York, 1964), 192.

²¹Ellen G. White, "Diary," Jan. 11, 1873, Ms. 3, 1873, in *Selected Messages*, Book 3 (Washington, D. C, 1980), 90.

²²Mary K. White to W. C. White, Sept. 14, 1887; W. C. White to L. J. Rousseau, Apr. 9, 1893; W. C. White to L. E. Froom, Jan. 8, 1928, in Ellen G. White, *Selected Messages*, Book 3, 456-459.

²³Robert Peel, *Mary Baker Eddy: The Years of Discovery*, 281

²⁴Ellen G. White to Edson and Emma, Aug. 4, 1895, Letter 125 1895.

²⁵Ellen G. White to J. H. Kellogg, Aug. 29, 1895, Letter 44, 1895.

²⁶W. C. White to Julia Malcolm, Dec. 10, 1894; Ellen G. White to G. A. Irwin, July

22, 1897; Ellen G. White to Children, Dec. 11, 1895, Letter 127, 1895.

[27]Ellen G. White to Mary Foss, Aug. 10, 1902, Letter 133, 1902, in *Selected Messages*, Book 3, 91-92.

[28]Ellen G. White to O. A. Olson, Feb. 5, 1894, Letter 59, 1894, quoted in Ellen G. White Estate, *The Fannie Bolton Story: A Collection of Source Documents* (Washington, D.C.: 1982), 11.

[29]Fannie Bolton, "A Confession Concerning the Testimony of Jesus Christ," c. April, 1901, quoted in Ellen G. White Estate, *The Fannie Bolton Story: A Collection of Source Documents*, 104.

[30]Ellen G. White, "Record of Writing," 1886, Ms. 74, 1886.

[31]Ellen G. White to Whom it May Concern, July 19, 1894, Letter 3, 1894.

[32]Ibid.

[33]Arthur L. White, *Ellen G. White: The Early Elmshaven Years* (Washington, D.C., 1981), 264-267.

[34]Carl H. Scheele, *A Short History of the Mail Service* (Washington, D.C., 1970)-; 88, 91, 105.

[35]Helmutt Lehmann-Haupt, *The Book in America* (New York, 1951), 77; James White, "Power Press," *Review and Herald*, vol. 10 (July 2, 1857), 72; "The Cause," vol. 16 (Aug. 28, 1860), 116.

[36]Daniel J. Boorstin, *The Americans, The Democratic Experience* (New York, 1973), 398-400; Richard N. Current, *The Typewriter and the Men Who Made It* (Urbana, Ill., 1954), 110,113.

[37]Winston Ferris, "Literary Production of Ellen G. White, A Statistical Survey" (typewritten, Andrews University, 1976).

[38]Susan Geary, "The Domestic Novel as a Commercial Commodity Making a Best Seller in the 1850's," *Papers of the Bibliographic Society of America*, vol. 70 (July-Sept, 1976), 366-370.

[39]Don F. Neufeld, ed., *Seventh-day Adventist Encyclopedia*, rev. ed., s.v. "Colporteurs."

[40]Arthur L. White, *The Ellen G. White Writings* (Washington, D.C., 1973), 114-115.

[41]H. L. Hastings, *The Great Controversy Between God and Man: Its Origin, Progress, and End* (Rochester, N.Y., 1858).

[42]Ruth Burgeson, "A Comparative Study of the Fall of Man as Treated by John Milton and Ellen G. White," (Master's Thesis, Pacific Union College, 1957).

[43]Arthur L. White, *Ellen G. White: Messenger to the Remnant* (Washington, D.C., 1969), 55.

[44]Ellen G. White, *Spiritual Gifts*, (Battle Creek, Mich., 1858).

[45]James White, "Book Notice," *Review and Herald*, vol. 11 (Mar. 18, 1858), 144.

[46]Ellen G. White, *The Spirit of Prophecy: The Great Controversy Between Christ and Satan from the Destruction of Jerusalem to the End of the Controversy* (Battle-Creek, Mich., 1884).

[47]Jonathan Butler, "The World of Ellen White and the End of the World,"

Spectrum, vol. 10 (Aug. 1979), 2-13. Butler places the predictions in the context of their late-nineteenth century times, when anti-Catholic sentiment was much more prevalent, and suggests their lack of continued relevance. His view was attacked by Leonard Brand and Don S. McMahon in *The Prophet and Her Critics* (Nampa, ID., 1984), 30-33.

[48]Ellen G. White to F. M. Wilcox, July 25, 1911, Letter 56, 1911, quoted in *Colporteur Ministry*, 128.

[49]Ellen G. White, "Diary," Nov. 24, 1890, Manuscript 23, 1890.

[50]Ellen G. White to D. H. Kress, Oct. 10, 1905, Letter 281, 1905, quoted in *Colporteur Ministry*, 127.

[51]This work is summarized in Donald R. McAdams, "Shifting Views of Inspiration: Ellen G. White Studies in the 1970's," *Spectrum*, vol. 10 (Mar., 1980), 27-41; and in the preface to the third edition of Ron Numbers' book, cited below.

[52]Ronald L. Numbers, *Prophetess of Health: A Study of Ellen G. White* (New York, NY., Harper and Row, 1976). The book is now in its third edition, having been republished in 1992 and 2008. It is now part of the Library of Religious Biographies, a series published by William B. Eerdmans Publishing Company in Grand Rapids, Michigan.

[53]"Prophet of Plagiarist," *Time*, vol. 108 (Aug. 2, 1976), 43; Ellen G. White Estate, *A Critique of Prophetess of Health* (Washington, D.C., 1976).

[54]Walter T. Rea, *The White Lie* (Turlock, Calif., 1982); John Dart, "Plagiarism Found In Prophet Books," *Los Angeles Times*, (Oct. 23, 1980); Kenneth L. Woodward, "A False Prophetess?" *Newsweek*, vol. 101 (Jan. 19, 1981), 72; Richard N. Ostling, "A Church of Liberal Borrowings," *Time*, vol. 114 (Aug. 2, 1982), 49; Kenneth A. Briggs, "7th-Day Adventists Face Change and Dissent," *New York Times*, Nov. 6, 1982; James C. Hefley, "Adventist Teachers are Forced Out in a Doctrinal Dispute," *Christianity Today*, vol. 27 (Mar. 18, 1983), 23-25.

[55]Ronald L. Numbers, *Ellen G. White: Prophetess of Health*, 3rd Edition (Grand Rapids, MI., Eerdmans, 2008), 83-84, 95, 155-156. [2019 note: revised to 3rd edition pagination)

[56]Ellen G. White, "Questions and Answers," *Review and Herald*, vol. 30 (Oct. 8, 1867), 260-261.

[57]Ibid.

[58]James White, "The Precious Youth," *Review and Herald*, vol. 57, (June 21, 1881), 392.

[59]Smith condemned the plagiarism of his sister's poem in "Plagiarism," *Review and Herald*, vol. 24, (Sept. 6, 1864), 120; Ron Graybill, "Ellen White as a Reader and Writer" *Insight*, vol. 12 (May 19, 1981), 8-10.

[60]Arthur L. White, "A Review and Ellen White's Unique Experience in Conducting 'Mrs. White's Department' in *The Health Reformer*, 18711874" (duplicated, Washington, D. C.,1983).

[61]Arthur L. White, "The Health Reformer: The Resuscitation of a Dying Health Journal," (unpublished manuscript, Washington, D.C., 1983).

[62]Ellen G. White, *Selected Messages*, Book 1 (Washington, D.C., 1958), 36.

[63]Uriah Smith to Ellen G. White, Aug. 10, 1882. Max Weber has warned, of course, that charisma depends on the prophets' continued ability to deliver miracles. S. N. Eisenstadt, ed., *Max Weber on Charisma and Institution Building* (Chicago, 1968), 49-55.

[64]Ellen G. White, "Looking Back on Minneapolis," Nov.-Dec., 1888, Ms. 24, 1888.

[65]Ellen G. White, *Testimonies for the Church*, vol. 5, 65, first published 1882.

[66]Ibid., 686, first published 1889.

[67]Ibid., 67, first published 1882.

[68]Ellen G. White to E. J. Waggoner and A. T. Jones, Feb. 18, 1887, Letter 37, 1887.

[69]Arthur L. White, *The Ellen G. White Writings*, 124; Willie White, "Seventh-day Adventism, Mrs. White and Her Visions, An Answer," c. Mar. 1894, Letter Book 4, 191; W. C. White to W. W. Eastman, Nov. 4, 1912.

[70]Ron Graybill, Analysis of Ellen G. White's Luther Manuscript (duplicated, Washington, D. G.-,1977); Donald R. McAdams, "Ellen G. White and the Protestant Historians," (typewritten, Keene, Texas, 1977).

[71]Walter F. Specht and Raymond Cottrell, "The Literary Relationship Between *The Desire of Ages* by Ellen G. White and The Life of Christ by William Hanna," Parts I and II (duplicated, Washington, D.C., n.d.).

[72]Warren H. Johns, "Ellen G. White Prophet or Plagiarist?" Ministry, vol. 55 (June, 1982), 2-19; Walter Rea, The White Lie, 222-409.

[73]Robert Peel, Mary Baker Eddy: The Years of Authority, 106-108.

[74]Robert Peel, *Mary Baker Eddy: The Years of Discovery*, 9-10, 17, 25, 28, 47.

[75]Robert Peel, *Mary Baker Eddy: The Years of Authority*, 190.

[76]Bruce F. Campbell, *Ancient Wisdom Revived: A History of the Theosophical Movement* (Berkeley, Calif., 1980), 33-34.

[77]Ellen G. White to G. I. Butler, Jan. 16, 1886, Letter 73, 1886.

[78]Ellen G. White to Brother Colcord, Mar. 10, 1890, Letter 60, 1890.

[79]William York Tindall, *John Bunyan, Mechanick Preacher*, 208.

[80]"A Valuable Book," *Signs of the Times*, vol. 9 (Feb. 22, 1883), 96.

[81]Ellen G. White, "Holiday Gifts," *Review and Herald*, vol. 5 (Dec. 26, 1882), 789.

[82]D. M. Canright, *Seventh-day Adventism Renounced* (New York, 1889), 37-58; Arthur L. White, ""The Story of Two Men," *The Youth's Instructor*, vol. 14 (May 3, 1966), 13-21.

[83]Ron Graybill, "D. M. Canright in Healdsburg, 1889: The Genesis of the Plagiarism Charge," *Insight*, vol. 11 (Oct 21, 1980), 7-10.

[84]"Adventism Renounced by Elder D. M. Canright," *Healdsburg Enterprise* (Feb. 13, 1889); "Some of Mrs. White's Revelations," "The Committee Report," *Healdsburg Enterprise* (Mar. 6, 1889).

[85]J. N. Loughborough, "False Charges Refuted," *Healdsburg Enterprise*, (Mar. 13, 1889).

[86]Ellen G. White, *The Great Controversy* (Battle Creek, Mich., 1888), iv.

[87]"An Authentic Interview Between Elder G. W. Amadon, Elder A. C. Bourdeau,

and Dr. John Harvey Kellogg in Battle Creek, Mich., on Oct. 7, 1907," 32-33.

[88]Ron Numbers, *Ellen G. White: Prophetess of Health*, 166

[89]John Harvey Kellogg, "Preface," in Ellen G. White, *Christian Temperance* (Battle Creek, 1890), iii; that Kellogg authored the preface is established in John Harvey Kellogg, "Christian Help Work," *General Conference Bulletin*, vol. 1, (March 8, 1897), 309.

[90][Charles E. Stewart], *A Response to an Urgent Testimony from Mrs. Ellen G. White Concerning Contradictions, Inconsistencies and Other Errors in Her Writings* (Battle Creek, Mich., 1907), 73-79.

[91]Willie White, "The Great Controversy,—1911 Edition," in Ellen G. White, *Selected Messages*, vol. 3, 433-444.

[92]C. Crisler to Guy Dail, Jan. 3, 1911, quoted in Arthur L. White, *Ellen G. White: The Later Elmshaven Years* (Washington, D.C., 1982), 317.

[93]Willie White, "The Great Controversy,—1911 Edition," in Ellen G. White, *Selected Messages*, vol. 3,437.

[94]Willie White to W. W. Eastman, Nov. 4, 1912, in Ellen G. White, *Selected Messages*, vol. 3, 446.

[95]S. N. Haskell to Ellen G. White May 30, 1910.

[96]Tim Poirier, "Survey Conducted at the General Conference Advanced Bible School," (unpublished manuscript, Washington, D. C., 1982).

[97]W. C. White, "Addresses to the Faculty and Students at the 1935 Advanced Bible School, Angwin, California," (duplicated, Washington, D. C., 1982).

[98]M. E. Devereux to "Sister White," *Review and Herald*, vol. 8 (May 8, 1856), 32.

[99]Milton S. Kellogg to "Brother Smith," *Review and Herald*, vol. 11 (Jan. 21, 1858), 87.

[100]A. S. Hutchins to "Brother Smith," *Review and Herald*, vol. 11 (Nov. 26, 1857), 24.

[101]John J. Curtis, to "Brother Smith," *Review and Herald*, vol. 12, (Oct. 28, 1858), 183.

[102]Arthur L. White, "Ellen White's Last Four Books, Part I," *Review and Herald*, vol. 158 (June 11, 1981), 3-5; "More Than 'One More Book,'" Ibid., (June 18, 1981), 8-10; Ibid., "The Story of *Prophets and Kings*," Ibid., (June 25, 1981), 10-13.

[103]Ellen G. White, *Selected Messages*, Book 1, 55.

[104]"Last Will and Testament of Ellen G. White," in Francis D. Nichol, *Ellen G. White and Her Critics* (Washington, D.C., 1951), 677.

[105]James R. Nix, "The Ellen G. White Estate," *Adventist Review, General Conference Bulletin Supplement*, June 30, 2005, p. 14.

Bibliographic Note

2019 note—The bibliographic essay and selected bibliography of sources relating to Ellen G. White in my 1983 dissertation are now much more extensively and reliably replaced by bibliographic essays in Denis Fortin and Jerry Moon, eds., *The Ellen G. White Encyclopedia* (Hagerstown, MD: Review and Herald Publishing Association, 2013). Similarly, readers can find more extensive and more current bibliographic notes on Alma White, Mary Baker Eddy, and Catherine Booth by consulting the Wikipedia articles about them.

Bibliography

Allen, James B. and Glen M. Leonard, *The Story of the Latter-day Saints* (Salt Lake City, Utah, 1976)

Anderson, David D., *Robert Ingersoll* (New York, 1972)

Anderson, Godfrey, *Outrider of the Apocalypse* (Mountain View, Calif., 1972)

Andrews, Edward Deming, *The People Called Shakers* (New York, 1963)

Andrews, J. N., et. al., *Defense of Eld. James White and Wife; Vindication of Their Moral and Christian Character* (Battle Creek, Mich., 1870)

Andrews, J. N., *The History of the Sabbath* (Battle Creek, Mich., 1859, 1862, 1873, 1887);

Arrington, Leonard J. and David Bitton, *The Mormon Experience: A History of the Latter-day Saints* (New York, 1979, 30-32.

Ballenger, Albion F., *Cast Out for the Cross of Christ* (Tropico, Calif., 1909)

Banner, Lois W., *Elizabeth Cady Stanton: A Radical for Woman's Rights* (Boston, 1980)

Bates, Joseph, *The Autobiography of Elder Joseph Bates* (Battle Creek, Mich., 1868)

Benedict, Louise C., *The Bible vs. Christian Science* (Los Angeles, 1927)

Bention, Arthur L., ed., *Behavioral Change in Cerebrovascular Disease* (New York, 1970)

Boorstin, Daniel J., *The Americans: The Democratic Experience* (New York, 1973)

Booth, Bramwell, *These Fifty Years* (London, 1929)

Booth, Catherine, Female Ministry; or, Woman's Right to Preach the Gospel (first published, 1859, reprinted, London, 1975).

Booth, Catherine, *Life and Death* (London, 1883)

Booth, Catherine, *Papers on Practical Religion* (London, 1891)

Booth, Catherine, *Popular Christianity* (London, [1887])

Booth, William, *Orders and Regulations for Field Officers of the Salvation Army* (London, 1891)

Booth-Tucker, F. L., *The Life of Booth, Catherine*, vol. 1 (New York, 1892)

Booth-Tucker, Frederick L., *The Life of Catherine Booth*, vol. 1 (New York, 1892)

Bramwell-Booth, Catherine, *The Life of Catherine Booth* (London, 1970)

Brand, Leonard and Don S. McMahon, *The Prophet and Her Critics* (Nampa, ID., 1984)

Campbell, Bruce F., *Ancient Wisdom Revived: A History of the Theosophical Movement* (Berkeley, Calif., 1980)

Canright, D. M., *Seventh-day Adventism Renounced* (New York, 1889)

Carpenter, Gilbert C., Jr., *The Visions of Mary Baker Eddy: As Recorded by Her Secretary, Calvin A. Frye, From 1872-1894 with Interpretations Written by Her Sometimes Assistant Secretary, Gilbert C. Carpenter* (Rumford, R.I., 1935)

Carson, Gerald, *Cornflake Crusade* (New York, 1977)

Carter, Paul, *The Spiritual Crisis of the Gilded Age* (DeKalb, Ill., 1971)

Caskey, Marie, *Chariot of Fire: Religion and the Beecher Family* (New Haven, Conn., 1978)

Clifford, Doborah Pickman, *Mine Eyes Have Seen the Glory* (Boston, 1978)

Cornell, M. E., *Miraculous Powers: The Scripture Testimony on the Perpetuity of Spiritual Gifts* (Battle Creek, Mich., 1862)

Cott, Nancy F., *The Bonds of Womanhood: "Woman's Sphere" in New England, 1780- 1835* (New Haven, Conn., 1977)

Coutts, Frederick, *No Discharge in This War* (New York, 1974)

Current, Richard N., *The Typewriter and the Men Who Made It* (Urbana, Ill., 1954)

Davies, John P., *Phrenology, Fad and Science: A 19th Century American Crusade* (New Haven, Conn.: 1971)

Davis, Allen F., *American Heroine: The Life and Legend of Jane Addams* (London, 1973)

Degler, Carl, *At Odds: Women and the Family in America from the Revolution to the Present* (New York, 1980)

Dillon, Mary Earhart, *Francis Willard: From Prayer to Politics* (Chicago, 1944)

Durand, Eugene, *Yours in the Blessed Hope, Uriah Smith* (Washington, D.C., 1980)

Eddy, Mary Baker, *Manual of the Mother Church* (Boston, 1936)

Eddy, Mary Baker, *No and Yes* (Boston, 1919)

Eddy, Mary Baker, *Retrospection and Introspection* (Boston, 1920)

Eddy, Mary Baker, *Rudimental Divine Science* (Boston, 1919)

Eddy, Mary Baker, *Science and Health with Key to the Scripture* (Boston, 1934)

Edwards, Jonathan, *Images or Shadows of Divine Things* (New Haven, Conn., 1948)

Eisenstadt, S. N., ed., *Max Weber on Charisma and Institution Building* (Chicago, 1968)

Ellen G. White Estate, *A Critique of Prophetess of Health* (Washington, D.C., 1976).

Ellen G. White Estate, *Comprehensive Index to the Writings of Ellen G. White* (Mountain View, Calif., 1962)

Ffirth, John, *Experience and gospel labours of the Rev. Benjamin Abbott : to which is annexed a narrative of his life and death* (New York, 1832).

Fielder, Fred E. and Martin M. Chemers, *Leadership and Effective Management* (Glenview, Ill.; 1974).

Foy, William E., *The Christian Experience of William E. Foy Together with the Two Visions He Received in the Months of Jan. and Feb., 1842* (Portland, Maine, 1845)

Froom, LeRoy E., *Movement of Destiny* (Washington, D.C., 1971)

Froom, Leroy E., *The Prophetic Faith of Our Fathers* (Washington, D.C., 1950- 1959)

Froom, Leroy, *Conditionalist Faith of Our Fathers* (Washington, D.C., 1965-1966).

Garrison, Winfred and Alfred T. DeGroot, *The Disciples of Christ: A History* (St. Louis, 1948)

Gaustad, Edwin, ed., *The Rise of Adventism* (New York, 1974)

Gottschalk, Steven, *The Emergence of Christian Science in American Religious Life* (Berkeley, Calif., 1973)

Graybill, Ron, *Mission to Black America: The True Story of James Edson White and the Riverboat Morning Star* (Mountain View, CA: 1971).

Haldeman, Isaac M., *Christian Science in the Light of Holy Scripture* (New York, 1909)

Harris, Barbara, *Beyond Her Sphere: Woman and the Professions in American History* (Westport, Conn., 1978)

Haskell, S. N., *Bible Handbook* (Washington, D.C., 1919)

Hastings, H. L., *The Great Controversy Between God and Man: Its Origin, Progress, and End* (Rochester, N.Y., 1858).

Henry, G. W., *Shouting: Genuine and Spurious, in All Ages of the Church* (Oneida, N. V., 1859).

Hetzell, Carol, *The Undaunted: The Story of the Publishing Work of Seventh-day Adventists* (Mountain View, CA: 1967).

Hodge, Charles, *Systematic Theology*, vol. 1 (New York, 1873)

Hook, Milton, *Flames Over Battle Creek* (Washington, D.C., 1977)

Humez, Jean McMahon, ed., *Gifts of Power: The Writings of Rebecca Jackson: Black Visionary, Shaker Eldress* (n.p., 1981)

Ingersoll, Robert, *About the Bible* (New York, 1894)

Jacquet, Jr.,Constant H., ed., *Yearbook of American and Canadian Churches*, 1982 (Nashville, Tenn., 1982)

James, Edward T., ed., *Notable American Women*, 1607-1950 (Cambridge, Mass., 1971)

Johnson, Allen W. *The Bible and Christian Science* (New York, 1924)

Johnson, Lelia A. Clark, *Sullivan and Sorrento Since 1760* (Ellsworth, Maine., 1953)

Knight, George, *Joseph Bates: The Real Founder of Seventh-day Adventism* (Hagerstown, MD 2004)

Larsson, Flora, *My Best Men are Women* (New York, 1974).

Lehmann-Haupt, Helmutt, *The Book in America* (New York, 1951)

Lerner, Gerda, *The Grimke Sisters from South Carolina* (New York, 1971)

Lewis, I M., *Ecstatic Religion: An Anthropological Study of Spirit Possession and Shamanism* (London, 1971)

Loughborough, J. N., *The Great Second Advent Movement* (Washington, D.C., 1905)

Loughborough, J. N., *The Rise and Progress of the Seventh-day Adven-*

tists (Battle Creek, Mich., 1892)

Lowance, Jr,.Mason I., *The Language of Canaan: Metaphor and Symbol in New England from the Puritans to the Transcendentalists* (Cambridge, Mass., 1980)

Lumpkin, Katherine DuPre, *The Emancipation of Angelina Grimke* (Chapel Hill, N.C., 1974)

Marsden, George, *Fundamentalism and American Culture* (New York, 1980)

Melvill, Henry, C. P. McIlvaine, ed., *Sermons*, 3rd edition (New York, 1844)

Moore, Henry, *The Life of Mrs. Mary Fletcher, Consort and Relict of the Rev. John Fletcher ... Compiled from Her Journal and Other Authentic Documents*, 3rd ed. (London, 1818).

Moore, James, *The Post-Darwinian Controversies* (New York, 1979); Paul

Moore, R. Laurence, *In Search of White Crows: Spiritualism, Parapsychology, and American Culture* (New York, 1977)

n. a., *Memoir of Jemima Wilkinson* (Bath, N.Y., 1844)

n.a. *Testimonies of the Life, Character, Revelations and Doctrines of Mother Ann Lee*, second edition (Albany, New York, 1888, Reprinted New York, 1975)

Neufeld, Don F., ed., *Seventh-day Adventist Encyclopedia*, rev. ed. (Washington, D.C., 1976)

Nichol, F. D., *The Midnight Cry* (Washington, D.C., 1944)

Nichol, Francis D., *Ellen G. White and Her Critics* (Washington, D.C., 1951)

Noorbergen, Rene, *White, Ellen G., Prophet of Destiny* (New Canaan, CT: Keats Pub., 1972)

Numbers, Ronald L., *Ellen G. White: Prophetess of Health* (New York, 1976)

Nye, Russel B., *William Lloyd Garrison and the Humanitarian Reformers* (Boston, 1955)

Olson, A. V., *Thirteen Crisis Years, 1888-1901*, rev. ed. (Washington, D.C., 1981)

Palmer, Walter and Phoebe, *Four Years in the Old World* (New York, 1866)

Papashvily, Helen, *All The Happy Endings: A Study of the Domestic Novel in America* (New York, 1956)

Pea,cLawrence h, *John Smedley of Matlock and his Hydro* (London, 1954)

Peel, Robert, *Mary Baker Eddy: The Years of Authority* (New York, 1977)

Peel, Robert, *Mary Baker Eddy: The Years of Discovery* (New York, 1966)

Peel, Robert, *Mary Baker Eddy: The Years of Trial* (New York, 1971)

Perry, Lewis, *Radical Abolitionism: Anarchy and the Government of God in Anti-Slavery Thought* (Ithaca, New York, 1973)

Powell, Lyman, *Christian Science, The Faith and its Founder* (New York, 1917)

Primer, Ben, *Protestants and American Business Methods* (Ann Arbor, MI: 1979)

Prince, Raymond, ed., *Trance and Possession States* (Montreal, 1966)

Rea, Walter T., *The White Lie* (Turlock, Calif., 1982)

Reuther, Rosemary Radford and Rosemary Skinner Keller, eds., *Women and Religion in America*, vol. 1 (San Francisco, Calif., 1981)

Robinson, Dores, *The Story of Our Health Message* (Nashville, Tenn., 1943)

Robinson, Virgil, *James White* (Washington, D.C., 1976)

Rogers, H[ester] A[nn], *A Short Account of the Experiences of Mrs. H. A. Rogers... with Brief Extracts from Her Diary* (Dublin: 1803)

Rupp, Daniel, ed., *An Original History of the Religious Denominations at Present Existing the United States* (Philadelphia, 1844)

Salvation Army, *The Salvation Army: Its Origin and Development* (London, 1945)

Sargant, William, *The Mind Possessed: A Physiology of Possession, Mysticism, and Faith Healing* (London, 1973)

Saxton, Martha, *Louisa May: A Modern Biography of Louisa May Alcott* (Boston, 1977)

Scheele, Carl H., *A Short History of the Mail Service* (Washington, D.C., 1970)-; 88, 91, 105.

Schwarz, Richard W., *John Harvey Kellogg, M.D.*, (Nashville, Tenn., 1970)

Sklar, Katherine Kish, *Catherine Beecher: A Study in American Domesticity* (New York, 1973)

Smith, Timothy L., *Revivalism and Social Reform* (New York, 1957)

Smith, Uriah, et. al., *Vindication of the Business Career of Elder James White* (Battle Creek, Mich, 1863).

Stanton, Elizabeth Cady, *The (Original) Feminist Attack on the Bible: The Woman's Bible* (N. Y., 1974)

Stewart, Charles E., *A Response to an Urgent Testimony from Mrs. Ellen G. White Concerning Contradictions, Inconsistencies and Other Errors in Her Writings* (Battle Creek, Mich., 1907)

Stowe, Calvin, *Origin and History of the Books of the Bible* (Hartford, Conn., 1867)

Summerhill, N., *History of the Christian Church* (Cincinnati, 1873).

Thomas, John L., *The Liberator: William Lloyd Garrison, A Biography* (Boston, 1963)

Tindall, William York, *John Bunyan: Mechanick Preacher* (New York, 1964)

Turner, R. Edward, *Proclaiming the Word* (Berrien Springs, Mich., 1980)

Vande Vere, Emmett K., *The Wisdom Seekers* (Nashville, Tenn., 1972)

Warren, Sidney, *American Freethought, 1860-1914* (New York, 1943)

Wesley, John, *The Works of John Wesley*, vol. 1 (London, 1872, Reprint, Grand Rapids, Mich., n.d.)

Wheatley, Richard, *The Life and Letters of Phoebe Palmer* (New York, 1876)

White, Alma, *Heroes of the Fiery Cross* (Zarephath, N.J., 1928)

White, Alma, *Klansmen: Guardians of Liberty* (Zarephath, N.J., 1926)

White, Alma, *Looking Back from Beulah* (Denver, Colorado, 1902, Zarephath, N.J., 1929).

White, Alma, *My Heart and Husband* {Zarephath, N.J., 1923)

White, Alma, *The Ku Klux Klan in Prophecy* (Zarephath, N.J., 1925).

White, Alma, *The Story of My Life*, 5 vols. (Zarephath, N.J., 1935-1943)

White, Alma, *Why I Do Not Eat Meat* (Zarephath, N.J., 1915)

White, Arthur K., *Some White Family History* (Denver, Col., 1948)

White, Arthur L., ed., *Witness of the Pioneers Concerning the Spirit of Prophecy* (Washington, D.C., 1981)

White, Arthur L., *Ellen G. White: Messenger to the Remnant* (Washington, D.C., 1969)

White, Arthur L., *Ellen G. White: Messenger to the Remnant* (Washington, D.C., 1969)

White, Arthur L., *Ellen G. White: The Early Elmshaven Years, 1900-1905* (Washington, D.C., 1981)

White, Arthur L., *Ellen G. White: The Later Elmshaven Years* (Washington, D.C., 1982)

White, Arthur L., *Ellen G. White: The Later Elmshaven Years, 1905-1915* (Washington, D.C., 1982)

White, Arthur L., *The Ellen G. White Writings* (Washington, D.C., 1973)

White, Ellen G., (Battle Creek Mich., 1880)

White, Ellen G., (Nashville, Tenn., 1921)

White, Ellen G., *Acts of the Apostles* (Mountain View, Calif., 1911)

White, Ellen G., *Adventist Home*, (Washington, D. C., 1952)

White, Ellen G., *Christ's Object Lessons* (Nashville, Tenn., 1941)

White, Ellen G., *Christian Temperance* (Battle Creek, 1890)

White, Ellen G., *Colporteur Ministry* (Mountain View, Calif., 1953)

White, Ellen G., *Counsels on Diet and Foods* (Washington, D. C., 1946)

White, Ellen G., *Counsels on Health*, (Mountain View, Calif. 1951)

White, Ellen G., *Counsels to Parents, Teachers, and Students* (Mountain View, Calif., 1943)

White, Ellen G., *Early Writings* (Washington, D.C., 1945)

White, Ellen G., *Gospel Workers*, (Washington, D.C., 1915, 1948)

White, Ellen G., *Life Sketches* {Mountain View, Calif., 1915).

White, Ellen G., *Ministry of Healing* (Mountain View, Calif., 1905, 1942)

White, Ellen G., *Patriarchs and Prophets* (Mountain View, Calif., 1958)

White, Ellen G., *Selected Messages*, Book 1 (Washington, D.C. 1958)

White, Ellen G., *Selected Messages*, Book 3 (Washington, D. C, 1980)

White, Ellen G., *Spiritual Gifts*, (Battle Creek, Mich., 1858).

White, Ellen G., *Spiritual Gifts*, vol. 2 (Battle Creek, Mich., 1860)

White, Ellen G., *Spiritual Gifts*, vol. 3 (Battle Creek, Mich., 1864)

White, Ellen G., *Supplement to Christian Experience and Views* (Rochester, N.Y., 1854)

White, Ellen G., *Testimonies for the Church*, vol. 1 (Mountain View, Calif., 1948)

White, Ellen G., *Testimonies for the Church*, vol. 2 (Mountain View, Calif., 1948)

White, Ellen G., *Testimonies for the Church*, vol. 3 (Mountain View, Calif., 1948)

White, Ellen G., *Testimonies for the Church*, vol. 4 (Mountain View, Calif., 1948)

White, Ellen G., *Testimonies for the Church*, vol. 5 (Mountain View, Calif., 1948)

White, Ellen G., *Testimonies for the Church*, vol. 6 (Mountain View, Calif., 1948)

White, Ellen G., *Testimonies for the Church*, vol. 7 (Mountain View, Calif., 1948)

White, Ellen G., *Testimonies for the Church*, vol. 8 (Mountain View, Calif., 1948)

White, Ellen G., *Testimonies for the Church*, vol. 9 (Mountain View, Calif., 1948)

White, Ellen G., *The Adventist Home* (Washington, D.C., 1980)

White, Ellen G., *The Great Controversy* (Battle Creek, Mich., 1888)

White, Ellen G., *The Great Controversy* (Mountain View, Calif., 1911)

White, Ellen G., *The Judgement* (Battle Creek, Mich., 1879)

White, Ellen G., *The Spirit of Prophecy: The Great Controversy Between Christ and Satan from the Destruction of Jerusalem to the End of the Controversy* (Battle-Creek, Mich., 1884).

White, Ellen G., *Thoughts from the Mount of Blessing* (Washington, D.C., 1956)

White, Ellen G., *Welfare Ministry* (Washington, D.C., 1952)

White, James and White, Ellen G., *Life Sketches* (Battle Creek, Mich. 1880)

White, James, *A Solemn Appeal to the Ministry and the People* (Battle Creek, Mich., 1873)

White, James, *A Word to the "Little Flock"* (Brunswick, Maine, 1847)

White, James, *Life Incidents in Connection with the Great Second Advent Movement* (Battle Creek, Mich., 1868)

Whittier, John Greenleaf, *The Writings of John Greenleaf Whittier*, Riverside ed., vol. 5: Prose Works, (Boston, 1889)

Wiggins, Arch P., *The History of the Salvation Army* (London, 1968)

Wisbey, Jr,.Herbert A., *Pioneer Prophetess, Jemima Wilkinson, The Public Universal Friend* (Ithaca, New York, 1964)

Wise, Daniel, *The Young Lady's Counselor* (Boston, 1852)

Yost, Donald, comp., *120th Annual Statistical Report—1982* (Washington, D.C., 1982)

Index

Vita

Ron Graybill was born March 25, 1944, in St. Helena, California. He received a bachelor's degree in theology from Loma Linda University in 1966 and a master of divinity degree from the Seventh-day Adventist Theological Seminary in 1968. Since 1970 he has been employed as a research assistant and archivist at the Ellen G. White Estate, Washington, D. C. He is the author of *Ellen G. White and Church Race Relations* (Washington, D.C., 1970), and a consultant on religious history to the Montgomery County, Maryland, 350 Committee, a group established at the request of Maryland Governor Harry Hughes to help in the celebration of the state's 350th anniversary.

2019 note—A more recent biographical sketch says: Ronald D. Graybill holds PhD degree in American Religious History from The Johns Hopkins University. He has worked as a university professor, historical researcher, corporate communications specialist, journalist, and editor during his career. He spent 13 years as an Associate Secretary at the Ellen G. White Estate at General Conference Headquarters where he assisted Arthur White in writing a portion of the six-volume biography of Ellen G. White. He wrote the introduction to the current *Seventh-day Adventist Hymnal* and the original draft of the Preamble to the Seventh-day Adventist Statement of Fundamental Beliefs. His many articles on Adventist history made him one of the most frequently cited sources in the new *Ellen G. White Encyclopedia*.

CPSIA information can be obtained
at www.ICGtesting.com
Printed in the USA
BVHW031828011020
590110BV00001B/162